Property, Family and the Irish Welfare State

Michelle Norris

Property, Family and the Irish Welfare State

palgrave
macmillan

Michelle Norris
School of Social Policy
Social Work and Social Justice
University College Dublin
Dublin, Ireland

ISBN 978-3-319-44566-3   ISBN 978-3-319-44567-0 (eBook)
DOI 10.1007/978-3-319-44567-0

Library of Congress Control Number: 2016948410

Cover illustration: © Justin Hannaford / Alamy Stock Photo

Printed on acid-free paper

This Palgrave Macmillan imprint is published by Springer Nature
The registered company is Springer International Publishing AG
The registered company address is: Gewerbestrasse 11, 6330 Cham, Switzerland

Acknowledgements

This book is the result of many years of thinking about housing policy in Ireland and Europe and its relationship to the welfare state. I would like to thank everyone who contributed to refining my thinking on these issues. This includes colleagues I have collaborated with from universities across the world, particularly those I have met through my involvement with the European Network for Housing Research and my students and colleagues at the School of Social Policy, Social Work and Social Justice, University College Dublin.

Among my students, Dr Aideen Hayden deserves special mention because supervising her PhD thesis on the history of sales of local authority social housing to tenants was one of the factors which inspired my interest in the history of Irish housing policy and ultimately led me to write this book.

Among these, my long-time UCD colleague and friend Professor Tony Fahey has played a particularly important role in informing my thinking, so I would like to single him out for particular thanks. This book includes several ideas I have "borrowed" from him and numerous others which have been inspired by the many debates about Irish social policy which have managed to fit in between debates on Irish party politics, academic politics and even some academic work.

I would also like to thank Dr Gerard Mills from the UCD School of Geography for drawing the maps included in the book and Dr Aidan

Kane from the Economics Department at the National University of Ireland Galway who very kindly generated data for me from his Duanaire database of Irish historical public spending data and answered all of my queries with great patience. His work in compiling this database is really valuable and will enable historians, economists and policy analysts to systematically trace trends in public spending in Ireland.

This book would not have been possible without the constant encouragement I have received from my family throughout my career. I would particularly like to thank parents Nell and Billy Norris, and my husband Colm for their unfailing support.

This book is dedicated to my much missed grandfather Dennis Kinsella and father-in-law Jerry O'Shea, who both passed away during its completion.

Contents

Abbreviations and Terminology

Ireland experienced three changes of currency during the period under review in this book. Prior to Irish independence, pounds sterling were used; after independence, the Irish pound (called the punt) was adopted which was replaced by the euro in 1999. In the interests of simplicity, the currency employed in the particular period under discussion is used throughout this book and all financial data are presented in current prices. Where foreign currencies are used, these are clearly identified in the text.

Also for simplicity, the different elements of the Irish local government system (local authorities) are referred to throughout this book using the modern nomenclature (city councils, which are responsible for cities; county councils, which have mainly rural operational areas; and town councils, which managed small urban centres until their abolition in 2013).

In Ireland, ministries are generally referred to as government departments (Department of Finance is the finance ministry, etc.), and this convention is adhered to in this book.

The following abbreviations and Irish-language terms are used in the text:

CDB   Congested Districts Board
DDDA   Dublin Docklands Development Authority.

Dáil Éireann	lower house of the Irish parliament.
EU	European Union.
EU15	The 15 countries which were European Union members prior to 2004. These are Austria, Belgium, Denmark, Finland, France, Germany, Greece, Ireland, Italy, Luxembourg, Netherlands, Portugal, Spain, Sweden and the UK.
EU27	The 27 countries which were European Union members prior to 2013. These are the EU15 and Bulgaria, Cyprus, Czech Republic, Estonia, Hungary, Latvia, Lithuania, Malta, Poland, Romania, Slovakia and Slovenia.
ICMSA	Irish Creamery Milk Suppliers' Association.
IFA	Irish Farmer' Association
IFSRA	Irish Financial Services Regulatory Authority.
IMF	International Monetary Federation.
MITR	mortgage interest tax relief
NFU	National Farmers' Union.
PDs	Progressive Democrats political party.
RAS	Rental Accommodation Scheme.
Táiniste	equivalent to deputy prime minister.
Taoiseach	equivalent to prime minister.
TD	equivalent to member of parliament.
SDA	Small Dwellings Acquisition Act mortgages.
TTL	Town Tenants' League.

List of Figures

List of Tables

1

Introduction

The Start of the Story

Every story has to start somewhere and like many stories about Ireland the story presented in this book starts in a conflict regarding land. This conflict is the mass revolt against the landownership system by tenant farmers, which began in 1879, petered out by 1902 and is popularly known as the "Land War". Conflicts between the (mainly Protestant and unionist in political orientation) landlords who owned most of the land and the (mainly Catholic and increasingly nationalist) farmers who rented it had of course shaped Irish history for a long period prior to this. However, between the late 1870s and early 1890s, this conflict was manifested in an unprecedented mass agrarian tenants' movement, which was led initially by the Irish National Land League and subsequently by a series of successor organisations. Irish nationalist members of the UK parliament realised that taking up the cause of land reform had the potential to unite the bulk of the population behind their banner and provide clear evidence of the practical benefits of supporting the nationalist movement (Clark, 1987). While, depending

© The Author(s) 2016
M. Norris, *Property, Family and the Irish Welfare State*,
DOI 10.1007/978-3-319-44567-0_1

on their political hue, different UK governments supported Irish land reform in order to procure nationalist support in parliament, smother nationalist sentiment or simply because they could see no alternative way to foster a sustainable agricultural economy in Ireland (Hudson, 2003).

These political pressures inspired a series of radical legislative interventions (the Land Acts) which first regulated the letting of land and then enabled and finally subsidised the transfer of landownership from landlords to tenant farmers (Clark, 1987). When the first major Land Act was introduced in 1870, only 3 per cent of Irish farmers owned their land and fewer than 800 landlords owned half the country. By the time Ireland seceded from the UK and an independent Irish state was founded in 1922, some two-thirds of tenant farmers had bought their holdings and the ownership of over 316,000 holdings, comprising 11 million acres, had been transferred from landlords to tenant farmers (Aalen, 1993).

The Irish land reform policies were not unique. Governments in many European countries introduced measures to support the replacement of previously widespread large capitalist farms with small family farms in the late nineteenth and early twentieth centuries. This action was inspired primarily by the widespread depression in agriculture triggered by imports from the new world which undermined the economic viability of the farming model (see Koning, 1994). However, compared to Britain and the rest of Europe, the Irish land reform experiment was unparalleled in terms of its scale, cost to the exchequer and long-term impact (Swinnen, 2002). Land redistribution in many Central and Eastern European countries was rolled back by communist regimes, and Swinnen's (2002) study of land redistribution in Ireland, England, Scotland, Belgium, France and the Netherlands since 1880 demonstrates that this policy was historically most ambitious in Ireland with the result that, by the late 1990s, far more Irish farmland was owner occupied (rather than leased) than in any other of these countries.

Despite its significance, the Land War is just the starting point of the story presented here. The primary focus of this book is on the long-term development and (until recent decades) distinctive character of Ireland's social policies and system of welfare provision. Therefore, this story's starting point in the 1870s reflects not only the emergence of the land reform movement, but also of the government interventions in the economy and society which would provide the foundations for the comprehensive welfare states which emerged in Europe and several other developed countries during the twentieth century. Around this time in Germany, Bismarck established the first system of social insurance benefits, encompassing: health insurance (introduced in 1883), accident insurance (1884) and old age and disability insurance (1889), and this model was subsequently copied across Western Europe (Balier, 2010). Concurrently, Western European governments began to intervene in housing provision by regulating private rented housing, clearing urban slums and, in some cases, making provision for the construction of replacement social rented housing for the poor (Pooley, 1992). Also in the late nineteenth century, government funding of health care was introduced or significantly extended in Britain (non-paupers gained access to public hospitals from 1886), Sweden (health insurance system established in 1891) and France (medical assistance provided to the poor from 1893) (Freeman, 2000).

European Stories

Stories about European welfare state development do not typically commence in agrarian politics and land redistribution policy. This is because most historians and social policy analysts link the establishment and expansion of public welfare systems to the emergence and growth of the urban labour movement – working-class agitation, trade unions and social democratic parties – which followed industrialisation, urbanisation and also the extension of the franchise to non-property owners during the late nineteenth and early twentieth centuries (e.g. Esping-Andersen, 1999; Castles, 1978; Korpi, 1978, among many others: Baldwin, 1990, is an exception). The imprint of these urban labourist influences is evident both in the long-run development of European welfare systems and also in the academic research which examines them.

For instance, early public health and housing policies in Europe were strongly focused on urban slums; examples of significant government intervention in rural housing are rare (Pooley, 1992). Furthermore, access to early social insurance schemes (such as Bismarck's 1883 and 1884 programmes) was generally limited to industrial employees and often to employees of businesses above a certain size. These arrangements benefitted many urban males but excluded self-employed farmers, the large number assisting relatives who also worked on farms and the female-dominated domestic service workforce. Land redistribution policies are not typically included within the remit of social policy and thus are largely ignored by welfare state historians. Indeed, public spending on capital goods such as housing is also largely excluded from comparative studies of welfare systems, which are heavily focused on current public expenditure on the redistribution of income (by means of taxes, social security benefits) and, to a lesser extent, on social services such as health care and education (Kemeny, 2001). This tendency is exemplified by Esping-Andersen's (1990) highly influential typology of welfare states in OECD countries which is derived mainly from analysis of social security policies. On this basis, he categorises Ireland and other Anglophone countries as "liberal welfare regimes" where households rely mainly on the market to maintain their standard of living (or his parlance living standards are not "decommodified") and government income support is minimalist and strongly targeted at the poorest households. However, this current spending bias in the social policy literature and the associated focus on social security benefits and social services does reflect the structure of most modern welfare states. Housing policy is often described as the "wobbly pillar under the welfare state" on the grounds that government spending on housing never came close to expenditure on the other elements of welfare and, unlike health care, education and social security, in all European countries most housing is provided by the private sector (Malpass, 2008; Torgersen, 1987). In 2009, OECD members devoted an average of only 0.7 per cent of gross domestic product (GDP) to public spending on housing, but they devoted 7.3 per cent of GDP to old-age pensions and 6.6 per cent to health care (OECD, various years).

A Distinctive Irish Story

As its unusual beginning in agrarian politics and land redistribution policy suggests, this book tells a story about the development of the Irish welfare system which differs significantly from the dominant narrative in the literature about Western European welfare states. The key insight offered here is that the land reform policies which emerged in Ireland in the late nineteenth century were not only highly significant progressively redistributive and decommodifying social policies in their own right, they had a defining influence on the welfare and broader social system which developed in Ireland during the twentieth century. This is because, by conceding the principle of significant government involvement in the redistribution of landownership from landlords to tenant farmers, the Land Acts opened a floodgate of knock-on demands firstly for the provision of higher and higher public subsidies for peasant proprietorship and subsequently for subsidisation of the redistribution of other types of property, principally dwellings, with the result that property redistribution became a major focus of government activity for most of the twentieth century.

Thus, rather than developing *weakly*, this book suggests that for most of the twentieth century the Irish welfare system developed *differently* from most other North Western European countries. Ireland's regime was distinctive firstly in terms of focus – which was primarily on property redistribution while the redistribution of incomes and provision of social services were relegated to a less important role than in neighbouring countries (Castles, 2002). The Irish welfare system was also distinctive in terms of purpose. Whereas welfare states in most other European countries were intended to operationalise the "grand bargain" between capital and the urban labour movement, Ireland's system of State subsidised property redistribution was intended to support a familist social order in which individual interests, values and prerogatives were subordinated to those of the family (Fahey, 2002; McCullagh, 1991).

The atypical early focus of the Irish welfare system is illustrated by the scale of spending on property redistribution prior to the foundation of the independent Irish state in 1922. By 1921, UK government loans to enable Irish tenant farmers purchase their farms amounted to £101 million, whereas Irish GDP in 1914 has been estimated at £135 million (Fahey, 2002). The extent of the government support enjoyed by tenant farmers inspired knock-on demands centred on providing social housing for large population of landless farm labourers who were excluded from the benefits of land reform but sufficiently numerous to merit the attention of politicians particularly as the franchise was extended to include all non-property-owning men. Consequently, in the early twentieth century, social housebuilding rates in rural Ireland far exceeded output in Britain and Western Europe (Fraser, 1996; Fahey, 2002).

After Irish independence, land reform spending declined because most of the landed estates had been broken up and redistributed by this time, but this policy was radicalised in terms of objectives because it now focused not only on the redistribution of land title (i.e. from landlords to the tenants who rented it) but redistribution of the land itself (from large landowners to smallholders and the landless) and the redistributive character of this policy was further amplified when the government increased the public subsidies available to peasant proprietors in the 1930s (Dooley, 2004). Therefore, land reform was a core social policy in the new State and, usually in this case, the welfare system focused on the consolidation of a "permanent" rural smallholder class, rather than on supporting the urban working class. As was the case before independence, these developments in land policy inspired knock-on claims for similar concessions from rural social housing tenants – in 1936, they were granted the right to buy their dwelling (for 75 per cent of the previous rent) and, in the interests of equity, their urban counterparts were granted the same right by the 1966 Housing Act (Norris and Fahey, 2011). Obviously, the urban middle classes could not be excluded from this largesse, so, during the final phase in the extension of property redistribution subsidies from land into other asset classes, numerous homeownership supports were introduced, including tax reliefs, grants, provision of mortgages by local government and subsidisation of mortgage provision by building societies. These exchequer supports and the associated public spending were gradually expanded until they equated to a "socialised" system of homeownership. This was not the same as the socialist system of state-owned housing operated by the communist regimes which governed Central and Eastern Europe at this time because Irish homeowners enjoyed unfettered property rights. Rather, it means that unlike the norm in Western Europe, homeownership in Ireland was not primarily a marketised tenure (supported by market forces such as commercial mortgages and private builders) because most capital for home purchase and construction came from the Irish government and many homeowner dwellings were also government constructed (Norris, 2016). By the mid-1950s, the United Nations (1958) calculated that state housing subsidies in Ireland were the highest among 15 Western European countries examined both in terms of the proportion of housing capital derived from the exchequer (75 per cent) and of new dwellings which received public subsidies (97 per cent). This policy regime also expanded owner occupation to "super normal" levels – well above what could be supported by the market alone (Norris, 2016). In 1971, 70.8 per cent of Irish households were homeowners, compared to 50 and 35 per cent of their counterparts in the UK and Sweden, respectively (Kemeny, 1981; Central Statistics Office, various years).

As exemplified by the legal recognition of "the family as the natural primary and fundamental unit group of Society" in the Constitution adopted by the Irish government in 1937, familism enjoyed wide political and societal as well as religious support in this country during the first half of the twentieth century (Government of Ireland, 1937). This book argues that a key reason for the expansion of property redistribution subsidies provided social support for this social order by reinforcing familial (in practice usually patriarchal) authority, because under the Irish common law legal system further redistribution of farms and dwellings to inheritors was at parental discretion. Subsidies for the purchase of family farms and low debt also foster the economic viability of the familist model, particularly the stem (or three-generational) family system which became widespread in Ireland after the Great Famine of the 1840s (Gibbon and Curtin, 1978). Commonly heirs designate worked unpaid on the family farm and marriage was delayed until they were deemed fit to inherit, the farm income could support an additional family and the patriarch was sure he would not be edged out by the new generation. The unpaid labour of heirs and other assisting relatives made subsistence farming viable and provided a valuable form of welfare in the context of limited alternative employment options in Ireland during the first half of the twentieth century.

However, the drivers which had inspired the growth of this property-based welfare system slowly weakened from the late 1960s as the number and political power of small farmers declined; developmentalism and a hunger for modernisation replaced familism as the dominant ideology and the generous public subsidies required to maintain this welfare regime became increasingly unaffordable in the face of demands for increased spending on mainstream welfare services such as social security and education. In tandem with the fiscal crisis which was sparked by the 1970s oil crises but grew more acute by the early 1980s, these developments enabled the rolling back of most key elements of the property-based welfare regime such as land reform, universal public subsidies for homeowners and government-provided mortgages during these decades (Honohan, 1992).

Most analysts take the view that Irish welfare, urban and housing policy subsequently converged with the neo-liberal norm in Anglophone countries (e.g. MacLaran and Kelly (Ed.), 2014; Kitchin et al., 2012), but this book disputes this thesis. While acknowledging the clear imprint of neo-liberalism on some aspects of the contemporary Irish welfare system, the analysis presented here highlights the strong continued influence of the legacy of the property-based welfare system. This legacy is evident in a number of remaining policy and socio-economic vestiges of this welfare regime such as the large number of government subsidies for low-income homebuyers and the large number of small farms which require continuing public subsidies to remain economically viable (Norris et al., 2007). The weak banking and mortgage lending regulation exposed following the acute Irish economic crisis which commenced in 2007–2008 are at least partial institutional legacies of property-based welfare because, until the 1980s, the vast majority of mortgages were provided by government (directly by local government or indirectly by building societies which tolerated ongoing government interference in return for generous tax subsidies); therefore, sophisticated structures for regulating commercial providers were not required (Norris and Coates, 2014).

This book also demonstrates that the withdrawal of the expensive public subsidies used to promote property-based welfare did not mean that policymakers also abandoned all of the objectives of this regime – rather, they devised alternative, marketised methods to achieve these objectives. In particular, the tradition of using property to promote economic and employment growth which was integral to property-based welfare has remained influential but since the 1980s has been operationalised primarily by the private sector with significant help from government in the form of banking deregulation, permissive land use planning and some public subsidies (tax incentives for property development and public spending on infrastructure) (Brenner 2006 offers a similar analysis of the USA). Thus the most recent phase in the history of the Irish welfare system has not encompassed merely the "rolling back" of the state as some authors have implied but rather the "rolling out" of government into new spheres of activity and ways of working which aim to support the market rather than replace it (Peck and Tickell, 2002).

Parallel International Stories

Although the focus of the Irish welfare system is unusual in North Western Europe, this book explains that this case is not without international parallels. For instance, Ireland's familistic, property-based welfare system shares key features with the "property-based" welfare states which emerged in developed South East Asian countries. In these countries, governments were willing to support the widespread accumulation of assets, particularly dwellings, in order to enable households to supplement the comparatively ungenerous system of public services and social security by liquidating assets if necessary; reinforce loyalty to the State, support the extended family model and underpin economic growth by animating construction (Groves et al., 2007; Ronald and Doling, 2010). Notably large-scale land reform programmes were successfully implemented in Japan, Taiwan and South Korea after World War II (Dore, 1959; Fei et al., 1979; Shin, 1998). Significant parallels also exist between Ireland's welfare regime and the residential capitalism system employed in the USA, where Prasad (2012) argues that government developed a "Keynesian credit state", focused on enabling asset accumulation, in contrast to the income redistribution-focused Keynesian welfare states of North Western Europe (Allen et al., 2004; Groves et al., 2007; Schwartz and Seabrooke, 2009; Ronald and Doling, 2010).

As well as the extent of the parallels between Ireland and these countries, their causes and significance are examined here. In relation to the former, the role of rural conflicts around access to land and the capital required to develop it and agrarian social movements driving the emergence of property-focused welfare systems in these countries is considered (Prasad 2012 suggests that these factors were also formative influences on the US welfare system). The extent to which Ireland and the other countries which operate property-based welfare systems constitute a distinct social policy regime type – to modify Esping-Andersen's (1990) phrase, they are "fourth world of welfare capitalism" – is also discussed. Notably many of the countries which employ property-based welfare regimes or have done so historically have been among those worst affected by economic and fiscal crises in recent decades, including the global financial crisis of 2007–2008 to date (which had a particularly marked impact on Ireland, the USA and some countries of Southern Europe) and the Asian financial crisis of the late 1990s (Kaufman et al., 1999; Rhodes (Ed.), 2013). The relationship between these economic and fiscal crises and the property-based welfare system is also examined here.

Data and Analysis

One of the reasons why comparative analysis of social policies focuses so heavily on social security benefits and health services which (at least in Western Europe) are funded mainly by direct public spending is that these expenditures are recorded in public spending statements and collated into a comparative database by international organisations such as the OECD and Eurostat, so that they can be easily accessed by researchers. In contrast, the instruments governments can employ to intervene in the provision or redistribution of capital goods such as land

and dwellings are often more numerous, varied and complex and, therefore, difficult for researchers to capture. Taking the example of housing provision, Fahey and Norris (2010) point out that housing is both a service (the accommodation that housing provides) and a capital asset (the dwelling that produces this service); therefore, governments can intervene on the capital side (for instance, by extending homeownership) or the service side (by regulating rented housing) and these interventions can be direct (providing housing or mortgages) or indirect (enabling others to provide housing or mortgages); monetary (grants, subsidies and taxes) or non-monetary (rent control, land use planning).

In an effort to examine all of these potential interventions, this book draws on a wide variety of sources including public spending and survey data, parliamentary debates, government policy statements, the media and existing research to assemble the first comprehensive picture of changes in the scale and nature of the Ireland's property-based welfare state over more than a century. However, this book is not a standard history text based primarily on archival research; rather, the analysis presented here draws heavily on the work of other scholars of Irish history and social policy and reinterprets a fresh interpretation of their arguments. Among these scholars, the work of Daly (1981, 1984, 1997), Dooley (2004), Fahey (2002), Fraser (1996), Garvin (2004, 2005), Carey (2007) and Ó Rian (2014) was particularly influential, and it is important to acknowledge that the analysis offered there stands on the shoulders of these giants.

Unlike most books on Irish history, this book is written by a social scientist and therefore draws on relevant social-scientific theories to explain the policy developments it examines. As explained earlier, this book links the initial focus of government intervention in property subsidisation and redistribution to distinctive socio-economic and political context in late-nineteenth-century and early-twentieth-century Ireland, particularly to the largely rural population and agricultural economy; disquiet about the particular inequities generated by Irish version of agrarian capitalism and the interlinking of these concerns with the nationalist politics and the nation building project. The analysis draws on a number of theories from the sociology, political science and social policy literature to explain why once this capital-oriented focus was established it remained the focus of government welfare policies for almost a century.

This development is related first of all to what historical sociologists call "path dependence" – that is, the tendency for policies to remain stable rather than to change except during periods of acute crisis called "critical junctures" (Mahoney, 2000). The first half of Chaps. 2–5 present a chronological account of path dependence in relevant policy fields between the late nineteenth and late twentieth centuries, which is followed by an account of significant policy change which took place between 1990 and 2007 in Chap. 6. Unlike most history texts, in this book the description of policy developments is presented separately from the analysis of why they occurred. The latter issue is examined in the second half of Chaps. 2–6, and this part of the analysis draws on three of the most prominent themes in the extensive literature on the factors which shape policy decisions (Bengtsson, 2008). Firstly, policy decisions are related to the extensive literature on power which suggests that policies remain stable because their focus reflects the interests of the powerful in society and the social distribution of power rarely changes radically (see Baldwin, 1990; Esping-Andersen, 1985; Lukes, 1974 among many others). Here this issue is examined with reference to the size of different social classes or other social groups, their economic power and effectiveness at mobilising to promote their own interests and electoral competition between parties to secure their votes. Second, the influence of moral or political legitimacy on policy decisions, because certain approaches may be accepted as the best or only way of doing things or complement a specific ideological agenda, is explored using information from parliamentary debates and policy documents. However, assessing the influence of legitimacy is challenging in the Irish context because the political party system does not adhere to the conventional European left/right divide; Irish politicians rarely offer explicitly ideological rationales for policy decisions and many of the rationales which they have offered (such as familism, Catholic social teaching and peasantism) are unusual in the Western European context where social and Christian democracy and liberalism have been the primary ideological influences on welfare state development. Finally, the role of efficiency considerations in driving path dependency is considered. This line of argument suggests that once a particular policy direction is selected it is often adhered to in the long term because of the administrative and political ease of building on existing arrangements and the high transaction costs of changing them (Bengtsson, 2008). In this book, the efficiency drivers of path dependency are also examined from the perspective of economics and public finances and it is argued that the property-based welfare system had key advantages in this regard in the Irish context. Financing poses particular challenges for property redistribution because property and construction is a "lumpy good" which requires high upfront investment; therefore, this issue in examined in significant depth in this book.

Historical developments often gain an air of inevitably in the retelling. This is a particular risk when analysing the factors which contributed to these developments as is done in this book and also a common criticism analysis which employs path dependency as an organising concept (Mahoney, 2000). No social, economic or policy development is enviable of course, and in acknowledgement of this, the analysis presented in this book also takes account of the factors which might have retarded the growth of the Irish property-based welfare system and promoted more investment in a more mainstream model and considers why this did not occur.

Parts of the Story

The analysis of the relationship between property, family and welfare in Ireland presented in this book is organised chronologically into five core chapters, preceded by an introduction and followed by a concluding chapter. The periodisation of the discussion in these core chapters broadly reflects the phases of housing policy development proposed in Bo Bengtsson and colleagues' comparative, historical institutionalist analysis of Nordic countries (see Bengtsson, 2008). These phases are

- establishment (when housing was transformed from a field of periodic crisis management to a permanent item on the policy agenda);
- construction (when the housing policy apparatus and many dwellings were constructed);

- saturation (when housing needs were largely met and the focus of policy moved away from new building) and
- retrenchment (when government housing subsidies and institutions were cut back).

To bring Bengtsson's (2008) typology up to date and tailor it to reflect developments in Ireland, an additional "marketisation" phase is added to capture the most recent stage in the development of the Irish welfare system in which mainstream welfare services expanded but policymakers remained committed to achieving many of the objectives of the property welfare system remained but by supporting the market to achieve these rather than by using exchequer investment to replace the market.

Thus the next chapter focuses on the establishment phase of the property-based welfare system in late nineteenth and early twentieth centuries. It examines the influence of Land War and nationalist politics on rural land and homeownership and also on early social housebuilding activity and government support for urban homebuyers prior to 1922 and government involvement in social services and social security benefits provision. In order to confirm the property-based nature of this system, this chapter first details the relevant policy and public expenditure developments. It then examines the power, legitimacy and efficiency factors which influenced these policy choices and the relationship between the property-based welfare system and spending on "mainstream" welfare activities such as social security benefits and social services. The next three chapters of the book (Chaps. 3–6) adhere to the same structure. Chapter 3 examines the construction phase which stretched from 1922 to 1950. During this time, the socialised homeownership system was established in rural areas; the land redistribution project was radicalised and urban social housing output increased, but the social security and education systems expanded only modestly. Chapter 4 focuses on the saturation phase which took place during the 1950s and 1960s. During this time, the socialised homeownership system was expanded to include urban areas and the first signs of weakness in Ireland's property-based welfare model became evident, but radical expansion occurred in other aspects of the welfare system, particularly social security. The fiscal crisis of the late 1970s and the 1980s and associated retrenchment phase are examined in Chap. 5. This chapter describes how the financing challenges which had slowly accumulated within the property-based welfare system came to a head in the mid-1980s in the context of a severe fiscal crisis and the weakening of the power and legitimacy pillars which had previously supported this welfare regime. In response, the land redistribution and socialised homeownership systems were largely dismantled in the middle of this decade and arrangements for public subsidisation of social housing were also radically reformed (although exchequer support for this housing tenure remained larger for longer) while spending on social security and social services proved much more resilient and continued to grow during the period. Chapter 6 examines the most recent marketisation phase in government intervention in capital redistribution. This commenced in the second half of the 1980s and was characterised by more minimal direct government and greater market involvement in capital redistribution, albeit enabled by significant indirect government support. It was accompanied initially by economic and house price stagnation; then by an unprecedented boom in house prices and in housebuilding and subsequently by a housing and economic bust. This chapter focuses in particular on the challenges associated with transitioning from the property-based welfare system to a more conventional income and services-based system during this period and the impact of the policy, social and ideological legacies of the previous regime. The conclusions to the book are set out in Chap. 7. This chapter sets out the key findings of the book regarding the nature and development of the Irish welfare state and considers their wider implications for the analysis of systems of welfare provision internationally.

References

Aalen, F. (1993). Constructive unionism and the shaping of rural Ireland, c 1880–1921. *Rural History, 4*(2), 137–164.

Allen, J., Barlow, J., Leal, J., Maloutas, T., & Padovani, L. (2004). *Housing and welfare in southern Europe.* London: Wiley-Blackwell.

Baldwin, P. (1990). *The politics of social solidarity.* Cambridge: Cambridge University Press.

Balier, B. (2010). Ordering change: Understanding the 'Bismarckian' welfare reform trajectory. In B. Balier (Ed.), *A long goodbye to Bismarck?: The politics of welfare reforms in continental welfare states* (pp. 19–43). Amsterdam: Amsterdam University Press.

Bengtsson, B. (2008). Why so different? Housing regimes and path dependence in five Nordic countries". *Paper presented to the European Network for Housing Research Conference*, 6–9 Dublin.

Brenner, R. (2006). *The economics of global turbulence: The advanced capitalist economies from long boom to long downturn, 1945–2005*. New York: Verso.

Carey, S. (2007). *Social security in Ireland, 1939–1952: The limits to solidarity*. Dublin: Irish Academic Press.

Castles, F. (1978). *The social democratic image of society*. London: Routledge.

Castles, F. (2002). Developing new measures of welfare state change and reform. *European Journal of Political Research, 41*(5), 613–641.

Central Statistics Office (various years). *Census of population: Housing volume*. Dublin: Stationery Office.

Clark, S. (1987). The political mobilisation of Irish farmers. In A. O'Day (Ed.), *Reactions to Irish nationalism, 1865–1914* (pp. 61–78). London: Hambleton Press.

Daly, M. (1981). *Social and economic history of Ireland since 1880*. Dublin: Educational Company of Ireland.

Daly, M. (1984). *Dublin: The deposed capital: A social and economic history 1860–1914*. Cork: Cork University Press.

Daly, M. (1997). *The buffer state: The historical origins of the Department of the Environment*. Dublin: Institute of Public Administration.

Dooley, T. (2004). *'The Land for the people': The land question in independent Ireland*. Dublin: University College Dublin Press.

Dore, R. (1959). *Land reform in Japan*. London: Oxford University Press.

Esping-Andersen, G. (1985). Power and distributional regimes. *Politics & Society, 14*(1), 223–256.

Esping-Andersen, G. (1990). *Three worlds of welfare capitalism*. Princeton: Princeton University Press.

Esping-Andersen, G. (1999). *The social foundations of post-industrial economies*. Oxford: Oxford University Press.

Fahey, T. (2002). The family economy in the development of welfare regimes: A case study". *European Sociological Review, 18*(1), 51–64.

Fahey, T., & Norris, M. (2010). Housing. In F. Castles, S. Leibfried, J. Lewis, H. Obinger, & C. Pierson (Eds.), *The Oxford handbook of the welfare state* (pp. 479–494). Oxford: Oxford University Press.

Fei, J., Ranis, G., & Kuo, S. (1979). *Growth with equity: The Taiwan Case.* New York: Oxford University Press.

Fraser, M. (1996). *John Bull's other homes: State housing and British policy in Ireland, 1883–1922.* Liverpool: Liverpool University Press.

Freeman, R. (2000). *The politics of healthcare in Europe.* Manchester: Manchester University Press.

Garvin, T. (2004). *Preventing the future: Why was Ireland so poor for so long?* Dublin: Gill and Macmillan.

Garvin, T. (2005). *The evolution of Irish nationalist politics: The reconstruction of nationalist politics, 1891–1910.* Dublin: Gill and Macmillan.

Gibbon, P., & Curtin, C. (1978). The family in social context: The stem family in Ireland. *Comparative Studies in Society and History, 20*(03), 429–453.

Government of Ireland (1937). *Bunreacht na hÉireann/Constitution of Ireland,* Dublin: Stationery Office.

Groves, R., Murie, A., & Watson, C. (2007). *Housing and the new welfare state: Examples from East Asia and Europe.* Aldershot: Ashgate.

Honohan, P. (1992). Fiscal adjustment in Ireland in the 1980s. *Economic and Social Review, 23*(3), 258–314.

Hudson, D. (2003). *The Ireland that we made: Arthur and Gerald Balfour's contribution to the origins of modern Ireland.* Akron: University of Akron Press.

Kaufman, G., Krueger, T., & Hunter, W. (1999). *The Asian financial crisis: Origins, implications and solutions.* New York: Springer.

Kemeny, J. (1981). *The myth of home ownership.* London: Routledge.

Kemeny, J. (2001). Comparative housing and welfare: Theorising the relationship. *Journal of Housing and the Build Environment, 16*(1), 53–70.

Kitchin, R., O'Callaghan, C., Boyle, M., Gleeson J., & Keaveney, K. (2012). Placing neoliberalism: The rise and fall of Irelands Celtic Tiger. *Environment and Planning A, 44*(1), 1302–1326.

Koning, N. (1994). *The failure of agricultural capitalism: Agrarian politics in the United Kingdom, Germany, The Netherlands and the USA, 1946–1919.* London: Routledge.

Korpi, W. (1978). *The working class in welfare capitalism.* London: Routledge and Keegan Paul.

Lukes, S. (1974). *Power: A radical view*. London: Macmillan.

MacLaran, A., & Kelly, S. (Eds.) (2014). *Neoliberal urban policy and the transformation of the city: Reshaping Dublin*. Basingstoke: Palgrave Macmillan.

Mahoney, J. (2000). Path dependence in historical sociology. *Theory and Society, 29*(4), 507–548.

Malpass, P. (2008). Housing and the new welfare state: Wobbly pillar or cornerstone? *Housing Studies, 23*(1), 1–19.

McCullagh, C. (1991). A tie that binds: Family and ideology in Ireland. *Economic and Social Review, 22*(3), 199–211.

Norris, M. (2016). Varieties of home ownership: Ireland's transition from a socialized to a marketised regime. *Housing Studies, 31*(1), 81–101.

Norris, M., & Coates, C. (2014). How housing killed the Celtic Tiger: Anatomy and consequences of Ireland's housing boom and bust. *Journal of Housing and the Built Environment, 29*(2), 299–315.

Norris, M., & Fahey, T. (2011). From asset based welfare to welfare housing: The changing meaning of social housing in Ireland. *Housing Studies, 26*(3), 459–469.

Norris, M., Coates, D., & Kane, F. (2007). Breeching the limits of owner occupation? Supporting low-income buyers in the inflated Irish housing market. *European Journal of Housing Policy, 7*(3), 337–356.

Ó Rian, S. (2014). *The rise and fall of Ireland's Celtic Tiger: Liberalism, boom and bust*. Cambridge: Cambridge University Press.

OECD (various years). *OECD social expenditure database*. Paris: OECD.

Peck, J., & Tickell, A. (2002). Neoliberalizing space. *Antipode, 34*(3), 380–404.

Pooley C. (1992). Housing strategies in Europe, 1880–1930: Towards a comparative perspective. In C. Pooley (Ed.), *Housing strategies in Europe, 1880–1930*, pp. 325–348. Leicester: Leicester University Press.

Prasad, M. (2012). *The land of too much: American abundance and the paradox of poverty*. Harvard, MA: Harvard University Press.

Rhodes, M. (Ed.) (2013). *Southern European Welfare States: Between crisis and reform*. London: Routledge.

Ronald, R., & Doling, J. (2010). Shifting East Asian approaches to home ownership and the housing welfare pillar. *International Journal of Housing Policy, 10*(3), 233–254.

Schwartz, H., & Seabrooke, L. (Eds) (2009). *The politics of housing booms and busts*. Basingstoke: Palgrave Macmillan.

Shin, G.-W. (1998). Agrarian conflict and the origins of Korean capitalism. *American Journal of Sociology, 103*(5), 1309–1351.

Swinnen, J. (2002). Political reforms, rural crises, and land tenure in Western Europe. *Food Policy, 27*(4), 371–394.

Torgersen, U. (1987). Housing: The wobbly pillar under the welfare state. In B. Turner, J. Kemeny, & L. Lundqvist (Eds.), *In between state and market: Housing in the post-industrial era* (pp. 116–127). Gavle: Almqvist and Wiksell International.

United Nations (1958). *Financing of housing in Europe.* Geneva: UN.

2

Establishment: 1870–1921

Introduction

From the starting point of 1870, this chapter examines the establishment phase of Ireland's property-based welfare system, when property redistribution was transformed from a field of periodic crisis management to a permanent item on the policy agenda (Bengtsson, 2008). This choice of starting point reflects the timing of the first significant attempt at land reform – the Landlord and Tenant (Ireland) Act, 1870. Politically the opening decades of this phase coincided with the foundation of the Land League and the start of the Land War in 1879 and the intensive phase of the parliamentary campaign for Irish home rule which was dominated by the Irish Parliamentary Party (commonly known as the Irish Party, which evolved from the Home Rule League founded in 1973). Its final decade coincides with the displacement of this constitutionalist nationalist movement by violent nationalism following the 1916 Rising and War of Independence (1919 to 1921) and of the Irish Party and the home rule cause by the Sinn Féin party and the demand for full independence for Ireland which attracted huge public support in the 1918 general election. The end of this establishment phase logically coincides with Ireland's

© The Author(s) 2016   **21**
M. Norris, *Property, Family and the Irish Welfare State*,
DOI 10.1007/978-3-319-44567-0_2

secession from the UK in December 1921 which was followed by the establishment of the independent Irish state and new policy-making apparatus in early 1922. However, most of the policy developments examined here were in fact introduced prior to 1914 because the outbreak of World War I and the period of Irish nationalist conflict which followed it severely constrained both social spending and policymaking.

The next section focuses on the evolution of land reform policy through three phases: regulation of tenant farmers' rents and security of tenure and then first enabling and finally subsidising these farmers to purchase their farms from landlords. The discussion then proceeds to examine how the example of government action on land redistribution inspired knock-on demands for public subsidisation of the redistribution of other types of capital assets. This precedent was initially most influential in the field of rural social housing which enjoyed extremely generous exchequer support in pre-independence Ireland by international standards. Although this tenure was not a mechanism for capital redistribution during the period examined in this chapter, it ultimately evolved in this direction in the mid-twentieth century. This chapter also argues that the precedent of land reform has significantly less impact on urban policy, as evidenced by the far less generous public subsidisation of urban social housing and home-ownership prior to the 1920s. As Ireland was part of the UK until 1921, Irish-specific policy developments are compared with policies applied to England/Wales or to Scotland only and to UK-wide developments in an effort to assess the distinctiveness of Irish policies and the factors which shaped them. In keeping with the format of the other core chapters of this book, the second half of this chapter relates the property-based welfare system policies to the drivers of power, legitimacy and efficiency.

The Establishment of the Property-Based Welfare System

Land Reform

The 1870 Landlord and Tenant (Ireland) Act was introduced by the Liberal Party government led by William Gladstone (see Table 2.1) but met with strong opposition from within his own party. Therefore, by the time the land bill was presented to parliament, it fell considerably short of the demands of the embryonic Irish tenant farmers' rights movement, led at this time by the Tenant Right League which emerged in 1850 to campaign for the "three Fs" – "fair rent, fixity of tenure and free sale" (Steele, 1974). However, the 1870 Act did increase Irish tenant farmers' security considerably by legally underpinning the so-called "Ulster Custom" (which afforded tenants of this province security of tenure so long as they paid their rent, and to sell the right to occupy their holding to another tenant acceptable to the landlord) and granting tenants in other parts of the country the right to be compensated by landlords for improvements made to their farm on the surrender of their lease and if they were evicted for any reason other than non-payment of rent. Furthermore, by extending these rights only to Ireland, this act signalled that separate arrangements would be applied to tenant farmers in this part of the UK. In another signal of the things to come, the 1870 Act also enabled tenant farmers to borrow two-thirds of the purchase price of their farms from government, but take-up was negligible because few farmers could afford the loan repayments (which were repayable at 5 per cent interest over 35 years), and landlords faced neither obligations not inducements to sell (see Table 2.2) (Aalen, 1993).

Despite the conservative nature of the 1870 Act, tenant agitation diminished in its wake mainly because a boom in agricultural prices across the developed world helped to raise farmers' incomes and reduce evictions. This changed in the second half of the 1870s when the international agricultural depression, coupled with crop failures in Ireland, precipitated a dramatic decline in farm incomes and rise in rent arrears and evictions. This inspired the resurgence of tenant agitation in the form of targeted violence, rent strikes and boycotts and more commonly mass meetings, which evolved into local land leagues. It was these local groups which were organised by Michael Davitt into the Irish National Land League in 1879. Significantly, Davitt had previously been jailed for his work with the Fenians – the primary movement in the physical force/violent tradition of Irish nationalism during this period – but the Land League's first president was Charles Stewart Parnell, a Member of Parliament (MP) in

Table 2.1 Key policy milestones in the establishment of Ireland's property-based welfare system, 1870–1921

Date	Land Reform and Provision of Housing for Farmers	Rural Social Housing	Urban Social Housing	Supports for Homebuyers and Regulation of Private Renting
1866			Labouring Classes (Lodging Houses and Dwellings) Act: provided public loans (at 4 per cent interest, over 40 years) for up to half the cost of building urban social housing	
1868			Artisans and Labourers Dwellings Act: empowered local authorities across the UK powers to repair or demolish insanitary dwellings if owners failed to do so	

Table 2.1 (continued)

Date	Land Reform and Provision of Housing for Farmers	Rural Social Housing	Urban Social Housing	Supports for Homebuyers and Regulation of Private Renting
1870	Landlord and Tenant (Ireland) Act: increased tenant farmers' security of tenure and enabled them to borrow two-thirds of the purchase price of their farms from government (at 5 per cent interest over 35 years)			
1875			Artisan's and Labourers' Dwellings Improvement Act: provided public loans (at 3.5 per cent over 50 years) to build replacement dwellings following urban slum clearance	

(continued)

Table 2.1 (continued)

Date	Land Reform and Provision of Housing for Farmers	Rural Social Housing	Urban Social Housing	Supports for Homebuyers and Regulation of Private Renting
1881	Land Law (Ireland) Act: increased tenants' security of tenure; set up a Land Court (to adjudicate on rent disputes and fix rents for up to 15 years); a Land Commission (to organise the sale of farms to tenants) and provided up to three-fourths of the money tenants needed to buy (at 5 per cent interest over 35 years)	Landlord and Tenant (Ireland) Act: provided public loans for social housing for farm labourers (commonly known as labourers' cottages)		
1882	Arrears of Rent (Ireland) Act: provided grants to enable 100,000 tenants pay their rent arrears and thereby qualify to apply to the Land Courts for rent reductions	Arrears of Rent (Ireland) Act: extended these loans to fund labourers' cottage building		

Table 2.1 (continued)

Date	Land Reform and Provision of Housing for Farmers	Rural Social Housing	Urban Social Housing	Supports for Homebuyers and Regulation of Private Renting
1883		Labourers (Ireland) Act: enabled 12 or more ratepayers to ask their local authority to construct labourers' cottages, funded by a public loan, repayable over 60 years using rents and rates		
1885	Purchase of Land (Ireland) Act: provided £5 million to enable tenants borrow the full purchase price of their farms to be repaid at 4 per cent over 49 years	Labourers' Act: streamlined procedures for approving labourers' cottage schemes and made the loan terms more attractive	Housing Act: offered public loans (at 3.5 per cent over 50 years) to all urban authorities for social housebuilding	
1887	Land Purchase Act provided a further £5 million to extend the land purchase activities of the 1885 Act			

(continued)

Table 2.1 (continued)

Date	Land Reform and Provision of Housing for Farmers	Rural Social Housing	Urban Social Housing	Supports for Homebuyers and Regulation of Private Renting
1890			Housing Act provided loans at 3.125 per cent over 60 years for urban social housing and allowed its construction on greenfield sites for the first time	
1891	Purchase of Land (Ireland) Act: set up the Congested Districts Board and provided £33 million for 100 per cent land purchase loans, repayable over 49 years	Land Act: provided the first central government subsidy for building of labourers' cottages Labourers' Act: included farm labourers' among the 12 proposers required to initiate a labourers' cottage scheme and enabled the Local Government Board to build schemes if local authorities wouldn't		

Table 2.1 (continued)

Date	Land Reform and Provision of Housing for Farmers	Rural Social Housing	Urban Social Housing	Supports for Homebuyers and Regulation of Private Renting
1896		Labourers (Ireland) Act: allowed the sale of labourers' cottages if rental demand was low		
1899				Small Dwellings Acquisition Act: empowers local government to provide SDA mortgages to enable private renting tenants buy their dwellings (if below a specified price) from their landlords
1903	Land Act: provided 100 per cent loans (over 68 years at 3.25 per cent interest) to enable tenants buy and a 12 per cent "bonus" to landlords who sold			

(continued)

Table 2.1 (continued)

Date	Land Reform and Provision of Housing for Farmers	Rural Social Housing	Urban Social Housing	Supports for Homebuyers and Regulation of Private Renting
1906		Labourers' Act: extended the loans provided under the 1903 Land Act to fund rural social housing, specified central government would meet 36 per cent of loan repayments and set-up a dedicated labourers' cottage loan fund		
1908			Housing Act: established the first central government fund to subsidise urban social housebuilding, removed the borrowing limit and increased social housing loan repayment period to 80 years	

Table 2.1 (continued)

Date	Land Reform and Provision of Housing for Farmers	Rural Social Housing	Urban Social Housing	Supports for Homebuyers and Regulation of Private Renting
1908	Land Act: corrected difficulties which hindered the 1903 Act and gave the Land Commission the power to acquire land compulsorily to relieve "congestion"			
1919			1919 Housing Act: equalised subsidies for urban social housing provision in Britain and Ireland	Housing (Ireland) Act 1919: doubled maximum value of dwellings which can be bought using SDA loans, increased repayment periods and introduced grants for building and renovating home-owner dwellings.

Table 2.2 Land sales under the pre-independence land acts, 1870–1909

Date of Act	Number of Farms Bought	Area of Land Bought (ha)	Percentage of Total Land Area Bought	Price (£/ha)
1870	877	21,418	0.2	40.1
1881	731	12,411	0.1	28.7
1885–1888	25,367	381,621	4.6	26.6
1891–1896	46,834	600,290	7.2	22.3
1903	204,341	2,642,190	31.8	26.9
1909	18,658	253,190	3.1	21.9
Total	296,808	3,911,051	47.0	25.9

Source: Swinton (2002).

Westminster and the leader of the Irish Party (Marley, 2007). Thus from early on in its history, the Land League was strongly integrated into the wider Irish nationalist movement.

The combination of pressure from the Irish Party and the Land League created a strong momentum behind land reform. This was one of the factors which inspired the second Irish Land Act in 1881 which effectively legally underpinned the three Fs by extending the Ulster Custom throughout the country and granting compensation to tenants for improvements and creating a Land Court (with the power to adjudicate on rent disputes and fix rents for a period of up to 15 years) and an Irish Land Commission (tasked with organising the purchase of holdings by tenant farmers and provided up to three-quarters of the loan finance they required to do) (see Table 2.1). These measures undermined landlords' absolute rights over their property and implied a measure of "dual ownership" between landlords and tenant farmers (Aalen, 1993). The land purchase provision of this legislation had little impact; it enabled just 731 tenants to become proprietors (see Table 2.2); however, its "fair rent" clause was much more radical in terms of both intent and impact. In relation to the former, this clause marked a radical break with the Liberal Party's traditional *laissez-faire* economic philosophy. In terms of impact, the vast majority of tenants who appealed to the Land Court under the terms of this clause were granted a reduction in rent, mostly of 15–20 per cent. This radically increased the burden of landlord debt, and by 1884, over 1,000 Irish landlords were bankrupt and the financial situation of smaller landlords was particularly weak (Daly, 1981; Curtis, 1980).

The Liberals lost power in 1885 and were replaced by a minority Conservative administration, which lost power after a year but regained it in 1894 and enjoyed an unbroken spell in government until 1905. This change of government ushered in a new phase in land reform policy. The key contribution of the Liberal administrations was to improve the rights of Irish tenant farmers which, in tandem with the widespread depression in agriculture during this period triggered by imports from the new world, undermined the financial viability of landlordism (Koning, 1994). The Liberal's efforts to enable tenant farmers to purchase their farms had minimal impact in the absence of a significant accompanying subsidy to reduce purchase costs. The Conservative governments radically increased government subsidies to enable tenants to purchase their farms and thereby ushered in a third phase in the land reform project which brought an end to the era of mass agricultural landlordism in Ireland.

This process began in 1885 when the Purchase of Land (Ireland) Act (also known, after its sponsor, as the Ashbourne Act) was introduced which allowed tenants to borrow the full purchase price of their farms from government and repay this at lower interest rates and over a longer period than preceding Land Acts (see Table 2.1). Five million pounds were made available to fund its implementation and this Land Act enabled the first large-scale transfer of farm ownership as 25,400 tenants purchased their holdings up to 1888 (see Table 2.2).

A further Land Purchase Act in 1887 provided an additional five million pounds to extend the land purchase activities of the Ashbourne Act. Arthur Balfour, who was chief secretary for Ireland (effectively the UK government minister with responsibility for Ireland) between 1887 and 1891, sponsored both the 1887 Act (known as the Balfour Act) and the follow-up legislation in 1891, which provided £33 million for 100 per cent loans to be repaid over 49 years. The latter measure had a smaller impact than envisaged, probably because the government bonds ("land stock") landlords received in return for selling their estates fluctuated in line with the stock market (O'Riordan, 2011). Nevertheless, this legislation enabled 47,000 tenants to purchase their farms under its auspices (see Table 2.2).

The process of land transfer was largely completed following George Wyndham's appointment as chief secretary for Ireland in 1900. He supported an unprecedented Land Conference between landlords' and tenants' representatives which was held in Dublin in 1902. The unanimous report it produced formed the basis of the 1903 Land Act which provided tenant purchasers with 100 per cent loans from government and, by lengthening repayment periods and further reducing interest rates, cut the cost of repayments to approximately 80 per cent of the previous rent (O'Riordan, 2011) (see Table 2.1). In addition to the purchase price paid by tenants, government funded a 12 per cent bonus payment to landlords who were willing to sell and covered the legal costs of the transfer. These provisions provided landlords with a lump sum sufficient to generate an income similar to that provided by their former holdings. The initiative proved an immediate success, and by 1909, a total of 270,000 tenants had bought their farms and a further 46,000 were in the process of completing the purchase (O'Riordan, 2011). This amounted to a total of 3.9 million hectares of 4.7 per cent of Irish agricultural land which had been purchased from landlords by tenants (see Table 2.2).

The Congested Districts Board

The land reform project received an additional boost in the West of Ireland from the work of the Congested Districts Board (CDB) – a quasi-autonomous government agency, established by the 1891 Land Act to alleviate poverty and "congestion" (i.e. farms which were too small and/or infertile to support the resident household) and stimulate economic growth in this region. According to the board's first annual report, in order to achieve this "its efforts as regards agriculture are to be directed towards increasing the size of small holdings and towards improving livestock and . . . towards aiding and developing all industries including fishing" (Congested Districts Board for Ireland, 1983: 5). Initially its operational area was limited to the poorest rural areas where land values were lowest, which incorporated 3,500,000 acres and 500,000 people in Connaught. The 1909 Land Act doubled the board's operational area to cover nearly one-third of Ireland, encompassing most of the provinces of Connaught and parts of Munster (Fraser, 1996) (see Fig. 2.1). Following its establishment, the board was given a yearly income of between £50,000 and £95,000 per year, but the 1909 Act increased this to £250,000 per annum (Dooley, 2004). The board was shut down in 1923 by the first government of the independent Irish State.

The CDB's first chairman (and it historian) Micks (1925: 12) claimed that it was based on the principle that "it was the duty of the state to attempt to relieve in a durable way widespread poverty, lapsing periodically into absolute destitution", which was a particularly radical departure from the dominant *laissez-faire* economic philosophy of the time. Aalen (1993: 154) points out that the CDB was also a radical departure in governance terms, because it was

> ... the earliest clear example of regional planning in the British Isles, and perhaps in Europe. The policies and procedures of the Board anticipate those of advanced twentieth-century planning in striking ways. They include, for example, the recognition of the need for special co-ordinated treatment of a problem lagging area through an independent regional administration with wide discretionary powers; the idea of preliminary survey and monitoring of progress (Base-Line Reports); a degree of community involvement (parish housing committees), and the search for self-generating growth rather than transient relief measures.

Lee's (1973: 124–125) classic study of *The Modernisation of Irish Society, 1848–1918* dismisses most of the board's economic development activities, which included land drainage, road building and the development of fisheries and cottage industries, as an "extensive waste of time and money" which created little sustainable employment. Breathnach's (2005) more recent comprehensive study of the CDB contradicts this view. In her assessment, the board's achievement was solid in view of its difficult operational context and this analysis is supported by the sustained economic decline the target regions experienced in the decades following the CDB's disillusion.

The Congested Districts
Ireland 1909

Fig. 2.1 Map of the operational area of the Congested Districts Board (1909) and the Irish counties

Land redistribution was also a key economic development strategy of the CDB, but early in its lifetime this work was constrained by the fact that the board could only redistribute "untenanted lands" (in practice mainly land let out on 11-month leases but also mountain pasture, bog land and the demesnes surrounding landlords' mansions). Following the Congested Districts Board (Ireland) Act 1899, land redistribution became the board's principal function and, anticipating this development, its annual report for the preceding year emphasised the below:

> We regard the improvement and enlargement of holdings, through the purchase and re-sale of estates to tenants, as likely to prove . . . the most permanently beneficial of the measures it is in our power to take for bettering the condition of the small occupiers in certain of the congested districts.
>
> (Congested Districts Board of Ireland, 1898: 19)

Its work in this regard was greatly aided by the 1909 Land Act which granted the CDB compulsory powers of land purchase for the relief of congestion (Breathnach, 2005). Furthermore, although not envisaged when the board was founded, the implementation of this land redistribution strategy often necessitated the provision or improvement of dwellings for the farm families (Breathnach, 2005).

By 1923, the CDB had purchased around 1,000 landlords' estates, which contained 60,000 holdings, at a total cost of £10.4 million (Aalen, 1993). Half of these holdings were "improved" by the board (which provided for drainage, fencing, roads, etc.) and 750,000 acres were redistributed for "the relief of congestion" (i.e. to enlarge existing smallholdings or to provide new holdings to cottiers whose existing farms were too small). During this period, the board spent £2.25 million on the improvement of holdings, of which roughly half was devoted to housing. It built around 3,000 new dwellings and provided grants for the refurbishment of 6,000 more, mainly for small farmers or cottiers rather than landless labourers (Aalen, 1993, Fraser, 1996). Occupants of the holdings purchased and redistributed by the board could remain CDB tenants or purchase their holdings under the terms of the relevant Land Acts and, as the purchase subsidies became more generous, most chose to buy (Breathnach, 2005).

Rural Social Housing

Another important step in the establishment of Ireland's property-based welfare system commenced in the early 1880s when local government became involved in enabling the construction of social housing for farm labourers (commonly known as labourers' cottages) in rural Ireland. This development was initiated by the 1881 Land Act, but subsequently extended through a series of "Labourers' Acts" separate from the legislation which governed social housing provision in large towns and cities (the Housing of the Working Classes Acts, which are described later) (see Table 2.1). These segregated legislative codes make it possible to identify variations in the administrative arrangements and public subsidies for urban and rural social housing as is done in Figs. 2.2 and 2.3. These graphs reveal that between 1887 (the first date for which data are available) and 1914 (when output diminished significantly due to wartime public spending restrictions) Irish local authorities built a total of 44,055 social rented dwellings at a cost of £1.6 million.

Crossman's (2006) history of the administration of public welfare supports in late nineteenth-century Ireland paints a vivid picture of how local politics (particularly the influence of the Irish Party on

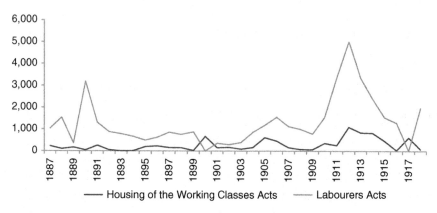

Fig. 2.2 Numbers of social housing units built by local government under the Housing of the Working Classes Acts and the Laborers' Acts, 1998–1918. *Source:* Minister for Local Government (1964)

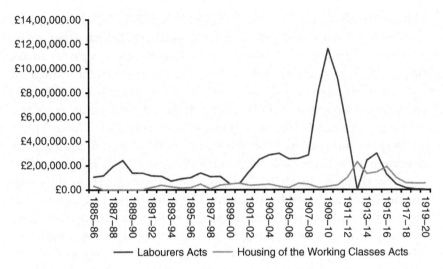

Fig. 2.3 Expenditure on social housing built by local government under the Housing of the Working Classes Acts and the Labourers' Acts, 1887–1918. *Source*: Fraser (1996)

local government, the willingness of ratepayers to fund building programmes and the strength of the local economy which influenced local authorities' income from local property taxes called rates) undermined the implementation of the Labourers' Acts in some districts and increased their use in others, thereby contributing to a spatially uneven pattern of output. Fraser's (1996) history of early Irish social housing identifies the generosity of subsidies from central government as the primary influence on chronological variations in labourers' cottage output.

In terms of the generosity of central government subsidies, Fraser (1996) identifies two distinct periods in the development of the Labourers' Acts: an initial, exploratory phase from the initiation of the programme in 1881 until 1906 and a second, more comprehensive phase after 1906. As mentioned earlier, the 1881 Act (and further legislation in 1882) introduced pubic loans for labourers' cottages, but the terms were too limited and take-up was minimal (Fraser, 1996) (see Table 2.1 and Fig. 2.1). In 1883, the Irish Party proposed a private members bill to parliament which, later that year, became the Labourers' (Ireland) Act. The Irish legislation was closely modelled on early British urban social housing legislation, and it enabled 12 or more local ratepayers to ask their rural local authority to construct a housing scheme which (if sanctioned by regional and central governments) would be eligible for a public loan, repayable over 60 years with the help of tenants' rents and a levy on rates (i.e. local property taxes) (see Table 2.1). The complexity of the administrative procedures and the high cost of servicing the development loans meant that output under the 1883 Labourers' Act was low; therefore in 1885, the new Conservative government passed an amending act which streamlined administrative procedures for approval of building schemes and made the loan terms more attractive to local authorities. It effected a marked increase in output of labourers' cottages to 1,537 dwellings in 1888 (see Fig. 2.2). However, output declined again because the agricultural depression of the late 1880s reduced local authorities' income from rates. In response, in 1890 Arthur Balfour suggested that the unused monies from the land purchase fund established to implement the Land Acts could be used to fund a temporary, experimental subsidy for labourers' cottage building. Irish Party lobbying persuaded him to turn this subsidy into a more permanent feature. As a result, the 1891 Land Act made available an initial grant of £40,000 to subsidise labourers' cottage building and it was agreed that the same amount should be provided in each of the following five years. Thus by 1896, a fund of over £200,000, which generated an annual income of close to £37,000 per annum, was available to subsidise building of labourers' cottages (Fraser, 1996). This measure resulted in a marked increase in output of labourers' cottages to 3,191 new dwellings in 1890 (see Figure 2.1), but Fraser (1996: 34) points out that this subsidy had a symbolic as well as a practical significance: "It was a purely *ad hoc* solution to a specific problem, but it qualifies as the first direct housing subsidy from central government" in Western Europe. Further minor amendments were made to the Labourers' Acts later in 1891 and 1896, but these proved insufficient to return building to its previous highs, and for the remainder of the nineteenth century output of labourers' cottages remained below 1,000 units per year (see Fig. 2.1).

This changed when the Liberal Party won a landslide election in 1905 and held power for the next decade. Their 1906 Labourers' Act extended to rural housing the generous public loan terms of the 1903 Irish Land Act (repayable at 3.25 per cent interest over 68.5 years), created a dedicated labourers' loan fund of £4,250,000 and, most significantly of all, specified that central government would meet 36 per cent of the loan repayments, thereby providing a high public subsidy. These particularly high subsidies enabled rural local authorities to increase the standard of labourers' cottages (three-bedroom cottages replaced two-bedroom units), while keeping rents low and also to increase output radically to over 1,000 united per year in the years following the legislation. Such was the scale of output that the initial fund was soon exhausted and, on foot of lobbying from the Irish Party, a new Labourers' Act was passed in 1911 which provided a further £1,000,000 for cottage building which enabled output to rise to a record 5,015 units in the following year. As a result, the supply of genuine farm labourers was soon exhausted and many cottages built after the 1906 Act were let to households with a marginal connection to agriculture (Fraser, 1996).

Urban Social Housing

In contrast to rural Ireland, the social housing legislation which applied to Irish towns and cities was not specifically tailored for Irish conditions and did not include additional Irish-specific subsidies. Rather, it was generally copied from British legislation (often a number of years later) and employed a subsidy regime which was almost identical to that provided for social housing in British cities.

Ireland's first urban housing legislation – the 1866 Labouring Classes (Lodging Houses and Dwellings) Act – was copied from 1851 British legislation (the two "Shaftesbury Acts" of that year) and applied to Ireland in response to a series of disease epidemics in Dublin (Fraser, 1996). The 1866 Act made public loans available to fund up to half the cost of building an urban social housing scheme. Output under this legislation was minimal and Irish authorities also made very little use of follow-up legislation introduced in 1868, which empowered local authorities across the UK powers to repair or demolish individual insanitary dwelling if owners failed to maintain them. Social housing output did increase under its successor – the 1875 Artisans' and Labourers' Dwellings Improvement Act (the Cross Act) – which was devised originally to clear London's slums but later extended to Ireland. It provided urban authorities with public loans to clear slums and envisaged that the land would then be sold or leased for building replacement new dwellings. The 1875 Act and all preceding urban social housing legislation in Britain and Ireland envisaged that social housing would be provided principally by non-governmental organisations and local authorities would be providers of "last resort". Therefore, none of the early social housing in the UK was municipal (see Table 2.1).

However, this non-governmental implementation strategy proved difficult to operationalise in the Irish context. In contrast to London, where the social campaigner Octavia Hill and charitable Peabody Trust provided substantial numbers of dwellings, the philanthropic housing sector failed to grow in Ireland (Power, 1993). The Iveagh Trust, which was established in 1890 with the help of a donation from the Guinness family, was the only substantial philanthropic housing body in Dublin. It had provided 586 dwellings in the south inner city by 1914 (Aalen, 1990). Daly (1984) links the weakness of this sector to the small size and politically fractured nature of Dublin's socio-economic elite (the only section of society with the resources to instigate major philanthropic projects). This view is echoed by Fraser (1996: 68–69), who argues: "Unionist reformers were often treated as would-be proselytisers . . . For their part, Catholic organisations preferred to deal with moral or temperance issues rather than concrete social problems." Semi-philanthropic organisations, which provided a modest return for investors in social projects, proved a better source of social rented housing in Irish cities – Fraser (1996) estimates that they provided 4,500 dwellings in Dublin by 1914, equivalent to around 15 per cent of the city's housing stock, and in Cork a semi-philanthropic organisation called the Improved Dwellings Company built several of the substantial schemes in the south inner city. However, compared to Britain, Irish semi-philanthropic housing activity was slow to get off the ground (the Dublin Artisans Dwellings Company, which provided 75 per cent of semi-philanthropic dwellings in Dublin, was established in 1876). Furthermore, in both countries, their business model proved unsustainable in the long run. In 1907, the pre-war housing slum ended the activities of Dublin Artisans Dwellings Company and the other Irish semi-philanthropic agencies (Fraser, 1996). These organisations were also criticised by politicians and social reformers because the rents they charged, in order to service development loans and pay investors' dividends, were unaffordable to all but the most comfortable sections of the working class (Power, 1993).

In Ireland, this practical concern to meet the housing needs of poor households, together with the increasingly nationalist-dominated city councils' desire to provide services for their voters following the extension of the franchise to non-property owners, encouraged urban local authorities to become involved in the direct provision of social housing, of which they subsequently became monopoly providers (Fraser, 1996). This municipal social housing provision began on a significant scale when the 1885 Housing Act offered subsidised public loans to all urban authorities; these supports had previously only been available to large cities which excluded many Irish municipalities on grounds of population size (see Fig. 2.2). Irish urban social housebuilding increased when the British 1890 Housing Act was extended to Ireland. This act improved the terms of the loans available for urban social housing provision and, for the first time, supported building on greenfield sites rather than slum clearance sites. As Fig. 2.1 demonstrates, urban local authorities continued to build social housing during the years which followed albeit at an uneven pace. However, despite intensive lobbying from the Irish Party and the introduction of additional subsidies under the Labourers' Acts, no further central government subsidies for urban social housing were provided during the closing years of the nineteenth century. Indeed, Ireland was covered by neither the 1900 Housing Act nor the 1903 Housing Act, which significantly improved British local authorities' access to sites and loans for social housebuilding. This was the first time in three decades when British urban housing legislation was not extended to Ireland, and it attracted vociferous complaints from Irish Party MPs.

This pattern was reversed following the Liberals' election in 1905. Protracted Irish Party lobbying resulted in the passing of a private members' bill proposed by their MP for North County Dublin, JJ Clancy. His Irish Housing Act, 1908, extended the provisions of the 1900 and 1903 Housing Acts to Ireland and established the first central government fund to subsidise urban social housebuilding. The subsidy available (around £6,000 a year) was substantially less than that envisaged in Clancy's original bill and much lower than that available for rural social housebuilding in Ireland at this time but it compares more favourably with those available to British cities (Fraser, 1996). No urban social housing subsidy was made available in Britain until the 1919 Housing Act equalised subsidies for Britain and Ireland (Cole and Furbey, 1994).

The public subsidies provided for in the various Housing of the Working Classes Acts enabled urban Irish local authorities to build 7,565 social rented dwellings by 1914 (see Fig. 2.2). In relative terms, this was a much higher level of output than in Britain where urban local authorities had constructed 23,520 social rented dwellings by 1914, for an urban population 22 times greater than Ireland's (Census Commissioners for Ireland, various years; Register General of England and Wales, various years; Register General of Scotland, various years). However, this building rate was insufficient to meet the scale of housing need in Dublin, where housing conditions were significantly worse than in British cities and where the lack of large industrial employers and the weakness of the Irish building industry impeded the emergence of market solutions to the problem (Daly, 1984).

Urban Private Rented Housing and Homeownership

The strongly rural nature of the early Irish property-based welfare state is further evidenced by the contrasting treatment afforded to urban private renting tenants and aspirant homeowners by government compared to their rural counterparts.

An urban version of the local land leagues, called Town Tenant Associations, emerged in the late nineteenth century and was particularly strong in the towns of Connaught and Leinster. These groups were organised into a national organisation called the Town Tenants' League (TTL) in 1904, and its demands were practically identical to the "three Fs" and the provisions of the 1881 Land Act (McNamara, 2010). They included increasing the security of tenure of urban private renting tenants (households and businesses) and limiting rent increases and ensuring they were compensated for improvements made when tenancies were sold (Fraser, 1996; Graham and Hood, 1996; McNamara, 2010). These demands were in large part granted by the 1906 Town Tenants' (Ireland) Act (see Table 2.1), but unlike their rural counterparts urban tenants' campaigns achieved no further concessions from government after this initial success.

Thus the next significant regulatory intervention in the urban private rented housing sector was entirely unrelated to TTL agitation. This was the Increase of Rent and Mortgage Interest (War Restrictions) Act 1915 which fixed rents on most dwellings across the UK at their August 1914 level and restricted landlords' powers of repossession. It was inspired by a mass rent strike in Glasgow about rent increases as a result of wartime restrictions in housing supply, coupled with an influx of people seeking work in munitions factories. The 1915 Act was intended to expire six months after the end of World War I, but was repeatedly extended and consequently had a significant impact on the private rented housing in the independent Irish state (Threshold, 1981).

The opening decades of the twentieth century also saw the introduction of the first public subsidies for homeownership in Britain and Ireland beginning with the Small Dwellings Acquisition Act (SDA) 1889 which empowered local authorities to provide mortgages to enable private renting tenants buy their dwellings. These SDA loans were only available for dwellings valued below £400, but further legislation in 1919 doubled this limit and also enabled local authorities to provide loans for the improvement of owner-occupied dwellings. The 1919 Act enabled Irish local authorities to provide support in the form of loans, loan guarantees or grants to public utility societies for the first time. These non-profit associations were tasked with building dwellings for sale or rent "to the working class and others" but in practice were mainly built for sale to the middle class (McManus, 1996: 28). Tax deductibility of loan interest was introduced along with the modern income tax system prior to World War I (Heywoon, 2011) (see Table 2.1). Although not designed specifically to subsidise mortgages during periods of high homeownership and high interest rates such as the 1970s, mortgage interest tax relief was a very significant (and costly for government) subsidy.

However, in Ireland (and to a lesser extent Britain), these early home-ownership supports had a minimal impact prior to 1922. Take-up of the SDA loans was low across the UK because local authorities had difficulty in borrowing to fund them and private landlords often proved unwilling to sell their dwellings to tenants (Town Tenants Commission, 1927). Public utility societies operated in Britain from the early 1900s, but take-up of the 1919 legislation in Ireland was impeded by the deteriorating political situation (Skilleter, 1993; McManus, 1999). In both countries, the financial benefits to homeowners of mortgage interest tax deductibility were largely cancelled out by the fact that the imputed rental value of their dwellings (i.e. of the amount which homeowners would have to pay to rent their homes) was liable for tax until the 1960s (Baker and O'Brien, 1979; Heywoon, 2011).

From the perspective of the discussion at hand, these homeowner subsidies are also notable for their lack of special provision for Ireland and minimal Irish input into their framing. The 1899 Act was applied without variation to Britain and Ireland and the only input from Irish MPs on the draft legislation related to removing initial proposals that SDA loans could only be provided in larger towns and cities (e.g. Haslett in House of Commons Debates, 3 July 1899, Vol 73, cols 1361 and Dillon in House of Commons Debates, 3 July 1899, Vol 73, cols 1360). The 1919 Act applied specifically to Ireland but was a straight copy of the British Housing, Town Planning Act of the same year, and Irish MPs' input into the debate on the former concentrated on ensuring that both measures would be identical (e.g. O'Neill in House of Commons Debates, 4 December 1919, Cols 122, 553).

Drivers of the Establishment of the Property-Based Welfare System

Among the factors which inspired the foundation of the property-based welfare system in the late nineteenth and early twentieth centuries, the growing power of the tenant farmers, particularly those who rented mid-sized farms, was the most significant. Their influence was in part numerical and in part due to their political skills at mobilising in their own interests and linking their cause with the Irish nationalist movement and gaining the support of the Catholic Church. The relative increase in the power of these middle-class farmers during the period under examination in this chapter, while the power of the urban working and middle classes failed to increase commensurately, is the key reason why this opening phase in the development of the Irish welfare system was overwhelmingly rural and focused on redistribution of property rather than of income or social services.

The numerical power of middle-class tenant farmers was augmented by the socially and spatially uneven pattern of population decline after the Great Famine of the mid-1840s (see Fig. 2.4). The Irish population contracted from almost 8.2 million people in 1841 to 4.3 million in 1911. The vast bulk of this decline was concentrated in the 1840s and 1850s (an estimated one million people died in the famine and a further 1.25 million emigrated in the years which followed), but the trend persisted over the longer term due to a combination of high migration

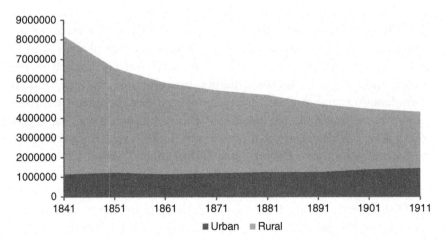

Fig. 2.4 Population of urban and rural districts of the Island of Ireland, 1841–1911. (*Source*): Census Commissioners for Ireland (various years).

Note: "Urban areas" refers to towns and cities with 2,000 or more inhabitants (these are termed "civic areas" in the census)

and a falling birth rate which was related to a low marriage rate (Census Commissioners for Ireland, various years; Guinnane, 1997).

Notably, from the perspective of the discussion at hand, this population decline was concentrated in rural areas and, due to the interlinking of demographic change and rural economic restructuring, was driven primarily by the loss of the poorer sections of the rural population (see Fig. 2.3). Before the famine, the land owned by Protestant Ascendancy landlords was let out to "middlemen", who would sub-let some or all to mainly Catholic sub-tenants, who would in turn sub-let sections to smaller farmers known as cottiers and these different levels of farmers were supported by a large population of (waged) landless farm labourers (Clark, 1982). That post-famine population decline was overwhelmingly concentrated among these economically weak cottiers and farm labourers. Numbers of farm labourers declined by 73 per cent between 1841 and 1891, the number of cottiers living on less than 1 acre declined by even more than this and small tenant farmers with holdings of between 5 and 15 acres also declined significantly, while the total male population declined by 38 per cent during this period. Concurrently, tenant farmers' holdings became larger (15–30 acres, or over) in most regions of the country, apart from in the West where subsistence farming persisted (Census Commissioners for Ireland, various years and see Fitzpatrick's 1981 definitive study of this period). Fitzpatrick (1980) points out that these developments resulted in the polarisation of the rural class structure, between the remaining landless farm labourers and medium to large tenant farmers, because the cottiers who were formerly in the middle of this rural class hierarchy largely disappeared. It also meant that tenants of middle-sized farms became the numerically dominant class in most Irish regions (Turner, 1996).

As Fig. 2.4 also reveals, in the Irish case, rural population decline was driven by migration abroad rather than to cities and towns in Ireland. In 1841, 86 per cent of the Irish population lived in rural areas, as did 75.9 per cent of the population in 1881. Urbanisation did accelerate in the closing decades of the nineteenth century and the early twentieth century (66.5 per cent of the population lived in rural areas in 1911), but in absolute terms the urban population increased by just under 200,000 people between 1881 and 1911. This strongly rural settlement pattern reflected Ireland's industrial underdevelopment and the associated short-age of employment in towns and cities. In the south of Ireland, urban areas were principally trading centres and the industry which did emerge was largely concentrated in around Belfast (at that time the largest city on the island) in the northeast (Bielenberg, 2009). This delayed pattern of urbanisation was highly significant from the perspective of the development of the property-based welfare system because it reduced urban dwellers' influence on the direction of policy developments, while amplifying the influence of rural tenant farmers.

As mentioned earlier, these disparities in numerical power of farmers and city dwellers were reinforced by urban/ rural imbalances in political power due to variations in the mobilisation skills of these different groups and in the extent to which their campaigns complemented other key contemporary political and social powers causes (Garvin, 2005). For instance, the Land League's success was helped by two political factors: unlike similar campaigns in the past, such as the Tenant Right League of the 1850s, the League was a truly mass agrarian movement which represented the vast majority of tenant farmers and it was strongly integrated in nationalist politics at a time when the influence of the nationalist movement was growing and crucially was also supported by the Catholic Church (Steele, 1974). In contrast, the concentration of unionist voters into urban areas (particularly Dublin and Belfast) and the failure of both working- and middle-class urban tenants to mobilise effectively in their own interests meant that, at least under Parnell's leadership, the Irish Party paid little more than lip service to urban housing concerns (Fraser, 1996).

Clark (1982) attributes the mass nature of the Land League movement to the changes in the rural class structure wrought by the famine. By the 1870s, he suggests:

> There remained important divisions amongst famers related to variations in the size of holdings. As a result of the decline in subletting, however, they were not divided as much as before . . . They were now in most cases simply tenants who had no under tenants and whose landlords were landowners.

> (Clark, 1982: 23)

In the southern part of Ireland, the Land League's political influence was also helped by support from the Catholic Church which, Larkin (1975) argues, played a key role in assuaging larger tenant farmers' initial wariness of the Land League, particularly of its violent and quasi-legal activities. This support was first expressed by the prominent Nationalist Archbishop Croke in a widely reported sermon in 1880 and subsequently came to be shared by the majority (but by no means all) of the Catholic hierarchy and almost all ordinary priests who were more closely acquainted with the plight of their parishioners and in many cases were themselves sons of tenant farmers and were active participants in the League's activities.

The Land League's integration into the wider Irish nationalist movement and complementarity of the aims of both movements also increased the League's influence. The extent of the integration between the two movements is evidenced by the politics of the League's first leaders – Davitt was a former Fenian activist and Parnell was the leader of the Irish Party – and also by the Irish Party's dependence on financial contributions from the Land League (Marley, 2007). The complementarity of the aims of both movements is evidenced by the "new departure" plan which Davitt had contributed to framing in 1878. This plan attempted to unite the parliamentary and physical force strands of Irish nationalism and (in part because both strands drew much of their support from urban areas) proposed that nationalists should afford priority to the land question in order to secure the allegiance of rural Ireland (Clark, 1971). Thus, according to Kane (2000: 245): "After decades of self-defeating struggle between conflicting nationalist factions, the Land War provided the 'political field' on which a unified national identity emerged from public discourse over landlordism and British domination".

In addition, the Land League's emergence coincided with (and propelled) the expanding influence of the Irish Party in the UK parliament in the 1870s and 1880s. This development reflected the slow extension of the franchise down the income scale (in 1884, all men who owned or rented property were granted the right to vote in UK parliamentary elections) and the fact that the Liberal Party was increasingly dependent on the support of the "Celtic fringes" of the UK to stay in power in

Westminster during this period (the Irish Party emerged from the 1895 general election holding the balance of power). This influence was further cemented by the Irish Party's unusually disciplined and professional nature, by the standards of the times. It was one of the first modern political parties which required candidates to promise to vote with the party in parliament, operated a strict whip system and paid MPs a salary from party funds to enable middle-class candidates run for office decades before the introduction of exchequer-funded salaries for MPs (Cruise O'Brien, 1946).

The decade long time lag between the first serious policy action on land reform (1870) and on labourers' cottage provision (1881) suggests that farm labourers were less powerful than tenant farmers which is not surprising in view of the shrinking numbers of the former and the Land League's domination by the latter (Clark, 1987). However, between 1881 and 1903, every Land Act was followed within five years by a Labourers' Act which introduced additional public subsidies for rural social housing provision, and this indicates that farm labourers' political power had increased by this period despite their continuing numerical decline (see Table 2.1). This development was partially the result of the extension of the franchise – the Irish Party (and rural local authorities) did not prioritise farm labourers' interests until the farm labourers gained the right to vote in local government elections in 1898. In addition, from this time farm labourers began to agitate more effectively for their own interests through political means like the Irish Labour and Industrial Association (founded in 1882) and the Land and Labour Association (founded in the early 1890s) and also sporadic violence (O'Connor, 2011). Farm labourers' political campaigning had the potential to fracture the Irish Party's carefully constructed pan nationalist alliance because the labourers were campaigning not for cottages but for farms, and meeting this demands would require the redistribution of land from the tenant farmers who were lynchpins of the Irish Party's support base. Fraser reports (1996: 27) that "Parnell tried to get round this problem by promising plots of unwanted semi-waste land to landless labourers, but it was hardly an appealing offer. Better housing was a far less controversial concession". On their part, Westminster governments were willing to concede further spending on labourers' cottage building in order to drive a wedge between the different elements of the Irish Party's rural support base (Hudson, 2003).

As mentioned earlier, during the decades after its foundation the Irish Party also exhibited limited interest in urban issues due to the small size of the urban electorate and its domination by unionist political interests. The situation changed marginally from the 1890s when the extension of the franchise inspired the party to try to dominate urban local authorities and the potential of the embryonic labour movement and urban housing campaigns to undermine this objective and its broader pan nationalist alliance forced it to devote more attention to urban housing. However, urban concerns were never afforded a similar priority to rural housing and the land question by the Irish Party and, in addition to the small size of the urban electorate, the fragmented nature of urban social movements was a key reason for this. The Irish labour movement was weak at this time and unlike the Land League was actively opposed by the Catholic Church and urban housing campaigns had emerged slowly and unevenly during the late nineteenth century (O'Connor, 2011). As mentioned earlier, Town Tenant Associations were established at this time, but were not organised into a national organisation (the Town Tenants' League) until 1904 and even then the TTL failed to grow into a truly mass movement (McNamara, 2010). Although the TTL founder – Councillor Coughlan Briscoe – was also a prime mover behind the growth of local authority housing provision in Dublin, analyses of the movement's membership indicate that it was overwhelmingly dominated by small businessmen and their activities focused primarily on the rights of urban private renters not on promoting urban social housing provision (Fraser, 1996; McNamara, 2010; Graham and Hood, 1996). These demands were granted by the 1906 Town Tenants' (Ireland) Act, but, unlike the Land League, McNamara (2010: 146) reports that after this initial victory "lacking clear leadership and direction. [the Town Tenants' League] ... embarked on a new phase of fragmented and dramatically less successful agitation". He also argues that the TTL members' concern about remaining respectable among other ratepayers prevented it from becoming sufficiently radical to attract working-class support or to achieve meaningful reform. Daly (1984) suggests that the Irish Party's commitment to resolving Dublin's housing problems was further weakened by the large number of nationalist sympathisers among the urban slum landlord class (several of whom were elected as councillors in Dublin) and the tendency of the party's councillors to use their position as a platform for nationalist agitation rather than to improve the administration of the city. Thus while the party was willing to campaign at Westminster for additional subsidies for urban social housing in Ireland, its elected members of the Dublin municipal government were "not in a position to adopt a critical stance on urban housing" (Daly, 1984: 318).

These power-related drivers of the foundation of the property-based welfare system were reinforced by its increasing legitimacy while alternative services and income redistribution-focused approaches to welfare promotion failed to garner the levels of legitimacy in Ireland they had secured in other European countries at this time. This occurred in part because land reform and rural social housing policies managed to simultaneously complement several, sometimes contradictory, ideological agendas promoted by different strands of Irish nationalism, large and small tenant farmers and Liberal and Conservative governments in Westminster.

From the period of the Land War, the project of freeing tenant farmers from the oppression of Anglo-Irish landlords and freeing the Irish nation from British domination came to be intrinsically linked in the mind of Irish nationalist voters and politicians to the extent that achieving the former was regarded as vital to securing the latter. However, this did not mean that the supporters of these causes had held uniform interpretations of the meaning of these freedoms. Just as the Irish nationalist movement included activists who would be satisfied with Irish home rule within the UK and republications who would settle for nothing less than full Irish independence, Kane (1997: 262) argues that land reform movement spoke to two distinct ideological agendas within he identifies in discourses of "retribution" and "conciliation" in Land League activists' speeches and press statements. The small tenant farmers of the West were intent on achieving retribution. They wanted to regain complete ownership of the land and by extension the nation back from their colonial "oppressors" and thereby gain proper compensation for past wrongs perpetrated on them. Their more comfortable counterparts who rented larger farms on better land in the south and east were interested in securing an arrangement which would enable them to increase their economic prosperity and secure their social status. They opposed the violent and quasi-legal methods employed by their Western counterparts and, at least during the initial stages of the land reform campaign, would have been satisfied with securing the three Fs (fair rent, free sale and fixity of tenure) and were not ideologically wedded to eradicating the landlord class (Kane, 1997). These differing agendas of course reflected the contrasting radical and conservative interpretations of fundamental purpose of land reform held by Davitt and Parnell. The former viewed land reform as a radical equalising project and favoured nationalisation of land to facilitate a type of agrarian socialism; the latter viewed land reform as a means to effect a much more conservative revolution and envisaged that peasant proprietorship would enable the emergence of a class entrepreneurial middle-class farmers who would be the economic, social and political backbone of Ireland post home rule (Marley, 2007; Garvin, 2005). In common with nationalist politics more broadly, the different land reform agendas generated tensions within the Land League, but its ability to unite proponents of these different agendas within a single organisation (at least until the end of the nineteenth century) enabled the League to become a mass organisation which was strong enough to push forward the land redistribution element of the property-based welfare state.

Among Westminster governments, the dominant ideology which shaped views on the role of the state at this time was of course *laissez-faire* economics and the property-based welfare state was a significant departure from this approach. The Conservatives' and Liberals' willingness to countenance such a departure in the Irish case was inspired by different factors. As explained later, for the Liberal Party political expediency, particularly the need to retain the Irish Party's support for its minority administrations, was a key driver. For the Conservative governments of the late nineteenth and early twentieth centuries, ideological factors, principally the policy of "constructive unionism" which was devised during the period of the Irish chief secretaryships of Arthur Balfour (1887–1891), his brother Gerard Balfour (1895–1900) and George Wyndham (1900–1905), were influential. This policy had the objective of "killing home rule with kindness" by eliminating the negative features of the union with Britain which was long exploited by nationalists for political gain (Hudson, 2003).

Constructive unionism was manifested in several policy arenas including reform of local government (the modern Irish local government system was established by the Irish Local Government Act, 1889) and of the university system and the establishment of Department of Agriculture and Technical Instruction in 1891. However, as evidenced by the sponsorship of the Land Acts by the Balfour brothers and Wyndham, the "second phase" of the land reform project which focused on the extension of peasant proprietorship in Ireland was the central plank of constructive unionism. According to Curtis (1963: 175):

> ... Balfour called it [peasant proprietorship] "the one permanent hope for Ireland"; most of the cabinet regarded purchase as the "final solution" to the land question; and Lord Salisbury who had been concerted to purchase by the act of 1881, argued that without this policy the clash of interests between landlords and tenants would go on forever ...

The establishment of the CDB was also a key plank of the Conservative's constructive unionist policy, but unsurprisingly, in view of the particularly radical nature of this initiative, this was not the sole inspiration for the board's establishment (Breathnach, 2005). Social conditions in the west of Ireland were very poor compared to the rest of the country and worsened considerably in the late 1880s due to the agricultural depression and poor harvests. These problems were energetically highlighted by the Quaker philanthropist James Hack Tuke in the newspapers and the pamphlet *Irish Distress and Its Remedies* which he published in 1881. This work inspired Gerard Balfour to seek Tuke's advice on the design of measures to address poverty in the west of Ireland and to undertake a tour of what would later be designated as the CDB's operational area in 1890 (Breathnach, 2005). Events subsequent to the demise of constructive unionism provide further evidence of the key influence of this approach. For instance, Fraser (1996: 84) links Ireland's exclusion from the 1900 and 1903 Housing Acts (which provided better loan terms for urban social housebuilding in Britain) to the fact that constructive unionism "was at this point being obstructed by those who were determined not to give increased spending powers to Nationalist municipalities" (Fraser, 1996: 82, 84).

For both Conservative and Liberal administrations, however, efficiency concerns were more significant drivers of their willingness to support the establishment of the property-based welfare system than ideology. In addition, efficiency issues played a central role in shaping the details of the design of property-based welfare system.

In the case of the Liberals, for instance, the practical political imperative of staying in power in Westminster was a key motivation for their willingness to support the first phase of land reform. The 1870 Landlord and Tenant (Ireland) Act was inspired by Gladstone's concern to undermine support for the Fenian violence in England in the 1860s and to unite the fractured Liberal party around the "Irish question" in the 1868 general election (Fraser, 1996). Further land reform legislation in 1886 and between 1892 and 1894 was necessitated by these minority Liberal administrations' reliance on Irish Party votes in Westminster. Liberal support for the labourers' cottage building programme in the early twentieth century was in part inspired by the party's ideological swing to the left during this period and also in part due to its continued dependence on Irish Party votes. During this period, labourers' cottages functioned as a "consolidation prize" to compensate for the Irish Party for the Liberals' failure to deliver home rule which had been repeatedly blocked by the House of Lords (Fraser, 1996).

The Conservatives' Pauline conversion to the cause of Irish peasant proprietorship from the mid-1880s and the equally surprising parallel *volte-face* among many Irish agricultural landlords (as evidenced by their willingness to participate in the 1902 Dublin Land Conference) reflect the increasing economic weakness of the agrarian capitalist model at this time. As mentioned earlier, by 1884 over 1,000 Irish agricultural landlords were bankrupt and many others were in financial difficulty (Daly, 1981). Their money troubles were in part related to global economic change – the globalisation of trade in food products which precipitated the agricultural depression in the 1880s had undermined the viability of large capitalist farms across Europe (Koning, 1994). However, in addition to these structural factors, Campbell (2002) points out that by 1900 landlords' rental incomes had been reduced by an average of 28 per cent as a result of the Land Courts' rent revisions and further revisions due in 1912 were likely to result in an overall reduction of close to half. Thus, he suggests: "By the turn of the century, the majority of Irish landlords had accepted that they would not be reinstated as the absolute owners of their estates, and recognized that their best option would be to sell their land under the Land Purchase Acts" (Campbell, 2002: 758). According to Curtis (1963: 175), the leaders of the Conservative party reached a similar view: "Minister saw in peasant proprietaries a means not only of ending the inequities of 'dual ownership' – which they blamed on Gladstone".

Thus in economic terms, the final phase of land reform during which peasant proprietorship was heavily subsidised by government was the logical conclusion of the first phase in which agricultural tenancies were regulated: the latter had helped to undermine landlords' financial position and the former came to be regarded by politicians and most landlords as the only economically viable solution to this. From this perspective, the government subsidised peasant proprietorship was as much as a "bail out" for the agricultural landlord class as a concession to the demands of their tenants. Indeed, Michael Davitt criticised the 1903 Act as a "financial God-send for the landlords" (cited in Marley, 2007: 273).

The Conservative's conversion to the cause of labourers' cottage building and willingness to sanction the establishment of the CDB was also influenced by similar practical concerns. As one Conservative member of the House of Lords put it, the 1881 Land Act "destroyed, to a great extent, in Ireland the only person who was in the habit of building cottages – namely, the landlord" (cited in Fraser, 1996: 26). Therefore in landlords' absence, the State was forced to step in and house farm labourers. The inadequacy of the existing Poor Law arrangements for poverty relief for conditions in Connaught also inspired the establishment of the CDB. Poor Law supports were funded by domestic rates paid by local property owners, but property values and therefore these local property tax payments and poor relief expenditure were much lower than average in this part of Ireland, and Gerard Balfour had strong concerns about the quality of Poor Law administration throughout the country (Breathnach, 2005).

Both the Conservatives' and the Liberals' willingness to support generous government spending on land reform and rural social housing in Ireland reflected the potential for these policies to be framed as "exceptional" on the grounds of the uniqueness of the scale of the problems in rural Ireland in the UK context and therefore not inspire knock-on claims for their extension to Britain. Arthur Balfour summarised this rationale as follows when he argued against the extension of Irish rural social housing subsidies to cities and towns in an 1891 parliamentary debate:

> The Act for providing agricultural labourers with cottages is a very exceptional one; but, then, it is admitted that the condition of the agricultural labourers in many parts of Ireland is exceptional, and there is no analogy between their condition and that of the agricultural labourers in England and Scotland.
>
> (Cited in Fraser, 1996: 81–82)

This analysis proved to be correct and, despite the emergence of a crofters' rights movement in Scotland (which was actively supported by Michael Davitt himself), land reform never progressed beyond regulation of agricultural tenancies in Britain (Marley, 2007). Thus, apart from the Scottish Congested Districts Board, which was founded in 1897 to deal with congestion in the Highlands, almost none of the exceptional policy supports for rural Ireland leaked into British policy (Breathnach, 2005).

In contrast, additional subsidies for urban social housing provision in Ireland were resisted on the grounds that they were very likely to inspire demands for their replication in more urbanised Britain. On this basis, for instance, the UK Treasury lobbied furiously to reduce the subsidies proposed in JJ Clancy's original version of the 1908, Irish Housing Act (Fraser, 1996). After the Clancy Act was passed, the chief secretary for Ireland dismissed lobbying from the Association of Municipal Authorities of Ireland for an increase in the urban housing subsidies it provided on the grounds that

> The rural problem in Ireland was a peculiar one requiring and certainly receiving very advantageous pecuniary assistance from the State. The

problem of urban slums however was not confined to Ireland, but involves the opening of the flood-gates of public grants to the other cities of Kingdom.

(Cited in Daly 1984: 312)

Daly's (1984) history of Dublin during this period reveals that this unwillingness to concede that exceptional support from central government was required to deal with the city's slums caused grave problems. The particularly low and insecure wages of Dublin's working class impeded their ability to pay rent, and the mass exodus of the middle classes to the new suburbs of Rathmines, Rathgar and Donnybrook (administered by separate local authorities at this time) reduced the city authority's income from local property taxes, called rates. In this context, the Dublin municipality experienced severe difficulties in funding social housing on the scale required to effect a significant improvement to the housing conditions of the city's poor.

Conclusions

This chapter has traced the slow, uneven but ultimately upward trajectory of government action to generate and redistribute capital assets in late-nineteenth-century and early-twentieth-century Ireland which was achieved primarily by transferring ownership of farmland from landlords to tenant farmers and providing social housing for farm labourers. In terms of *character*, these policy developments were not unique in the wider UK or international context of this time. Governments in several European countries supported the conversion of large capitalist farms which had previously dominated the agricultural economy into smaller family-owned farms and rural decline and poverty was a problem in Britain too, with the result that a Scottish Congested Districts Board similar to the Irish CDB was established in 1897 (Cameron, 1996; Swinnen, 2002). However, the *scale* of government spending on land reform and rural social housing provision in Ireland was unparalleled during this period. Between 1870 and 1903, Irish land reform policy progressed from regulating tenancies to enabling and then subsidising tenant farmers to purchase their holdings, whereas land reform policies in Britain failed to develop beyond the tenancy regulation stage (Swinnen, 2002). As a result, in 1870, 96 per cent of agricultural land in Ireland was leased (rather than owned) by farmers, but this had fallen to just 25 per cent by 1920, whereas the comparable figures for Scotland are 92 and 87 per cent, respectively (Swinnen, 2002). By 1914, Irish local authorities built 44,055 social rented dwellings, 82.8 per cent of which were located in rural areas (Fraser, 1996). In contrast, their counterparts in England, Scotland and Wales had built only half as many social rented dwellings (24,000) by 1914 and only 98 per cent of British social housing was in towns and cities (Malpass and Murie, 1999). Levels of social housebuilding in most other Western European countries were even lower at this time, and dwellings of this type were very rarely provided outside towns and cities (Pooley, 1992).

The scale of the government investment in the production and redistribution of capital assets indicates that a property-based welfare system had begun to emerge in late-nineteenth-century and early-twentieth-century Ireland. By 1921, UK government loans to enable Irish tenant farmers purchase their farms amounted to £101 million, whereas Irish GDP has been estimated at £135 million (Fahey, 2002). Public spending on social housing provision varied significantly year-on-year during the period under review in this chapter, but Fig. 2.3 demonstrates the board trend was one of increased spending to a peak of £1,189,657 in the 12 months to September 2010. The Congested Districts Board for Ireland (various years) also invested in housing provision; although its annual reports do not provide comprehensive longitudinal picture of trends in this spending, they indicate that its scale was significant – the CDB spent £142,202 on housing in the 12 months to September 1909 for instance. In contrast, direct spending on Poor Law administration, which was broadly equivalent to more conventional European benefits and services welfare state model (it included the entire social security benefits, health and social services prior to the introduction of old age pensions in 1908), was £1,063,567 in the year to September 1914 (Eason,1928).

Despite the very substantial spending on property-based welfare prior to Irish independence, this period also saw unprecedented expansion of the social services and benefits to the extent that the mainstream Irish welfare state was among the most comprehensive in the developed world at this time. However, almost without exception these new mainstream welfare services were initiated in Britain and extended to Ireland sometimes after considerable delay. The Poor Law system, subsidies for urban social housing provision, public education provision, unemployment insurance and old age pensions are all in this category (Crossman, 2006). The extension of these measures to Ireland was on occasions the result of lobbying Irish politicians or the Catholic Church, but in many cases it was not and the measures were applied to Ireland as a matter of course. Furthermore, in all cases the initiation of these measures was driven by socio-economic and political developments in Britain which concurrently inspired the establishment of welfare states across Europe – urbanisation and industrialisation and the related emergence of trade unions and of social democratic parties as the franchise was extended. Indeed, it is notable that the only major British social policy initiative which was not extended to Ireland prior to 1922 – the health insurance elements of the 1911 National Insurance Act – remained a British-only measure as a result of lobbying from the Irish Catholic Church and medical profession (Barrington, 1987).

In contrast, the analysis presented in this chapter has linked the emergence of this distinctive Irish property-based welfare model and its overwhelmingly rural focus to the influence of local factors which were unusual in the wider UK and Western European context. These are the numerical power and unparalleled mobilising ability of the tenant farmer lobby in late nineteenth century; the overwhelming national consensus in support of the legitimacy of their claims and some efficiency-related concerns which helped to reinforce these policy trends. The agricultural depression of the late 1880s had undermined the economic viability of the capitalist farming in Europe and inspired governments in several countries to support their replacement by family farms which had the key economic advantage of necessitating the provision of only a living for the owner occupier's household (which, if necessary, could be a subsistence lifestyle) rather than a profit for the owner and wages for workers (Koning, 1994). However, in Ireland, the combination of this economic context with the marked increase in the proportion of the population who were tenant farmers after the famine and interlinking of their campaign with the Irish home rule movement propelled government support for land reform to much greater levels than in Britain and the rest of Europe with the result that the scale of peasant proprietorship in Ireland expanded well above than the Western European norm (Swinnen, 2002).

When considered in retrospect, events can seem somewhat inevitable, but the halting expansion of land reform and rural social housing provision in Ireland demonstrates that this was far from the case. These policies faced consistent opposition from UK Treasury officials and uneven but sometimes overwhelming opposition from Westminster politicians which at times stymied their growth. However, as these policy reforms progressed, a type of self-reinforcing logic emerged as one reform necessitated complementary follow-up action. For instance, the first phase of land reform bankrupted large sections of the agricultural landlord class which inspired government to subsidise tenant farmers to purchase their farms and resolve this situation. The end of agricultural landlordism removed the potential that the aristocracy would provide housing for farm labourers and thereby inspired government intervention to provide rural social housing instead.

The other key argument proposed in this chapter is that the property-based welfare policies adopted at this time are not just an interesting historical footnote; rather, they marked a "critical juncture" in the Irish welfare system when particular institutional arrangements were adopted from a number of alternatives and these choices influenced long-term policy trajectories (Mahoney, 2000). By creating a large class of owner occupier farmers, for instance, the Land Acts ensured that the Irish society and the economy would remain strongly agrarian well into the twentieth century, and, due to their economic power, force of numbers and the moral authority afforded by their central role in the nation building project, this class would enjoy strong political influence in the independent Irish state (Garvin, 2005). Only two-thirds of tenant farmers bought their farms prior to independence, and the power of the agrarian lobby rendered it almost unthinkable that the leaders of the infant Irish state would not compete the peasant proprietorship project despite the very significant costs involved (Garvin, 2004).

The early property-based welfare policies described in this chapter also set an influential precedent. Once government had conceded the availability of public subsidies for land purchase and rural social housebuilding, this inspired lobbying for the deepening of these subsidies and their extension to previously excluded sections of the population. The concentration of early social housing provision on rural Ireland and the structural impediments to urban housing production, highlighted earlier, meant that the urban households, particularly the poor, were the section of the population in greatest need of government subsidies. The labourers' cottage building programme eliminated practically all of the one-roomed mud cabins in rural Ireland (categorised as "fourth-class" dwellings in the census) before World War I – the 1881 census recorded 38,804 rural dwellings in this category, but this declined to 4,828 by 1911. In contrast in 1881, 42.7 per cent of Dubliners lived in fourth-class dwellings (mainly "tenements" – the formerly grand upper-class houses which had been crudely converted for multi-occupancy), but 33 per cent did so in 1911 (Census Commissioners for Ireland, various years). The precedent established by the CDB was also particularly important in the development of the property-based welfare state because these policies signalled a marked radicalisation of the land reform project. The Land Acts had enabled the transfer of landownership from landlords to the tenants who rented the land, whereas the CDB redistributed the land itself from landlords and large tenant farmers to cottiers who previously had very limited access to this resource. From the early 1900s, the United Irish League (the successor to the Land League) commenced a vocal campaign for the extension of the latter policy and, following the practical eradication of the landlord class, their attentions focused on the mainly Catholic "grazier and "rancher" farmers who owned or rented large farms for cattle production (Higgins and Gibbons, 1982).

References

Aalen, F. (1990), *The Iveagh Trust: The first hundred years.* Dublin: Iveagh Trust.
Aalen, F. (1993). Constructive unionism and the shaping of rural Ireland, c 1880–1921. *Rural History*, 4(2), 137–164.

Baker, T., & O'Brien, L. (1979). *The Irish housing system: A critical overview.* Dublin: ESRI.

Barrington, R. (1987). *Health, medicine and politics in Ireland 1900–1970.* Dublin: Institute of Public Administration.

Bengtsson, B. (2008). Why so different? Housing regimes and path dependence in five Nordic countries. *Paper presented to the European Network for Housing Research Conference,* 6–9 July, Dublin.

Bielenberg, A. (2009). *Ireland and the industrial revolution: The impact of the industrial revolution on Irish industry, 1801–1922.* London: Routledge.

Boléat, M. (1982). *The building society industry.* London: Allen & Unwin.

Breathnach, C. (2005). *The congested districts board, 1891–1923.* Dublin: Four Courts Press.

Cameron, E. (1996). *Land for the people?: The British government and the Scottish Highlands, c. 1880–1925.* East Linton: Tuckwell Press.

Campbell, F. (2002). Irish popular politics and the making of the Wyndham Land Act, 1901–1903. *The Historical Journal, 45*(4), 755–773.

Census Commissioners for Ireland (various years). *Census of Ireland – 1841–1911.* Dublin: HMSO.

Clark, S. (1971). The social composition of the Land League. *Irish Historical Studies, 17*(68), 447–469.

Clark, S. (1982). The importance of agrarian classes: Agrarian class structure and collective action in nineteenth century Ireland. In P. J. Drudy (Ed.), *Ireland: land, politics and people* (pp. 11–36). Cambridge: Cambridge University Press.

Clark, S. (1987). The political mobilisation of Irish farmers. In A. O'Day (Ed.), *Reactions to Irish nationalism, 1865–1914* (pp. 61–85). London: Hambleton Press,

Cole, I., & Furbey, R. (1994). *The eclipse of council housing.* London: Routledge.

Congested Districts Board for Ireland (1983). *Annual reports.* Dublin: HMSO.

Crossman, V. (2006). *Politics, pauperism and power in late nineteenth-century Ireland.* Manchester: Manchester University Press.

Cruise O'Brien, C. (1946). The machinery of the Irish Parliamentary Party, 1880–85. *Irish Historical Studies, 5*(17), 55–85.

Curtis, L. (1963). *Coercion and conciliation in Ireland, 1880–1892.* Princeton: Princeton University Press.

Curtis, L. (1980). Incumbered wealth: Landed indebtedness in post-famine Ireland. *The American Historical Review, 85*(2), 332–367.

Daly, M. (1981). *Social and economic history of Ireland since 1880*. Dublin: Educational Company of Ireland.

Daly, M. (1984). *Dublin: The deposed capital: A social and economic history 1860–1914*. Cork: Cork University Press.

Dooley, T. (2004). *Land for the people: The land question in independent Ireland*. Dublin: University College Dublin Press.

Eason, C. (1928). Report of the Irish Poor Law Commission. *Journal of the Statistical and Social Inquiry Society of Ireland*, XIV(5), 17–43.

Fahey, T. (2002). The Family Economy in the Development of Welfare Regimes: A case study, *European Sociological Review*, 18(1), 51–64.

Fitzpatrick, D. (1980). "The disappearance of the Irish Agricultural Labourer, 1841–1912. *Irish Economic and Social History*, 8(1), 66–92.

Fraser, M. (1996). *John Bull's other homes: State housing and British policy in Ireland, 1883–1922*. Liverpool: Liverpool University Press.

Garvin, T. (2004). *Preventing the future: Why was Ireland so poor for so long?* Dublin: Gill and Macmillan.

Garvin, T. (2005). *The evolution of Irish Nationalist Politics: The reconstruction of nationalist politics, 1891–1910*. Dublin: Gill and Macmillan.

Graham, B., & Hood, S. (1996). Social protest in late nineteenth-century Irish towns – The House League Movement. *Irish Geography*, 29(1), 1–12.

Guinnane, T. (1997). *The vanishing Irish: Households, migration, and the rural economy in Ireland*. New Jersey: Princeton University Press.

Heywoon, A. (2011). *The end of the affair: Implications of declining home ownership*. London: Smith Institute.

Higgins, M.D., & Gibbons, J. (1982). Shop-keeper graziers and land agitation in Ireland. In P. J. Drudy (Ed.). *Ireland: Land, politics and people* (pp. 93–118). Cambridge: Cambridge University Press.

House of Commons (various years). *House of commons debates*. London: Hansard.

Hudson (2003). *The Ireland that we made: Arthur and Gerald Balfour's contribution to the origins of modern Ireland*. Akron: University of Akron Press.

Kane, A. (1997). Theorizing meaning construction in social movements: Symbolic structures and interpretation during the Irish Land War, 1879–1882. *Sociological Theory*, 15(3), 249–276.

Kane, A. (2000). Narratives of nationalism: Constructing Irish national identity during the Land War, 1879–82. *National Identities*, 2(3), 245–264.

Koning, N. (1994). *The failure of agricultural capitalism: Agrarian Politics in the United Kingdom, Germany, the Netherlands and the USA, 1846–1919*. London: Routledge.

Larkin, E. (1975). *The Roman Catholic Church and the creation of the modern Irish State, 1878–1866*. Philadelphia: The American Philosophical Society.

Lee, J. (1973). *The modernisation of Irish Society, 1848–1918*. London: Macmillan.

Mahoney, J. (2000). Path dependence in historical sociology. *Theory and Society, 29*(4), 507–548.

Malpass, P., & Murie, A. (1999). *Housing policy and practice*. London: Macmillan.

Marley, L. (2007). *Michael Davitt: Freelance radical and frondeur*. Dublin: Four Courts Press.

McManus, R. (1999). The "Building Parson" – The role of Reverend David Hall in the Solution of Ireland's early twentieth-century housing problems. *Irish Geography, 32*(2), 87–98.

McManus, R. (1996). 'Public Utility Societies, Dublin Corporation and the Development of Dublin, 1920–1940'. *Irish Geography*, 29(1), 27–37.

McNamara, C. (2010). A tenants' league or a shopkeepers' league?: Urban protest and the town tenants' association in the west of Ireland, 19096–1918. *Studia Hibernica, 36*, 135–160.

Micks, W.L. (1925). *An account of the congested districts board for Ireland, 1891–1923*. Dublin: Eason and Son.

O'Connor, E. (2011). *A labour history of Ireland, 1824–2000*. Dublin: University College Dublin Press.

O'Riordan, T. (2011). Home rule and the elections of 1885–6. In D. ÓCorráin, & T. O'Riordan (Eds.), *Ireland, 1970–1914: Coercion and conciliation* (pp. 68–87). Dublin: Four Courts Press.

Pooley C. (1992). Housing strategies in Europe, 1880–1930: Towards a comparative perspective. In C. Pooley (Ed.), *Housing strategies in Europe, 1880–1930* (pp. 325–348). Leicester: Leicester University Press.

Power, A. (1993). *Hovels to high rise: State housing in Europe since 1850*, London: Routledge.

Register General of England and Wales (various years). *Census of England and Wales, 1911*. Edinburgh: HMSO.

Register General of Scotland (various years). *Census of Scotland, 1911*. Edinburgh: HMSO.

Skilleter, K. (1993). The role of public utility societies in early British town planning and housing reform, 1901–36. *Planning Perspectives, 8*(2), 125–165.

Steele, E. (1974). *Irish land and British politics: Tenant-right and nationality 1865–1870*. Cambridge: Cambridge University Press.

Swinnen, J. (2002). Political reforms, rural crises, and land tenure in western Europe. *Food Policy, 27*(4), 371–394.

Threshold (1981). *Private rented: The forgotten sector.* Dublin: Threshold.

Town Tenants Commission (1927). *Interim report on the working of the Small Dwellings Acquisition Act 1899.* Dublin: Stationery Office.

Turner, M. (1996). *After the famine: Irish agriculture, 1850–1914.* Cambridge: Cambridge University Press.

3

Construction: 1922–1947

Introduction

Following the signing of the Anglo Irish Treaty, in January 1922 the southern two-thirds of the Island of Ireland gained independence (and was renamed the Irish Free State) while the northeastern corner (Northern Ireland) remained part of the UK. The Free State's establishment was preceded by a series of political and violent revolutions. These commenced in an armed uprising in 1916, which was followed by the trouncing of the Irish Party in the 1918 general election by a new nationalist party called Sinn Féin (which refused to attend Westminster but rather established a separate parliament called Dáil Éireann as well as a separate court and public administration system in southern Ireland) and then by the war of independence between 1919 and 1921. The signing of the Anglo Irish Treaty also prompted the fracturing of Sinn Féin into pro- and anti-treaty sides which engaged in a civil war between 1922 and 1923. The pro-treaty side took the reins of government and formed themselves into the Cumann na nGaedheal party, while the anti-treaty side initially

© The Author(s) 2016
M. Norris, *Property, Family and the Irish Welfare State*,
DOI 10.1007/978-3-319-44567-0_3

boycotted the independent parliament, until a significant rump formed the Fianna Fáil party in 1926, and fought its first general election in the following year.

The period from Irish independence until 1947 was the "construction phase" of Ireland's property-based welfare state, when government involvement in property redistribution was radically extended in terms of variety of policy measures employed, proportion of the population covered and (due to the enormous investment on land reform in the early 1900s), to a lesser extent, expenditure. This chapter examines this development in three policy fields: land reform, supports for home-ownership and social housing provision and sales of these dwellings to tenants. It examines the power, legitimacy and efficiency-related factors which inspired these policy developments.

In political terms, the period under examination here coincides with governments led by Cumann na nGaedheal between 1922 and 1932 (in 1933, this and a number of smaller parties merged to form Fine Gael) and by Fianna Fáil between 1932 and 1948. In economic terms, the first half of this period in particular was challenging. During its early years, the finances of the new State were precarious and the government faced marked difficulties in raising sufficient loans to finance its activities and meeting the crippling costs of maintaining the army and repairing damage to infrastructure which occurred during the civil war (Lee, 1989). Following an agricultural depression in the early 1920s, the economy stagnated for much of the remainder of this decade. Between 1932 and 1938, Irish exports were undermined by the Anglo Irish "economic war" which saw the introduction of trade tariffs by both governments (Ó Gráda, 1997). The approaches of these two political parties to spending on benefits and social services also contrasted significantly. Driven in part by the fiscal crisis and a concern to demonstrate their fiscal prudence and in part by inherent social and fiscal conservatism, Cumann na nGaedheal introduced swingeing public spending cuts to balance the national accounts (Ferriter, 2004). Public spending was reduced from £42 million in 1923 to £28 million in 1926, which in part reflected reduced military spending but was also related to the abolition of some subsidies for urban social housebuilding and reductions in public sector wages and old age pensions. Concurrently, the standard rate of income tax was also cut from five to three shillings in the pound in 1927/1928 (Powell, 1992; Lee, 1989). In contrast, the populist and more interventionist by inclination Fianna Fáil party increased social spending, particularly on social security benefits (Cousins, 2003). However, irrespective of these fluctuations in benefit and social services spending and in the scale of government intervention in the wider economy, this chapter will demonstrate that the property-based welfare system expanded steadily throughout this period.

Construction of the Property-Based Welfare System

Land Reform

The first evidence of the bright prospects for property-based welfare in independent Ireland came very soon after the State's establishment in the 1923 Land Act (see Table 3.1). This act enabled the Land Commission to compulsorily purchase and sell to tenants the landlords' remaining tenanted holdings and thereby rectified the situation of approximately 114,000 tenants who had not purchased their holdings under the terms of the pre-independence Land Acts (Dooley, 2004b). However, as well as completing the process of reassigning land title from landlords to tenant farmers which was initiated under British rule, this legislation significantly expanded and radicalised the land reform project and by extension property-based welfare. The 1923 Act also conferred the Land Commission with powers to compulsorily acquire untenanted (i.e. not let out to long-term tenants) land from large landowners and redistribute it to smallholders if this was required to relieve "congestion" (farms too small or infertile to generate a living). This potentially affected some two million acres which remained in the ownership of Anglo Irish landlords in 1922 (Dooley, 2004b). As explained in Chap. 2, prior to independence, the CDB had carried out similar work in the west of Ireland. The 1923 Act abolished the CDB, but transferred its land

Table 3.1 Key policy milestones in the construction of Ireland's property-based welfare system, 1922–1947

Date	Land Reform	Government Provided Mortgages for Homeowners	Universal Government Subsidies for Homeowners	Direct/Indirect Government Provision of Homeowner Dwellings
1922				Million Pound Scheme enabled local government to build 2,000 dwellings, most of which were sold to homeowners.
1923	Land Act empowered the Land Commission to compulsorily purchase and sell to tenants the landlords' remaining tenanted holdings and also redistribute landlords' untenanted holdings to relieve congestion.			

Table 3.1 (continued)

Date	Land Reform	Government Provided Mortgages for Homeowners	Universal Government Subsidies for Homeowners	Direct/Indirect Government Provision of Homeowner Dwellings
1924			Grants for owner occupiers building or reconstructing homes introduced by the 1919 Housing Act were increased and local authorities empowered to give new homeowners rates remission.	
1925				Eligibility for home owner grants extended from individuals to building cooperatives called Public Utility Societies.
1927	Town Tenants' Commission investigated low take-up of the Small Dwellings Acquisition Act (SDA) mortgages.			

(continued)

Table 3.1 (continued)

Date	Land Reform	Government Provided Mortgages for Homeowners	Universal Government Subsidies for Homeowners	Direct/Indirect Government Provision of Homeowner Dwellings
1929		Local authorities granted access to the Local Loans Fund to borrow for social housing and SDA mortgages. This fund was previously only used for other infrastructure. Cork and Dublin City Councils are excluded from access.	Housing Act made remission of rates mandatory for new homeowners and enabled local authorities to supplement central government grants to self-builders and public utility societies with extra grants or loans.	
1931	Land Act irons out difficulties in the implementation of the previous legislation.	Housing Act allows SDA mortgages to be used to buy new dwellings or for self-building. Increases the max cost of dwellings eligible for SDA mortgages from £800 to £1000.	Housing (Miscellaneous Provisions) Act reduced homeowner building grants to £20.	

Table 3.1 (continued)

Date	Land Reform	Government Provided Mortgages for Homeowners	Universal Government Subsidies for Homeowners	Direct/Indirect Government Provision of Homeowner Dwellings
1932			Homeowner building grants increased again, with higher grants payable to farmers and farm labourers and also limited eligibility for reconstruction grants to this cohort.	Public Utility Society grants increased to match rising homeowner grants.
1933	Land Act removed most restrictions on compulsory purchase of untenanted landlords' estates and farms which had been tenant purchased under the Land Acts.			
1935		The Local Loans Fund was significantly expanded. Cork and Dublin City Councils remained ineligible for access.		

(continued)

Table 3.1 (continued)

Date	Land Reform	Government Provided Mortgages for Homeowners	Universal Government Subsidies for Homeowners	Direct/Indirect Government Provision of Homeowner Dwellings
1936	Land Act closed legal loopholes used by land-owners to avoid lands being appropriated by the Land Commission.		Home purchase grants reduced for urban areas, but this reduction is not applied to rural areas.	Labourers Act afforded rural social tenants the right to buy their dwellings, with repayments set at 75 per cent of rents.
1946	Land Act enabled the Land Commission to repossess tenant-purchased farms which had been sub-let or ineffi-ciently farmed.			
1948		The maximum market value of a dwelling which can be purchased using an SDA mortgage was increased from £1750 to £2,000.	Housing Act increased homebuyer grants and introduced supplemen-tary grants for low income homebuyers.	Public Utility Society grants increased to match increases to homeowner grants.

Source: Department of Local Government and Public Health (various years); Dooley (2004b); O'Connell (2004).

redistribution responsibilities to the Land Commission and consequently extended the scope of these activities countrywide.

The majority of untenanted land was not really vacant but rented out on 11-month leases to commercial farmers known as graziers who generally used it to fatten cattle prior to sending them to market. Most other untenanted land (e.g. gardens, demesnes surrounding landlords' houses, land intermingled with woodland and stud farms) was exempted from compulsory purchase by the 1923 legislation (Jones, 2001). The 1923 Act also provided for the compulsory purchase of farms which had been tenant purchased under the previous Land Acts, but specified that this could only be done if untenanted land was not available locally to relieve congestion and obliged the Land Commission to provide farmers in this category with a replacement farm of similar value. Therefore, this provision was not widely used during the 1920s (Dooley, 2004b).

Under the terms of the 1923 Act, owners and also tenants whose land was compulsorily acquired were paid not market value but "fair value" and compensated not in cash but in "land bonds". These bonds yielded a fixed rate of return payable in biannual instalments, the level of which varied according to the year of issue (it was set at 4.5 per cent by the 1923 Act). Government periodically bought back a proportion of bonds for their original value (the bonds to be redeemed in this way were selected by lottery) and any remaining bonds were redeemed after 30 years at the discretion of the Minister for Finance (Jones, 2001; Kirk, 1991, in Dáil Éireann, various years, Vol. 414, No. 10, Col. 578). Bondholders who did not wish to wait for the government to buy their bonds could also sell them on the stock market, although those who did so had no guarantee that the bonds would be bought for their original value.

To enable allottees (as recipients of redistributed land were known) to purchase, they were given an advance by the State, which was repaid in instalments called annuities. This was a similar arrangement to that which applied to tenant farmers who purchased their farms under the pre-independence Land Acts and its continued use after 1922 reflected the lack of commercial credit available particularly to small farmers (Dooley, 2004b). Under the terms of the 1923 Act, annuity repayments generally extended over a period of 66 years, with an annual interest rate fixed at 4.75 per cent. Notably, arrangements for funding land redistribution provided a significant subsidy to allottees who usually purchased land for substantially less than the price at which the Land Commission had originally acquired it. In addition, the Land Commission often undertook improvements to allotted holdings which were funded by a (repayable) advance to the allottees or by a (non-repayable) government grant (Dooley, 2004b). The 1923 Act specified that farmers with inadequate holdings should receive first priority when redistributing land, former employees of the landlords whose estates were redistributed should be next in order of priority, followed by local tenants who had been evicted by landlords in the past and landless persons (Jones, 2001). This order of priority, particularly the low-priority-afforded landless persons, provoked much controversy during the early years of the State and was amended on a number of occasions by Fianna Fáil governments (Dooley, 2004b).

The architecture for implementing land redistribution put in place by the 1923 Act remained largely unchanged until the Land Commission was finally closed in the early 1990s but, the focus of the programme changed significantly and so did the level of the public subsidy. Within months of taking office in 1932, Fianna Fáil refused to pass on the annuity payments arising from the pre-independence Land Acts to the UK exchequer (as the Irish government was obliged to do by the 1923 Anglo Irish Finance Agreement). This policy stance reflected years of sporadic campaigning by agrarian and republican groups, which had intensified from 1931 when the Great Depression began to undermine the price of Irish agricultural products (Ryan, 2005). The land annuities dispute sparked off the Anglo Irish economic war – a retaliatory trade dispute with the Irish and UK governments introducing tariffs for the others' goods – which had a negative impact on Irish exports (Ferriter, 2004). However, the dispute yielded significant benefits for the Irish government because it continued to collect the annuity payments (despite opposition from farmers' representatives) and used them for general expenditure and to compensate those most negatively affected by the trade dispute.

Furthermore, under the terms of the 1938 Anglo Irish agreement which ended the economic war, the UK government not only removed the trade tariffs, it wrote off the land annuities in exchange for a once-off payment of £10 million – in view of the fact that the pre-independence annuity payments totalled around £5 million per annum at that time, this was a very good deal for the Irish side (Neary and Ó Gráda, 1991).

The retention of the land annuities also enabled the government to increase subsidies to the agricultural tenant purchasers, and Fianna Fáil's first Land Act in 1933 cut in half the annual interest payable by post pre- and post-independence allottees on land annuities and wrote off the arrears on annuities of more than 3 years (Dooley, 2004b). By decreasing the debt smallholders had to take on in order to purchase their holdings and increasing their equity, the 1933 Land Act radically extended the redistributive and therefore the property-based welfare element of the land reform programme. This progressive redistributive tendency was reinforced by other provisions of this act. For instance, it afforded landless persons (particularly veterans of the War of Independence) higher priority in the scheme for redistributing land and removed most of the restrictions on the purchase of untenanted landlords' estates. In addition, the act withdrew most restrictions on the Land Commission's powers to compulsorily acquire farms which had been tenant purchased under the Land Acts by stipulating that only residential owners who lived on or adjacent to their land and farmed it themselves would be eligible to receive alternative holdings if their lands were compulsorily acquired; that alternative holdings provided need no longer be of similar value to the compulsorily acquired lands (instead, the former owner would be compensated for the difference in land bonds) and repealing the veto on the compulsory acquisition of land if untenanted land was available locally to relieve congestion (Dooley, 2004b). These provisions were strengthened by additional legislation introduced by Fianna Fáil in 1946 (see Table 3.1).

Jones (2001) identifies graziers as the group most negatively affected both by the land redistribution measures introduced by the 1923 Land Act and their extension in 1933 and afterwards. The majority of the land let by landlords to graziers on short leases was redistributed to smallholders following the 1923 Land Act. The provisions of the 1933 Land Act further disadvantaged graziers who owned their holdings because they rarely lived on site (many had day jobs in urban areas) and the cattle rearing on which they concentrated was far less employment intensive than the tillage favoured by smallholders. However, Section 32(3) of the 1933 Act specified that only land that "is producing an adequate amount of agricultural products and is providing an adequate amount of employment" was exempt from compulsory acquisition. So as Dooley (2004a: 192) points out that these provisions raised the spectre that few were safe from the Land Commission's clutches:

> After 1933 farmers had to live with the fear that the Land Commission might resume their holding if it was large enough to be needed for the relief of local congestion, or if a land-hungry neighbour reported that it was not being worked in a satisfactory manner, or if the farmer fell on hard times and was unable to repay his annuities owing to any one of a variety of causes such as economic depression, illness or infirmity.

Due to the widening of eligibility for compulsory purchase, coupled with the completion of much of the time-consuming associated legal groundwork and appeals during the 1920s, the scale of land redistribution increased significantly in the 1930s. Between 1923 and Fianna Fáil's election in March 1932, the Land Commission acquired and divided 330,825 acres among 16,587 allottees (an average of 36,758 acres per annum) (Dooley, 2004b). In contrast, during the first five years of the Fianna Fáil administration (ending on 31 March 1937), almost 353,000 acres were divided among 25,802 allottees (i.e. 70,600 acres per annum) (Dooley, 2004a).

Finalising the process of redistribution of land title from landlords to tenants and commencing the nationwide process of land redistribution from large or smallholders in 1923 required enormous borrowing by the infant State. To generate the seed capital to fund the land bonds, the Irish government negotiated an STG£30 million loan facility which, due to the Free State's lack of creditworthiness, had to be backed by a British government guarantee (*Irish Times*, 1923, April 23). Patrick Hogan, Minister for Agriculture and Lands in the first Cumann na nGaedheal government, explained to his fellow parliamentarians that this:

> …is an enormous loan, when compared with ordinary development, say, with the development of the Shannon [reference to a major hydro-electric scheme], a gigantic scheme, but at the outset which is only going to cost about five million pounds. Thirty million pounds for land purchase is a very expensive matter very much more expensive than any other.
>
> (Hogan in Dáil Éireann, 1925, Vol. 10, No. 18, Col. 1543)

Once this seed capital was secured, the ongoing costs of maintaining the system were less onerous because many of the costs were transferred to those whose land was being appropriated. This is becuase, the available evidence indicates that the fair value price paid to vendors prior to 1950 was less than market value (Nunan, 1987). Furthermore, because vendors were paid in land bonds rather than cash upfront (prior to 1950), so as Ferriter (2004: 315) points out they were "in effect forced to lend to the state". The annuities paid by allottees accrued in a Land Bond Fund which funded the payment of interest on and redemption of land bonds. This substantially reduced the ongoing financing costs of the scheme, although Ferriter's (ibid.) assessment that "schemes cost little in terms of current expenditure" is a significant underestimation.

As Fig. 3.1 demonstrates, from the foundation of the State annuity payments were consistently insufficient to cover withdrawals from the Land Bond Fund, so to ensure the fund's adequacy the exchequer had to make additional contributions (Kirk, 1991, in Dáil Éireann, various years, Vol. 414, No. 10, Col. 578). After the reductions in annuity payments introduced by the 1933 Land Act, these exchequer contributions spiked, and although they subsequently declined, throughout the remainder of the 1930s and 1940s these contributions were on average more than double the level which had prevailed during the 1920s. In addition, grants for improvements to allottee's holdings and the administrative costs of the Land Commission and Department of Lands were also exchequer financed and the former also spiked in the mid-1930s on the back of the

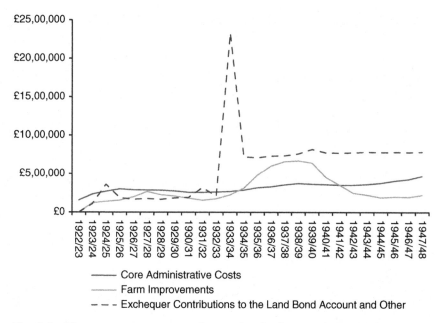

Fig. 3.1 Direct government spending on land reform, 1922/1923–1947/1948. *Source*: Generated from the annual appropriations account as collated in Duanaire economic history database held by the National University of Ireland, Galway.

Note: "Core administrative costs" include salaries and incidental expenses. Exchequer contributions to the Land Bond Account and Other relates mainly to spending on the former but it also includes minor spending on administration and farm improvements which could not be disaggregated from the total

energetic land redistribution activity which followed the 1933 Land Act (Dooley, 2004a).

As well as these direct costs, there is some evidence that the land reform programme generated significant indirect costs for the exchequer. A paper published by Charles Eason in 1931 links the high level of interest on the national debt to the high levels of additional government which was not formally defined as part of the national debt and his analysis places particular emphasis on the contribution of land bonds in this regard, which were reported separately from the national debt (albeit in the same column) in the national accounts of this period. Figure 3.2

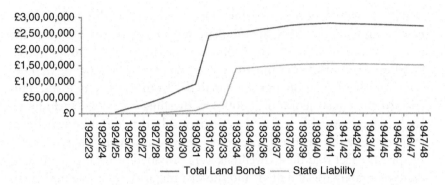

Fig. 3.2 Land bonds outstanding at the end of each fiscal year and the component of which were a direct state liability, 1922/1923–1947/1948. *Source*: Generated from the annual finance accounts as collated in Duanaire economic history database held by the National University of Ireland, Galway.

Note: Data on the State's liability between 1923/1924 and 1924/1925 are not available

reveals that land bonds' outstanding value was £24.2 million at the end of the 1931/1932 fiscal year, of which £2.4 million were a direct State liability, whereas the "formal" national debt was £20.89 at this time (Eason, 1931). Outstanding land bonds rose to around £27 million during the mid-1930s and 1940s and, following the De Valera government's partial write-off of the land annuities, the State was responsible for servicing approximately half of these (between £26 and £27 million) by means of its contributions to the Land Bond Fund (see Fig. 3.2). Notably, from the perspective of the discussion at hand, Eason's (1931) paper also highlights the contribution of another key element of the property-based welfare state to inflating the "unofficial national debt" – local government stock issues, which were mainly used to fund housing expenditure. These are examined in the two sections which follow.

Homeownership Subsidies

The Free State's early and energetic policy action on land reform was paralleled by a similar action on other key bulwark of the property-based welfare system – homeownership. Developments in this regard commenced immediately after the foundation of the State in 1922 when the new government established a "Million Pound Scheme" to fund housebuilding – half of which came from a central government grant, 12.5 per cent from local taxation and the remainder from short-term loans. This enabled the construction of 2,000 new dwellings by 1924, including a landmark estate at Marino in the northern suburbs of Dublin which was influenced by the British "garden city" design movement (Fraser, 1996). Despite the fact that these dwellings were provided by local government, they were rarely social rented, and the vast majority were sold directly to homeowners who paid off the purchase price in weekly instalments in a variation of the "annuity payments" system used in the land reform programme (Aalen, 1992). Fraser (1996) links the decision to sell the Mario houses to financial considerations – Dublin City Council has initially planned to rent them out, but could not afford to service the associated development loans if it did do so. However, the local authority employed this model to sell almost all of the suburban estates it built prior to World War II, and until the 1970s the construction of dwellings for immediate sale by local government continued at an uneven, but significant, pace at times and helped to bolster homeownership rates particularly during times of undersupply from the market in urban areas (National Economic and Social Council, 1977).

When the million pound fund was exhausted, the 1924 Housing Act significantly increased the existing grants for the self-building or reconstruction of owner-occupied dwellings which had been introduced prior to independence by the 1919 Housing Act (see Chap. 2). The generosity of the subsidies introduced in 1924 (they funded approximately one-sixth of average housebuilding costs at the time) provoked some controversy at the time because the same legislation set grants for social housing provision by local authorities at an identical level, while abolishing the exchequer interest subsidies on loans for social housebuilding which had been introduced prior to independence (O'Connell, 2007). The 1924 Act also empowered local authorities to grant homeowners remission from residential rates (local property taxes) for a number of years after the dwelling's purchase and further legislation in 1929 made the granting of rates remission compulsory (see Table 3.1).

The 1925 Housing Act extended the availability of these homeowner grants from individuals to public utility societies and empowered local government to provide and service land to enable these societies develop housing (McManus, 1996). Thus despite their slow start in the early 1900s (see Chap. 2), this cooperative movement grew rapidly after Irish independence. Four hundred public utility societies were established between the 1920s and 1960s, and though the scale of their output is unclear, it appears to have been very significant particularly prior to World War II and in Dublin (Acheson et al., 2004). They built 9 per cent of all new housing nationwide between 1922 and 1927 and 27 per cent of all private housing built in Dublin between 1933 and 1938 (ibid.; McManus, 1996). However, though mandated to build housing for sale or rent for the "the working class and others", McManus (1996: 28) reports that in practice "few of the public utility societies of the 1920s and 1930s seem to have had any philanthropic intent" and the vast majority of the dwellings they constructed were sold to homeowners.

As well as directly and indirectly developing housing for sale and providing grants and tax subsidies, government provided households with the credit necessary to purchase a dwelling using the system of mortgage loans established by the Small Dwellings Acquisition Act, 1899. As mentioned in Chap. 2, take-up of SDA loans was low in the early 1900s and this remained the case after Irish independence. No annual data on SDA loans are available for most of the 1920s, but Daly (1997) estimates that an only 100 SDA mortgages per annum on average were issued during this decade, and Fig. 3.3 reveals that only 16 were issued in 1931/1932. Daly (1997) attributes this low take-up to low demand and the Town Tenant's Commission (1927), which also investigated this issue in the 1920s, concurs with her analysis, but it suggests that lending was also constrained by qualification criteria for borrowers and financing arrangements. SDA loans were intended to enable private tenants purchase their dwellings, but landlords were often unwilling to sell. Furthermore, local government stock issues were traditionally used to fund SDA loans (and social housing provision) in urban areas, but in the 1920s and 1930s, concerns about local authorities' creditworthiness made it difficult to sell stock at affordable rates of interest (Town Tenants Commission, 1927; Corporation of Dublin, 1945). Thus,

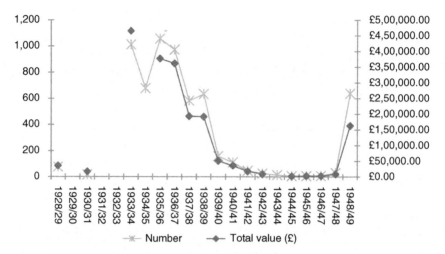

Fig. 3.3 Number and value of mortgages advanced under the Small Dwellings Acquisition Act, 1928/1929–1948/1949. *Source*: Department of Local Government and Public Health (various years).

Note: Data for 1929/1930, 1931/1932 are not available

after independence Irish local authorities, particularly in rural areas, were forced to rely on borrowing from commercial banks for housing-related finance. However, the banks employed a cartel-like structure (officially called the Irish Banks' Standing Committee) to coordinate their products, charges and lending terms and under these arrangements offered unattractively high interest rates and short repayment terms of 15 years for local government housing loans. Therefore, this source of finance also became unaffordable for local government and little commercial loan finance was available to support SDA mortgage lending (and social housebuilding) in the 1920s and early 1930s (see Fig. 3.4) (O'Connell, 2007).

During the late 1920s and early 1930s, the barriers to SDA mortgage lending were incrementally removed (see Table 3.1). This process commenced in 1929 when, on foot of determined lobbying from local authorities, Cumann na nGaedheal reluctantly granted sector access to the Local Loans Fund to finance social housebuilding and SDA Loans

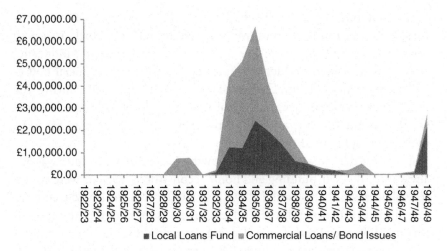

Fig. 3.4   Sources of finance for Small Dwellings Acquisition Act Mortgages, 1922/1923–1948/1949. *Source*: Generated from the Duanaire economic history database held by the National University of Ireland, Galway

and Fianna Fáil significantly expanded the fund in 1935 (Daly, 1997). The Local Loans Fund had originally only financed infrastructure spending and was financed by central government borrowing. The fund's availability to fund SDA mortgages, together with 1931 legislation which allowed SDA mortgages to be used to purchase new dwellings or for self-building, removed most of the barriers to providing and taking up these loans. Figs. 3.3 and 3.4 demonstrate that take-up of SDA loans and the amounts drawn from the Local Loans Fund to finance them (and therefore the costs to the exchequer and the national debt within which the Local Loans Fund was included) increased radically after these reforms. A total of 2,102 SDA mortgages were issued between the scheme's establishment in 1889 and 1933/1934, whereas 4,648 mortgages were issued between the latter date and 1943/1944 (Department of Local Government and Public Health, various years). Notably the municipalities responsible for Dublin and Cork cities were excluded from access to the Local Loans Fund until the 1950s, for reasons which were not explicated in any housing ministry policy statement, but are probably related to concerns about costs. Instead, these municipalities were forced to rely on stock issues to finance their housing activities. This precipitated regular fundraising crises and associated problems in funding SDA loans (and social house-building) particularly in Dublin (Daly, 1997). Although during the mid-1930s Dublin City Council managed several successful stock issues, which account for the vast bulk of the commercial borrowing for SDA mortgages highlighted in Fig. 3.4.

Table 3.1 demonstrates that the growth of exchequer subsidies was not always steady – self-building and home reconstruction grants were cut on several occasions between the 1920s and 1940s – but the broad trend was one of increasing expenditure. Indeed, such was the extent of this growth that by 1930 social transfers in Ireland accounted for the second highest proportion of national product (3.87 per cent of GNP) among the 30 developed countries studied by Lindert (1994). Ireland's position in this regard was primarily the result of investment in two fields: pensions (which reflected the high proportion of older people in the popula-tion due to high emigration among young people) and housing. His data do not include land reform spending, but if they did it is likely that Irish social transfers would have been the highest among his sample.

In Fig. 3.5, levels of direct central government subsidies for the purchase and reconstruction of dwellings for homeownership between 1923/1923 and 1948/1949 are compared to the direct subsidies available for social housebuilding. Although these data exclude some significant public subsidies for housing (most notably rates remission for homeowners and central government loans and additional local government subsidies for both social and owner-occupied housing), they do illustrate the extent to which government housing expenditure prioritised homeowners. Assuming most of the Million Pound Scheme and subsidies for public utility societies supported homeownership, Fig. 3.5 indicates that 76.2 per cent of central government direct spending on housing between 1922/1923 and 1929/1930 was devoted to supporting this tenure. Homeownership subsidies declined in rela-tive terms to 66 per cent of total direct exchequer housing expenditure between 1930/1931 and 1939/1940 as a result of increased spending on social housing and also the collapse in private housebuilding during

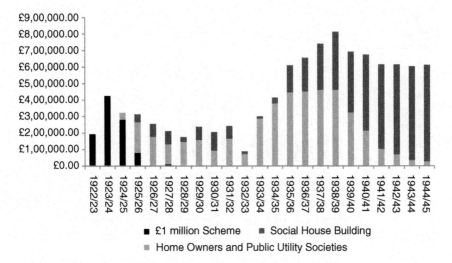

£1 million Scheme   ■ Social House Building
■ Home Owners and Public Utility Societies

Fig. 3.5 Direct government subsidies for homebuilding and reconstruction by tenure, 1922/1923–1944/1945. *Source*: Department of Local Government and Public Health (various years).

Note: Social housebuilding subsidies include both grants and interest subsidies

World War II. This concentration of public investment on home-ownership is evident in the inter-tenure variations in the housebuilding and reconstruction achieved with state aid between 1922/1923 and 1944/1945 which are sketched in Fig. 3.6. This graph reveals that homeowners and public utility societies built almost twice as many dwellings with state aid during the 1920s as local authorities and although local authority social housebuilding increased significantly during the 1930s, so did the use of state aid to fund the reconstruction of owner-occupied dwellings.

The high proportion of capital for homeownership derived from exchequer grants and SDA loans, their universal availability and the variety of policy instruments employed in the promotion of this tenure indicates that by the middle of the twentieth century homeownership in Ireland was not a market service, delivered and financed by the private sector, as is the norm in most developed, free market econo-mies. Rather, in the Irish case homeownership was largely a socialised tenure, which was financed not by the market primarily but rather by

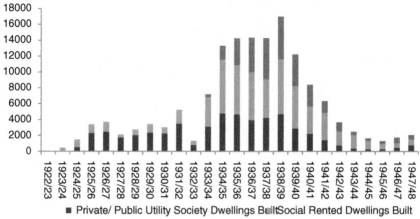

Fig. 3.6 Social rented, private and public utility society dwellings built and private dwellings reconstructed with direct state aid, 1922/1923–1944/1945. *Source*: Department of Local Government and Public Health (various years)

direct and indirect exchequer subsidies and local government mortgages was therefore a welfare service and a key part of the property-based welfare state.

The socialised nature of this tenure is further evidenced by Irish homeownership rates during the period under examination here which were high by Western European standards and well above what could have been sustained by market forces alone. Also, 52.6 per cent of Irish households were homeowners in 1946, whereas only 32.3 per cent of their English and Welsh counterparts owned their homes in 1953 (Central Statistics Office, various years; Holmans, 2005). This discrepancy is probably in part related to more rural nature of the Irish population (homeownership rates are usually lower in towns and cities) but is also linked to the much higher level of public subsidisation of homeownership in Ireland (SDA mortgages and home purchase grants were also available in the UK, but were much less widely used) and to the particular design of the Irish subsidy regime. This regime enabled Irish households to overcome the key barriers to accessing homeownership identified by researchers: access to credit and the need to accumulate a down payment (Ioannides, 1989; Duca and Rosenthal,

1994; Andrews and Sánchez, 2011). Provision of SDA mortgages addressed credit barrier and also the deposit barrier because these mortgages covered 90 per cent of the house purchase price in the 1940s, but government grants could make up half the remainder and a United Nations (1958) study revealed that deposits averaged 5 per cent for SDA mortgages compared to between 10 and 30 per cent elsewhere in Europe.

Social Housing as Property-Based Welfare

As mentioned in the preceding section, the decade after Irish independence saw a decline in construction of social housing by local authorities compared to output in the early 1900s. This was in part due to the difficulties which local authorities faced in raising loans to fund social housebuilding (which was constrained by the same factors which limited borrowing for SDA loans during this period) and in part due to reductions in central government building subsidies. As mentioned above, Cumann na nGaedheal's 1924 Housing Act abolished the subsidies towards the interest on social house construction loans introduced under British rule and replaced them with grants set at the same level as homebuyer grants. These loans were repaid using a mixture of income from rates and tenants' rents which reflected the cost of providing the dwellings. Therefore, the low level of subsidy meant that local authorities were unable to provide social housing at rents which were affordable for the lowest income families who more urgently required it.

An increase in the social housebuilding grant in 1925 proved insufficient to resolve this situation, and building rates did not increase until most local authorities were gained access to Local Loans Fund for social housing building finance (and SDA loans) in 1929 and subsidies towards the interest on these loans were reintroduced by Fianna Fáil's first Housing Act in 1932. Figure 3.6 demonstrates that social housing output increased significantly as a result of these reforms, and it accounted for 55.3 per cent of total housing output between 1930/1931 and 1939/1940. Although Cork and Dublin City Council's ineligibility for Local Loans Fund housing finance and their difficulties in raising alternative funding from stock issues meant that social housing output remained inadequate in these cities and progress in tackling the vast private rented slums which blighted their inner areas was painfully slow (Daly, 1997; Norris, 2003).

However, from the perspective of the discussion at hand, the most significant developments in the social housing sector during this period were not levels of new building, but rather its conversion from a rented tenure and therefore a part of the mainstream welfare state into an owner-occupied tenure and therefore form of property-based welfare, at least in rural areas. Like many elements of property-based welfare in Ireland, the roots of this development can be traced to land reform. When the Fianna Fáil government cut by half the outstanding annuities that farmers were obliged to pay arising from the land act settlements in 1933, this inspired a campaign by rural social housing tenants for the right to buy their dwellings on similar subsidised terms. Social housing was regularly sold to tenants prior to this – the 1919 Housing Act allowed sales – but these occurred only at the discretion of the relevant local authority and generally attracted no subsidy. The rural social housing tenants' campaign in the 1930s had strong echoes of the farm labourers' campaigns for additional spending on Labourers' Act dwellings which had followed each of the land acts prior to independence. This is evident in a submission to government commission established to investigate the rural social housing tenants' case which stated: "The rural tenants have in mind the land purchase schemes by which the farmer has become the owner of his holding at an annuity less than the rent and he sees no reason why he should not enjoy the same benefit" (Soarstát Éireann, 1933: 23). The commission's report recommended that the tenants' demands should be acceded to (although a minority report dissented from this view). As a result, the 1936 Labourers' Act afforded rural social tenants the right to buy their dwellings, initially using the system of payment in instalments employed by the land acts, with purchase annuities set at 75 per cent of pre-purchase rents and repayable for the same period as that out-standing on the loan the local authority had borrowed to construct the dwelling. Tenant purchase did not properly take off until annuities were reduced further to 50 per cent of rents in 1951, but by the mid-1960s, 80 per cent of rural social housing was owner occupied and according to the 1966 census they accounted for 11.6 per cent of all homeowners in the country at that time (Central Statistics Office, various years).

This development meant that a proportion of the exchequer housing expenditure detailed in Fig. 3.5 started life as a social housing subsidy, but functioned ultimately as a homeowner subsidy. However, calculating the scale of this homeowner subsidy is a complex matter. In the mid-1930s, local authority housing rents were calculated on the basis of the "all in" cost of providing the dwelling (i.e. land acquisition and construction costs plus the interest on the loans taken out to finance these) minus the subsidies from local government rates and central government. The commission on the sale of labourers' cottages reported that rents covered only 37 per cent of local authorities' housing development loans servicing costs (Soarstát Éireann, 1933). Therefore, setting the purchase annuities at 75 per cent of pre-purchase rents implies a public subsidy of 77.2 per cent of the costs of providing the dwelling. This is a minimum estimate because the 1936 Labourers' Act subsidies to tenant purchasers were further increased by the requirement that local authorities ensure that dwellings were in good repair prior to their sale (Department of Local Government and Public Health, various years). The requisite data are not available to calculate the subsidy with reference to the basis of the market value of the dwelling or the costs of its replacement by a new social rented dwelling, but the exchequer subsidy would most likely be significantly higher if calculated in this way.

Drivers of the Construction of the Property-Based Welfare System

The key driver of the continued growth of the property-based welfare state during the period under examination in this chapter was the increased power of the agrarian lobby after independence. Counterintuitively and contrary to the claims of some commentators (e.g. Larkin, 1994), in terms of policy influence, small farmers were more powerful than their larger counterparts. As Table 3.2 demonstrates, this phenomenon was due in large part to simple power of numbers because the already strong rural nature of Irish society was further amplified by partition and smallholders were the numerically dominant class. Belfast, which was the only

Table 3.2 Occupations and farm size in 1926, 1936 and 1946 (percentage of working population aged 14 years and over)

	1926 (%)	1936 (%)	1946 (%)
Occupations			
Farmers	20.6	19.3	19.2
Farmers' relatives assisting	20.1	18.2	15.7
Paid agricultural employees	10.6	10.5	10.8
Fishing, mining and quarrying	0.6	0.6	0.5
Industry	12.7	14.6	14.5
Transport and communications	5.0	5.2	4.6
Commercial finance and insurance	6.5	7.0	6.8
Public administration and defence	2.9	2.3	3.3
Professional occupations	4.2	4.6	5.5
Personal services	9.8	9.6	9.5
Clerks	2.3	2.8	3.4
Other	4.7	5.1	6.4
Farm size			
Farmers and relatives assisting living on more than 1 acre	0.03	0.03	0.02
Farmers and relatives assisting living on 1–5 acres	3.7	3.3	2.2
Farmers and relatives assisting living 5–10 acres	9.9	8.2	6.4
Farmers and relatives assisting living on 10–15 acres	12.0	10.5	9.2
Farmers and relatives assisting living on 15–30 acres	27.7	27.7	27.7
Farmers and relatives assisting living on 20–50 acres	19.9	21.5	23.1
Farmers and relatives assisting living on 50–100 acres	16.7	18.2	19.8
Farmers and relatives assisting living on 100–200 acres	6.9	7.5	8.2
Farmers and relatives assisting living over 200 acres	2.3	2.3	2.5
Farmers and relatives assisting farm size not stated	0.9	0.8	0.9

Source: Central Statistics Office (various years).

significant industrial centre on the Island, remained in the UK. The cities of the Irish Free State were small (in 1926, only 32 per cent of the population lived in urban centres with more than 1,500 inhabitants) and mainly centres of trade rather than industry (only 12.7 per cent of the population worked in industry in this year) and therefore could not provide large numbers of well-paid, steady, working-class jobs (Ó Gráda, 1997). In contrast, 51.3 per cent of the economically active population of the new Irish State worked in agriculture in 1926 and the majority of these were smallholdings (53 per cent of farmers and their relatives who also assisted them worked holdings of less than 30 acres) (see Table 3.2). Gaining access to land was the only route to a living and also to social status for the vast bulk of the population and this imperative drove the "land hunger" which inspired agrarian unrest and political campaigning (Dooley, 2004a).

The numerical power of the small farming class was amplified by their political skills. Garvin (1981) also argues that, drawing on a strong tradition of political mobilisation which stretched back to the land war, small farmers were far more skilled and effective advocates of their concerns than their urban class counterparts. Unlike many other European countries, in Ireland this mobilisation was not expressed primarily by establishing dedicated agrarian parties (although three parties of this type emerged and disappeared between the 1920s and 1950s, their effectiveness was limited) but rather by mobilising behind Cumann na nGaedheal/Fine Gael or Fianna Fáil and campaigning to influence these parties' policies and also by establishing non-party political campaign groups (Varley, 2010). Lee (1989: 72–73) links the disappearance of the farmers' parties to the fact that the interests of this section of population were well protected by the mainstream political system:

> There were streaks of peasantism in all major parties, but resentment at exclusion from the charmed circle of power, privilege and education never penetrated peasant consciousness sufficiently to form the effective basis of a national peasant party, simply because there was relatively little exclusion.

Thus, due to their numbers and strong political mobilisation, existing and aspirant small farmers' voting patterns had a key influence on the outcomes of elections during the early decades of the independent Irish State. This class was also not averse to using non-mainstream political methods to achieve its objectives during the early history of the State. Agrarian violence and violent "land grabbing" mainly by land-hungry landless labourers and small farmers emerged during the war of independence and became a widespread problem during the civil war (Dooley, 2004b).

The power of the small farmers' lobby (and the relative lack of political influence of large farmers, despite their economic importance) was a key factor behind the extension and radicalisation of land reform policy between 1922 and 1948. Furthermore, the uneven and changing distribution of this power across the political spectrum during the period under review at least partially explains the variations in the attitudes of the two main political parties to the land reform project and therefore differences in the policies they introduced.

Girvin (1989: 15) points out that "the social and regional basis of Cumann na nGaedheal support was not that dissimilar from Sinn Féin or Fianna Fáil during the 1920s", and this factor, together with the strong ideological commitment to finishing the process of redistributing land title from landlords to tenants shared by the vast majority of politicians this time, explains Cumann na nGaedheal's willingness to concede to extensive investment in land reform via the 1923 Land Act, despite their general antipathy to public spending (Dooley, 2004b). The limits the act placed on this process, in terms of the compulsory acquisition of untenanted estates, were primarily a *quid pro quo* for a British government land bond guarantees rather than a reflection of the views of the members of the Cumann na nGaedheal government. A further important motivation behind the 1923 Act was end to the agrarian violence associated with the civil war (Dooley, 2004b). This is evident in the parliamentary address proposing this legislation which was made by the first Irish Prime Minister W.T Cosgrave:

> Questions involving land matters that have been troublesome for the last 12 or 18 months have been intensified to an extraordinary extent by the fact that very great unrest has been evidenced in a great many parts of the country by reason of so many grievances existing, which it is hoped and believed this Land Bill will rectify. . . . [this] measure is one that will go far towards making for much more peaceful condi-tions and much more ordered conditions and for greater security and greater stability than perhaps any other measure we have had under

consideration here. We consider that the public peace is ensured by the passing of this Bill.

(Cosgrave in Dáil Éireann, 1923, Vol. 4, Col. 1983)

However, the radical extension of the land redistribution programme in 1933 was a Fianna Fáil policy, which was generally opposed by Cumann na nGaedheal and later by Fine Gael. This is confirmed by a contribution made by Patrick Hogan – the architect of the 1923 Land Act – to a parliamentary debate on amending legislation in 1926:

> ... I think land purchase has gone far enough. I think it should be our aim to limit it. It should apply to all ordinary agricultural tenancies. We all know that there are demands from all quarters, from fee-farm grantees as well as from the holders of long leases, from owners of plots in the very hearts of the cities, from owners of houses, that something should apply to them, comparable to the particular legislation applying to agricultural tenants. These demands are coming constantly upon us, but I suggest to anyone who values the security of property that we must set our face against that tendency somewhere. There were very special reasons for the Land Acts which go back a very long time. There was need for special legislation to deal with the agricultural tenants of the country. Our land legislation is probably the most drastic of any land legislation in Europe, and, as far as I am concerned, I am not anxious to extend its scope. ... We must draw the line somewhere.

(Hogan in Seanad Éireann, 1926, Vol. 6. Col. 494)

From the perspective of electoral power, during the 1920s at least this stance (and their introduction of unpopular public spending cuts) was related to the party's general lack of concern about popularity with the electorate. This unusual attitude reflects the atypical political context of the times – Cumann na nGaedheal has developed a government first of all which subsequently became a political party, and due to the anti-treaty side's parliamentary abstentionism, this party never needed a parliamentary majority to govern during its lifetime (Ferriter, 2004). Following Fianna Fáil's abandonment of parliamentary abstentionism in the late 1920s, Cumann na nGaedheal's opposition to extending land reform is likely to have been cemented by what Girvin (1989: 59) characterises as a period of "electoral realignment, primarily along a left-right axis". From this time, larger and commercially minded farmers and graziers gravitated towards Cumann na nGaedheal, while the working class, republicans and small farmer vote supported Fianna Fáil.

From its foundation, Fianna Fáil built an impressive electoral machine and its support for the extension of the land reform programme reflected a hunger for gaining and retaining power which in the Irish Free State required capturing the votes of current and aspirant small farmers. Dooley (2004a) suggests that Fianna Fáil's clear victory in the second election held in 1932 (they had failed to secure an overall majority in the first) was helped by small farmers attracted by their radical land reform proposals. Whereas he suggests that Fianna Fáil's defeat in the 1948 general election was in part related to "the party's ultimate failure to deliver upon its pre-1932 promises of land division" (Dooley, 2004a: 194). In support of this argument, he cites the sharp decline in this party's vote in small farmer-dominated regions and the emergence of a political party dedicated promoting the interests of this section of the farming population in the early 1940s (called Clann na Talmhan – literally: people of the land). Undermining the position of large farmers, landlords and graziers also reflected the approach of Fianna Fáil's precursors on the anti-treaty side of the civil war and chimed with the party's wider electoral strategy. The anti-treaty side had successfully exploited anti-grazier feelings to gain support from the small farmer class and, like many populist parties, an egalitarian inclination to favour the "common people" against the interests of the "elite" was central to Fianna Fáil's electoral appeal (Dooley, 2004b; Dunphy, 2005).

Rather than electoral competition between the parties which represented the pro- and anti-treaty sides of the civil war, the introduction of the right to buy rural social housing by the 1936 Labourers' Act was shaped by competition between Fianna Fáil and the Labour Party. Despite its strong links with the trade unions, during the opening half of the twentieth century, Labour failed to establish itself as a significant electoral force in urban centres and its parliamentary representatives remained heavily concentrated in the rural counties of east and the south where the party attracted a substantial vote from farm labourers

(O'Connor, 2011). Thus, between the 1920s and the 1940s, Labour members of parliament worked tirelessly to protect the interests of this class which encompassed around 10 per cent of the workforce at this time and also to protect the votes they provided from Fianna Fáil's charms (see Table 3.2). Hayden (2013: 166) assesses Labour's contribution to the parliamentary debate on the 1936 Act as "particularly vocal" and "bitter" – probably because the legislation "in effect stole Labour's clothes". The two decades which followed saw numerous attempts by Labour to have the terms of sales of rural cottages made even more generous to purchasers. For instance, a 1937 Labour private members bill proposed reducing the purchase price to 50 per cent of the previous rent and allowing tenants in arrears of rent to purchase (the latter provision was adopted by government in the 1937 Housing and Labourers' Act) (see Table 3.1). Two Labour Party private members' bills introduced in 1938 proposed reducing repayments to 50 per cent of rent and the party introduced a bill with the same objectives in 1944 which, for good measure, also proposed reducing the period for which tenant purchasers were required to make annuity payments. Notably these proposals were refused by a succession of Fianna Fáil housing ministers on grounds that they would place too great a burden on ratepayers (Hayden, 2013).

Apart from the 1936 Labourers' Act, the links between the power of the agrarian lobby and the other elements of the property-based welfare project were less obvious, but this does not mean that they were any less significant. Daly's (1997) history of the local government ministry highlights sustained efforts by senior civil servants to cut or abolish self-building and housing reconstruction grants during this period under review in this chapter. Table 4.1 reveals that their efforts, which were motivated by cost concerns, enjoyed only limited success, but it is notable that these successes applied only to urban areas. For instance, proposals to abolish these grants in 1929 were scuppered by the Minister for Local Government, General Richard Mulchay, on the grounds that "the absence of financial provisions for rural housing would be received very unfavourably" (Daly 1997: 218). The 1932 Housing Act limited eligibility for home reconstruction grants to farmers and farm labourers and the reductions in home purchase grants introduced in 1936 were only applied to urban areas (Daly, 1997). The agrarian lobby's interest in homeowner grants was related to their much higher take-up in rural areas due primarily to the shortage of mortgage credit at this time and the difficulty of self-building a home in a town or city. O'Connell (2007) estimates that 69 per cent of the new owner-occupied dwellings built with grant aid between 1922 and 1947 were constructed by farmers who had access to free or cheap sites.

Due to this discrepancy in the take-up of homeownership supports and the impact of land reform, this construction phase of Ireland's property-based welfare state was overwhelmingly rural in focus. In 1946, only 26 per cent of Dubliners were homeowners, as were 13.2 per cent of their counterparts in Ireland's second city of Cork, compared to 61 per cent of households outside the two largest cities (Central Statistics Office, various years).

In addition to the power of the agrarian lobby, the building industry lobby also had a significant influence on the introduction, persistence and expansion of homeownership subsidies. For instance, the increase in homebuyer subsidies introduced by the 1924 Act, in tandem with cuts to funding for social housing, was justified by W.T Cosgrave on the grounds that giving a small subsidy to a large number of homeowners would generate many building jobs, whereas the alternative solution of funding large-scale social housing building would place "...a very serious burden falls on the shoulders of the...taxpayers of this country, which they are not at the moment ready to bear" (in Dáil Éireann, 1924, Vol. 6 No 6, Col. 386). Not surprisingly, given the weakness of the economy and the chronic oversupply of labour during the period under examination, similar arguments were regularly used to justify exchequer subsidies for homebuilding. The introduction and maintenance of these subsidies also reflected more direct lobbying on the part of the building industry. Daly (1997) reports that homebuilders successfully lobbied the government to maintain homebuilding grants in urban areas which it had been announced would be abolished in 1938, while on a number of occasions similar lobbying was employed successfully to thwart Department of Finance efforts to reduce the maximum SDA mortgage available.

In tandem with the political power of the small farmers' lobby, the widespread political consensus regarding the legitimacy of their demands was also an important driver of the expansion and radicalisation of the land reform programme between the 1920s and the 1940s. Both of the main political parties which emerged during this period were strongly committed to finishing the process of redistributing land title from landlords to tenants; they viewed this as necessary to reverse the historic wrongs perpetuated on the Irish by colonial oppressors and therefore a central part of the nation-building process. Furthermore, they recognised the key role which the support of small farmers had played in the success of the nationalist movement and to ensure that very smallholdings were expanded to a sustainable size that some land would have be redistributed to smallholders (Dooley, 2004b).

However, Éamonn de Valera, Fianna Fáil's founder and leader until 1959 and the majority of his senior party colleagues, held a more radical interpretation of the purpose of land redistribution than the majority of Cumann na nGaedheal/Fine Gael politicians, and these differences in vision explain the more interventionist land redistribution policies pursued by the former party during the 1930s and 1940s (Jones, 2001). De Valera viewed land distribution as key social policy – a method of achieving his wider vision of a familist social order in which individual interests, values and prerogatives were subordinated to those of the family (see also Dooley, 2004b; Fahey, 2002; McCullagh, 1991). This vision was apparent in Fianna Fail's core objectives as enunciated at its inaugural meeting in April 1926, which committed it "to establish as many families as practicable on the land" (Dunphy, 1995). It was also evident in the 1937 Irish Constitution, largely drafted by de Valera, which recognised "the Family as the natural primary and fundamental unit group of Society, and as a moral institution possessing inalienable and imprescriptible rights, antecedent and superior to all positive law" and identified establishment "on the land in economic security as many families as in the circumstances shall be practicable" as a "directive principle of social policy" (Government of Ireland, 1937, Articles 41 and 45).

Familism and land reform were interlinked because the latter was crucial to the economic viability of the former – as Fahey (2002) argues, land reform was a method of fostering a "family economy" which would provide an alternative to an unfettered free market. Subsidies for the purchase of family farms were particularly useful from this perspective because they supported the stem (or three generational) family system which became widespread in Ireland after the Great Famine of the 1840s and as Table 3.2 demonstrates persisted well into the twentieth century (Gibbon and Curtin, 1978). Commonly heirs designate worked unpaid on the family farm and marriage was delayed until they were deemed fit to inherit, the farm income could support an additional family and the patriarch was sure he would not be edged out by the new generation. The unpaid labour of heirs and other assisting relatives made subsistence farming viable and provided a valuable form of welfare in the context of limited alternative employment options. Government subsidisation of property redistribution reinforced familial (in practice usually patriarchal) authority since further redistribution to inheritors was at parental discretion (Fahey, 2002; McCullagh, 1991). The emphasis on land reform also reflects de Valera's concerns about the social problems generated by urbanisation, and Garvin (2005) suggests a lack of confidence that sufficient industrial development could be achieved to support the population.

Although de Valera's land reform ideas were obviously conservative insofar as they aimed to preserve traditional lifestyles, family structures, gender roles and settlement patterns, in other respects this ideology was very radical. Rather than protecting the living standards of working-class households from the vagaries of the market by using social security to redistribute incomes ("decommodification" in policy analysis parlance), Fianna Fáil sought to achieve the same outcome by redistributing property. The decommodifying effects of this policy were obviously particularly strong in the case of land reform because a farm provided both a home and a living, whereas an owner-occupied dwelling usually provides only the former so it is a less effective (but still useful) decommodifying instrument. The decommodifying effect of land reform was amplified by the public subsidy to allottees and particularly by Fianna Fáil's decision to cut the land annuities in half and write-off most payment arrears in 1933 because this meant that most farms were encumbered by little or no debt. Land reform required government intervention in the property rights of landowners which was just as radical as the taxation applied to the incomes and assets of middle and higher earners to establish the social security and social service systems provided by other European welfare states. Indeed, the Fine Gael TD Patrick Belton's assessment that the 1933 Land Act as "could not be framed or conceived by anybody of men except men imbued with a communistic outlook" contains more than a grain of truth (Belton in Dáil Éireann, 1933, Vol. 49, No. 9, Col. 937).

Political support for land redistribution and the other aspects of property-based welfare was also reinforced by indirect ideological drivers, in the sense that this policy complemented causes which were close to politicians' hearts during the period under examination here. For instance, the redistribution of land from large farmers and graziers (who tended to concentrate on raising cattle for export) to smallholders (generally engaged in tillage and dairy farming which served local markets or supported a subsistence lifestyle) complemented Fianna Fáil's economic policy during the 1930s and 1940s which was strongly protectionist and focused on promoting national self-sufficiency (Ferriter, 2004). Housing was also used to support protectionism, as evidenced by Fianna Fáil's introduction of regulations in 1932 which made the receipt of subsidies for social housebuilding conditional on the use of materials of "Saorstát [Irish] manufacture" (Department of Local Government and Public Health, various years). In contrast, Cumann na nGaedheal's opposition to the further extension of the land reform programme beyond the parameters set out in 1923 Land Act reflected its reluctance to undermine the large farmers and graziers who were a cornerstone of its alternative plans to foster economic growth by liberalising trade and increasing exports and its general antipathy towards government intervention in any sector of the economy and society (Girvin, 1989).

As well as reinforcing the rural nature of Irish society, partition reinforced the dominance of Roman Catholicism in the Free State. Only 7 per cent of the population were not Catholics in 1926 and, as has been documented extensively elsewhere, the Church's influence on family, health and education policy was very strong between the 1920s and 1940s (Whyte, 1984). However, it is less widely appreciated that outside these "core" areas of Catholic interest politicians did not always follow the Church's views unless the interests of both in concert (Kelly, 1999, makes this point drawing on examples from social security policy) Land reform and home-ownership subsidies both fall into this category. Policy on these fields reflected the Catholic values of the primacy of the family and also the need for governments to protect the poor and promote social justice as set out in Papal encyclicals *Rerum Novarum* (1891) *Quadragesimo Anno* (1931). Land reform and homeownership sup-ports also complemented the "distributist" economic philosophy, popular during the 1920s and 1930s, which encouraged govern-ments to promote the widest possible distribution of property own-ership across society (Garvin, 1981). Distributism was largely devised by the English intellectuals Chesterton (1927) and Belloc (1912), drawing heavily on the principles of Catholic social teaching and the aforementioned encyclicals. In Ireland, it was promoted by Catholic intellectuals (e.g. De Blacam, 1944) as a "third way" between unfettered free markets and communism, which promoted social cohesion rather than class conflict and by a clergy which was strongly rooted in the farming and small business classes and there-fore intuitively sympathetic to this approach (O'Dowd, 1987). The term distributism rarely permeated Irish policy debates (although in 1937 Labour Party leader Tom Johnson delivered a lengthy lecture to his Dublin constituency council entitled: *A Workers' Republic: Socialist or Distributist?* which argued that Ireland should strive to achieve both ideals), but this ideology's equation of property ownership and Christian principles did influence the growth of property-based welfare policy in Ireland (Johnson, 1937). This was evident in the debate about the tenant purchase of labourers' cot-tages for instance. The commission of inquiry into this matter concluded

> The history of our country had been one of continuous struggle both on the land and in the town to gain the freedom and security that go with ownership. This we regard as a basic and essential principle in any Christian State that bases social order on justice.
>
> (Saorstát Éireann, 1933: 1)

Similarly, the minister who introduced the 1936 Labourers' Act suggested: "The principle is a good one of inducing the tenants to become the owners of their property. It is the best kind of Christian and Catholic philosophy" and this policy had the added benefit that it "is one way of defeating subversive social propaganda, propaganda subversive of the State and of religion" (O'Ceallaigh in Dáil Éireann, 1936: Vol. 62, No 1, Cols 199–200 and Vol 63, No. 3, Col, 419).

Despite the political power of the supports of the property-based welfare system and the strong consensus around the legitimacy of their remands, Dooley (2004b) reveals that civil servants raised concerns about the costs of land reform in the 1920s and 1930s. However, with the exception of the World War II period (when the Department of Finance pressure for reduced expenditure as part of an emergency programme of cutbacks brought land reform to a temporary halt), their views had little impact on policy. Similarly, Daly (1997) reports that consistent opposition by the Department of Finance to exchequer spending on homeownership supports between the late 1920s and the late 1940s resulted in three rounds of cuts to homebuyer grants (1929, 1936 and 1937) but on each occasion these reductions were reversed within a couple of years. The Department of Finance's lack of influence on property-based welfare policies during the period under examination in this chapter is surprising in view of the almost hegemonic influence it exercised on most other policy fields at this time (as highlighted by Garvin 1981, Girvin 1989 and Fanning 1978, among many others) and the fact that this influence was generally employed to dissuade politicians from increasing public spending particularly on social policies (Kelly, 1999). It also raises questions about the role of "efficiency" considerations as drivers of the expansion of the property-based welfare system. If, as Cousins (2003) argues, the Department of Finance's attachment to fiscal rectitude and deflationist economic policies was a key reason why Ireland's social security system failed to expand between independence and World War II, why were the same senior civil servants willing to concede to enormous expenditure on land reform?

The answer relates partially to land reform and housebuilding's wider socio-economic functions as employment generators, which could be justified on efficiency grounds and also to the distinctive arrangements for public funding of property-based welfare which raised fewer efficiency concerns than arrangements for funding the mainstream welfare state. Prior to the introduction of insurance-based benefits in the 1950s, social security payments were funded from direct public spending which had to be paid for through central government taxation and local government rates and were visible in the national accounts. In contrast, spending on land reform was less visible because it was funded by borrowing in the land bonds which were not considered part of the national debt during the period under examination in this chapter (Eason 1931 points out that this was not the case in Britain or Northern Ireland). Thus while the opening sections of this chapter argued that the ongoing costs to the exchequer of the landownership revolution were much greater than historians have generally acknowledged, they were less substantial in terms of their implications for tax rates and crucially less visible than the costs of effecting a revolution of similar scale in the provision of social security benefits. As a result, land reform has attracted less concerted opposition from the civil service than mainstream welfare spending and, unlike social security benefits, for instance, which were promoted by the relatively weak Labour Party and trade union movement, the power and legitimacy supports for land reform were sufficiently strong to overcome the bureaucrats' efficiency-related concerns.

Grants for home purchase and also most local authorities' borrowing from the local loans fund for SDA loans were funded directly by the exchequer from 1929, so homeowner supports do not fit as neatly into this analysis. However, Dublin and Cork City Councils were excluded from the local loans fund until the 1950s and funded their SDA lending by stock issues, so this major stream of investment in homeownership at least was not considered part of the national debt. In addition, most capital subsidies are "once off" costs which do not generate an ongoing liability for the exchequer and (unlike social services and benefits) are at least in theory easy to cut back in times of declining revenue. These factors may have influenced civil servants' willingness to accede to high spending on homeownership supports.

Conclusions

This chapter has documented the construction phase of the property-based welfare system which was distinguished by radical growth in the number of ownership supports compared to the pre-independence period. Most notably, the 1936 Labourers' Act effected the conversion of social housing in rural areas from a rented tenure (and therefore part of the mainstream welfare state) into a stepping stone to homeownership (and thus part of the property-based welfare system) (Norris and Fahey, 2011). The full scale of exchequer supports of homeownership is difficult to quantify because they were numerous and often indirect (e.g. tax relief, sales of social housing at below market value) rather than direct (public spending) subsidies. However, there is no doubt that public spending on homeownership supports expanded significantly during the period under examination in this chapter. Spending on land reform did not grow radically between the 1920s and the 1940s, largely because the "heavy lifting" phase of this project in terms of take-up and public subsidies was completed before the foundation of the State, but the aims of this policy were radicalised as the 1923 Land Act extended government powers to compulsorily acquire land for redistribution and further legislation in 1933 and 1936 removed the last remaining loopholes which enabled large landowners to evade compulsory purchase by the Land Commission. Thus the scope of the land reform project was extended as far as practicable between the 1920s and 1940s.

Although not conventionally defined as "social policies", the preceding analysis has made the case that these property redistribution policies shared key characteristics with the mainstream welfare state in terms of inputs, outcomes and objectives. They were intended to help achieve the social objective of supporting a familistic social order which enjoyed widespread support at this time. Like social security benefits, land redistribution in particular insulated low-income families from market forces and therefore enabled decommodification of labour. Operationalising this policy also required government intervention in the property rights of landowners which was just as radical as the taxation applied to the incomes and assets of middle and higher earners to establish mainstream welfare states. Therefore, the key argument proposed in this chapter is that between the 1920s and 1940s, rather than just establishing a weak version of the conventional European benefits and services welfare state as most accounts suggest, Ireland bolstered the property-based welfare system which had emerged in the late nineteenth century.

In terms of the factors which drove the growth of property-based welfare system during the period under examination here, the power of small farmers in terms of numbers and political mobilisation and to a much lesser extent farm labourers were particularly influential. Ideological factors, particularly the influence of nationalism, familism and Catholic economic philosophy of distributism, also played an important role in legitimating efforts to expand the property-based welfare system and the fact that land reform in particular complemented other important political objectives such as promoting protectionism was also helpful. The growth of the property-based welfare was also enabled by the fact that efficiency and affordability concerns were less of a concern for this policy area than for others. Land reform and housing subsidies inspired less worry among the many proponents of fiscal rectitude in the finance ministry because borrowing for these purposes was not formally categorised as part of the national debt and in theory were funded by loans which would be repaid (although in practice land redistribution and social housebuilding loans were rarely repaid in full by their beneficiaries). Housebuilding and small farms also provided employment which was particularly valuable in the context of chronic over supply.

In contrast, while the property-based welfare system expanded significantly between the 1920s and 1940s it is significant that the mainstream welfare system expanded only modestly during this period. As mentioned in the introduction to this chapter, the period of the Cumann na nGaedheal government in the 1920s and early 1930s saw the contraction rather than the expansion of public spending. The old age and blind pensions were reduced in 1924; in the same year, government subsidies to the national health insurance scheme were also reduced and notwithstanding Ireland's very high rate of tuberculosis the benefit paid to those who had been hospitalised with the disease was abolished in 1929. No new benefits or social services were introduced during this party's time in office and the few progressive reforms made to existing benefits were largely superficial as Poor Law institutions and benefits were renamed, but continued to treat clients in the same demeaning way as before (McCashin, 2004). The mainstream welfare system did start to expand following Fianna Fáil's election in 1932. In 1933, they introduced means tested unemployment assistance (thereby partially displacing the stigmatised Poor Law benefit called home assistance) and in 1935 the Widow's and Orphan's pension was introduced, followed by a new universal family allowance (called Children's Allowance) in 1944. However, compared to the UK in particular, the growth of the mainstream Irish welfare state during the period under examination in this chapter was modest. Only with the introduction of the Children's Allowance, which was launched in Ireland before many other countries, did Ireland exceed the Western European norm in welfare state development. Significantly, the rationale offered by policymakers for this development in many ways complements the familist rationale offered for property-based welfare – it was intended to bolster the economic basis of the family, particularly large families (it was initially only paid to third and subsequent children in each family) and it also reinforced the patriarchal family model because it was paid to fathers only until 1985.

References

Aalen, F.A. (1992). Ireland. In C. Pooley (Ed.), *Housing strategies in Europe, 1880–1930* (pp. 132–164). Leicester: Leicester University Press.
Acheson, N., Harvey, B., Kearney, J., & Williamson, A. (2004). *Two paths one purpose: Voluntary action in Ireland North and South.* Dublin: Institute of Public Administration.
Andrews, D., & Caldera Sánchez, A. (2011). *The evolution of homeownership rates in selected OECD countries: Demographic and public policy influences.* Paris: OECD.
Belloc, H. (1912). *The servile state.* London: The Liberty Fund.
Central Statistics Office (various years). *Census of population of Ireland.* Dublin: Stationery Office.

Corporation of Dublin (1945). *Dublin housing inquiry, 1939–1945.* Dublin: Corporation of Dublin.

Cousins, M. (2003). *The birth of social welfare in Ireland: 1922–1952.* Dublin: Gill and Macmillan.

Chesterton, C. (1927). *The outline of sanity.* London: IHS Press.

Dáil Éireann (various years). *Díospóireachtaí Dála [Parliamentary Debates].* Dublin: Houses of the Oireachtas.

Daly, M. (1997). *The buffer state: The historical origins of the department of the environment.* Dublin: Institute of Public Administration.

De Blacam, A. (1944). An outline of distributivism. *The Irish Monthly, 72*(856), 430–441.

Department of Local Government and Public Health (various years). *Department of local government and public health report.* Dublin: Stationery Office.

Dooley, T. (2004a). Land and politics in independent Ireland, 1923–48: The case for reappraisal. *Irish Historical Studies, 34*(134), 175–195.

Dooley, T. (2004b). *The land for the people: The land question in independent Ireland.* Dublin: UCD Press.

Duca, J., & Rosenthal, S. (1994). Borrowing constraints and access to owner occupied housing. *Regional Science and Urban Economics, 24,* 301–322.

Dunphy, R. (1995). *The making of Fianna Fáil power in Ireland, 1923–1948.* Oxford: Oxford University Press.

Dunphy, R. (2005). *Fianna Fáil and the working class, 1928–38.* In F. Lane, & D. Ó. Drisceóil, (Eds.), *Politics and the Irish Working Class, 1830–1945* (pp. 246–261). London: Palgrave.

Eason, C. (1931). Should the list of authorised trustee investments in the Irish free state be extended? *Journal of the Statistical and Social Inquiry Society of Ireland, XV*(2), 1–9.

Fanning, R. (1978). *The Irish department of finance, 1922–58.* Dublin: Institute of Public Administration.

Fahey, T. (2002). The family economy in the development of welfare regimes: A case study. *European Sociological Review, 18*(1), 51–64.

Ferriter, D. (2004). *The transformation of Ireland, 1900–2000,* London: Profile Books.

Fraser, M. (1996). *John Bull's other homes: State housing and British policy in Ireland, 1883–1922.* Liverpool: Liverpool University Press.

Garvin, T. (1981). *The evolution of nationalist politics.* Dublin: Gill and McMillan.

Gibbon, P., & Curtin, C. (1978). The stem family in Ireland. *Comparative Studies in Society and History, 20,* 429–453.

Garvin, T. (2005). *Preventing the future: Why was Ireland so poor for so long?* Dublin: Gill and Macmillan.

Girvin, B. (1989). *Between two worlds: Politics and economy in independent Ireland.* Dublin: Gill and Macmillan.

Government of Ireland (1937). *Bunreacht na hÉireann [Constitution of Ireland].* Dublin: Stationery Office.

Hayden, A. (2013). *Tenant purchase in Ireland: A study of path dependency.* Dublin: unpublished PhD thesis submitted to University College Dublin.

Holmans, A. (2005), *Historical statistics of housing in Britain.* Cambridge: Cambridge Centre for Housing and Planning Research.

Ioannides, Y. (1989). Housing, other real estate and wealth portfolios: An empirical investigation based on the 1983 survey of consumer finances. *Regional Science and Urban Economics, 19*(2), 243–263.

Irish Times (1923, August 1) Senators and the land bill: Criticism of the Commission's powers of 'confiscation'. *Irish Times,* p. 7.

Irish Times (1923, April 23), Text of the 1923 agreements: Land purchase annuities. Irish Times, p. 4.

Johnson, T. (1937). *A workers' republic: Socialist or distributist?, A lecture by Thomas Johnson in Dublin, October, 1937.* Dublin: Dublin City Constituencies Council, Labour Party.

Jones, D. (2001). Divisions within the Irish government over land distribution policy, 1940–70. *Eire-Ireland, XXXVI,* 83–109.

Kelly, A. (1999). Catholic action and the development of the Irish welfare state in the 1930s and 1940s. *Archivium Hibernicum, 53*(1), 107–117.

Larkin, E. (1994). Foreword. In W. Finegold (Ed.), *The revolt of the tenantry: The transformation of local government in Ireland, 1872–1886* (pp. xiv–xv). Boston: Northern University Press.

Lee, J. (1989). *Ireland, 1912–1985: Politics and society.* Cambridge: Cambridge University Press.

Lindert, P. (1994). The rise of social spending, 1880–1930. *Explorations in Economic History, 31*(1), 1–37.

McCashin, T. (2004). *Social security in Ireland.* Dublin: Gill and Macmillan.

McCullagh, C. (1991). A tie that binds: Family and ideology in Ireland. *Economic and Social Review, 22*(3), 199–211.

McManus, R. (1996). Public utility societies, Dublin corporation and the development of Dublin, 1920–1940. *Irish Geography, 29*(1), 27–37.

National Economic and Social Council (1977), *Report on housing subsidies*. Dublin: NESC.

Neary, P., & Ó Gráda, C. (1991). Economic war and structural change: The 1930s in Ireland. *Irish Historical Studies, 27*(10), 250–266.

Norris, M. (2003). The housing service. In H. Callanan, & J. Keogan (Eds.), *Local government in Ireland* (pp. 76–92). Dublin: Institute of Public Administration.

Norris, M., & Fahey, T. (2011). From asset based welfare to welfare housing: The changing meaning of social housing in Ireland. *Housing Studies, 26*(3), 459–469.

Nunan, D. (1987). Price trends for agricultural land in Ireland 1901–1986. *Irish Journal of Agricultural Economics and Rural Sociology, 12*, 51–77.

O'Connell, C. (2004). The housing market and owner occupation in Ireland. In M. Norris, & D. Redmond (Eds.), *Housing contemporary Ireland: Policy, society and shelter* (pp. 21–44). Dublin: Institute of Public Administration.

O'Connell, C. (2007). *The state and housing in Ireland: Ideology, policy and practice*. London: Nova Science.

O'Connor, E. (2011). *A labour history of Ireland 1824–2000*. Dublin: UCD Press.

O'Dowd, L. (1987). Town and county in Irish ideology. *Canadian Journal of Irish Studies, 13*(2), 43–53.

Ó Gráda, C. (1997). *A rocky road: The Irish economy since the 1920s*. Manchester: Manchester University Press.

Powell, F. (1992). *The politics of Irish social policy: 1600–1995*. New York: Edwin Mellen Press.

Ryan, R. (2005). The anti-annuity payment campaign. *Irish Historical Studies, 34*(135), 306–320.

Seanad Éireann (various years). *Díospóireachtaí Seanad Éireann [Parliamentary Debates]*. Dublin: Houses of the Oireachtas.

Soarstát Éireann (1933). *Final report of the commission of inquiry into the sale of Cottages and Plots Provided Under the Labourers (Ireland) acts*. Dublin: Stationery Office.

Town Tenants Commission (1927). *Interim Report on the Working of the Small Dwellings Acquisition Act 1899*. Dublin: Stationery Office.

United Nations (1958). *Financing of housing in Europe*. Geneva: UN.

Varley, T. (2010). On the road to extinction: Agrarian parties in twentieth-century Ireland. *Irish Political Studies, 25*(4), 581–601.

Whyte, J. (1984). *Church and state in modern Ireland, 1923–1979*. Dublin: Gill and Macmillan, 1984.

4

Saturation: 1948–1968

Introduction

Between 1948 and 1968, the system of socialised homeownership which had emerged between the 1920s and the 1940s and initially focused on rural dwellers was expanded to include urban areas and the process of land redistribution also increased from the lows seen during the wartime period. This was the "saturation" period in the development of Ireland's property-based welfare system, when demand for asset redistribution was almost completely satisfied or at least the limits of the distribution possible were reached but, concurrent with the peak of its development, the first signs of weakness in this welfare model also became evident. The latter was evidenced by growing criticism of this model by politicians, rather than any radical redirection in policy. The end of hegemonic support for property-based welfare reflected the weakening of the legitimacy and efficiency bulwarks which supported these policies as a result of a wider crisis within Ireland's socio-economic model and pressures on associated public expenditure. However, during the 1950s and 1960s, the power of farmers and the building industry proved sufficient to ensure the continued expansion of the property-based welfare system.

© The Author(s) 2016   **113**
M. Norris, *Property, Family and the Irish Welfare State*,
DOI 10.1007/978-3-319-44567-0_4

This chapter describes this expansion, the drivers of this development and the tentative signals of the weakening of these drivers which also emerged between 1948 and 1968.

In political terms, the late 1940s and 1950s in particular were a more volatile period than the 1930s and early 1940s. Fianna Fáil's iron grip on power was broken by the 1948 general election which saw it replaced by a coalition (known as the first inter-party government) of five parties led by Fine Gael. Fianna Fáil regained power in 1951 but as a minority government and was replaced by the second inter-party government in 1954 (led by Fine Gael and including Labour and Clann na Talmhan). This political volatility was strongly related to the low economic growth, high emigration and series of balance of payments crises Ireland suffered during the 1950s. Voters blamed the incumbent government for their plight and turned to the opposition to provide solutions (Murphy, 1997). Between 1957 and 1973, long-term electoral norms reasserted themselves and there was another uninterrupted stretch of Fianna Fáil government. Until 1959, these administrations were led by the veteran Fianna Fáil leader Éamonn de Valera, after which his long-time Industry and Commerce Minister Seán Lemass took over as party leader and Taoiseach. This long stretch of Fianna Fáil rule did not signal the end of electoral instability however. The 1960s were distinguished by particularly tight electoral contests, and the 1965–1969 Fianna Fáil government was a minority one.

Saturation of the Property-Based Welfare System

Land Reform

Clann na Talmhan was one of the five parties which made up the first inter-party government, and the party's leader Joseph Blowick was appointed Minister for Lands. Not surprisingly, in view of Clann na Talmhan's role as the representative of small farmers, Blowick was an ardent supporter of land division and in a speech to parliament soon after his appointment as minister he confirmed his commitment to "the relieving of congestion, the raising of uneconomic holdings to economic standard, and the placing of as many people as economically possible on the land and making each man complete owner of his own holding" (Blowick, 1948, in Dáil Éireann, Vol. 110 No. 16, Col. 2258). Thus he moved quickly to reanimate the activities of the Land Commission which had been severely restricted during World War II. A prohibition on the acquisition of lands in the midlands and east which had been introduced during the war was lifted by Blowick in 1948, and in 1949 he increased the target standard size of holdings outside the main congested areas from 25 to 35 acres to reflect changing views on the farm size necessary to generate an acceptable living (see Table 4.1) (Dooley, 2004b). His 1950 Land Act also gave the Land Commission stronger legal powers to push through "rearrangement schemes", that is, to compulsorily acquire and reallocate parts of neighbouring smallhold-ings to relieve congestion and resolve the intermingling of holdings owned by different farmers. Implementing this provision necessitated revival of "migration schemes" which enabled the transfer of farmers from congested holdings in the west to available land in the east. This policy had been extensively used in the 1930s but had ceased during World War II (Dooley, 2004b).

However, the lack of land eligible for compulsory acquisition by the Land Commission severely constrained the implementation of Blowick's plans. Most of the ascendancy landlord's estates had already been acquired by the late 1940s, so, to overcome this problem, the 1950 Land Act enabled the commission purchase land for cash on the open market if it was needed for rearrangement or migration schemes. This measure was not widely employed in the 1950s principally because, unlike land bonds, the full costs of cash purchase of land for redistribu-tion were explicit in the public accounts and therefore subject to the usual affordability constraints on direct public spending (see Childers, 1957, in Dáil Éireann, Vol. 161 No. 3, Cols 153). The 1950 Act also included some significant changes to arrangements for compensating those whose land had been compulsorily acquired under the Land Acts. It required the Land Commission to pay market value for land in this category rather than fair value (which was paid for compulsorily acquired land) and also removed the requirement that tenant-purchasers

Table 4.1 Key policy milestones in the saturation of Ireland's property-based welfare system, 1922–1948

Date	Land Reform	Government-Provided Mortgages for Homeowners	Universal Government Subsidies for Homeowners	Direct/Indirect Government Provision of Homeowner Dwellings
1948	Prohibition on the acquisition of lands in the midlands and east which had been introduced during the World War II was lifted.	The maximum value of a dwelling which could be purchased using an SDA mortgage was increased from £1,750 to £2,000.	Housing (Amendment) Act introduced grants of up to £275 for households and £285 for public utility societies building dwellings for homeownership and extra local government grants for those with incomes below £832 per annum.	
1949	Target standard size of holdings outside main congested areas raised from 25 to 35 acres.			

Table 4.1 (continued)

Date	Land Reform	Government-Provided Mortgages for Homeowners	Universal Government Subsidies for Homeowners	Direct/Indirect Government Provision of Homeowner Dwellings
1950	Land Act gave Land Commission stronger legal powers to enforce "rearrangement schemes" and enabled it to buy land for cash on the open market for rearrangement or migration schemes. It also required the commission to pay "market value" not "fair value" for compulsorily acquired tenant purchased land.		Housing Act made grants available for buying (as well as building) dwellings for owner occupation; made new homebuyers eligible for rates and stamp duty remission; enabled recipients of home purchase/building or reconstruction grant get a second reconstruction grant 15 years later and made urban dwellers eligible for reconstruction grants.	
1951				Minister allowed labourers' cottages to sell for 50 per cent of pre-purchase rents.

(continued)

Table 4.1 (continued)

Date	Land Reform	Government-Provided Mortgages for Homeowners	Universal Government Subsidies for Homeowners	Direct/Indirect Government Provision of Homeowner Dwellings
1953	Land Act removed the 4 per cent limit on land bond interest rates and linked them to market rates.			
1952			Housing (Amendment) Act reduced waiting time for receipt of a second housing reconstruction grant to 10 years for some works, removed limits on the size of dwellings eligible for this grant and introduced a new water and sewage grant for dwellings not on public mains.	Housing (Amendment) Act empowered local authorities to build dwellings directly for sale to homebuyers.

Table 4.1 (continued)

Date	Land Reform	Government-Provided Mortgages for Homeowners	Universal Government Subsidies for Homeowners	Direct/Indirect Government Provision of Homeowner Dwellings
1956		Dublin and Cork City Councils gain access to the local loans fund for SDA loan finance. Housing (Amendment) Act limited the max SDA loan to 95 per cent of market value and introduced government guarantees for some building society mortgages. The income limit for access to SDA loans was raised to £832 per annum.	Housing (Amendment) Act index linked all home-buyer and reconstruction grants.	
1957	The definition of "eco-nomic holdings" was amended so fewer farms were eligible for enlargement.			

(continued)

Table 4.1 (continued)

Date	Land Reform	Government-Provided Mortgages for Homeowners	Universal Government Subsidies for Homeowners	Direct/Indirect Government Provision of Homeowner Dwellings
1959	Land Commission is instructed to undertake a survey of the remaining "substantial holdings" with a view to compulsorily acquiring them.			
1965	Land Act removed restrictions on Land Commission purchase of land for cash; enabled it to offer elderly farmers a pension if they surrendered their land for redistribution and to offer loans to enable farmers in congested districts buy land on the market.	Income limit for eligibility for SDA mortgages was increased from £1,040 to £1,200 and the maximum loan available raised to £2,500 outside cites.		

Table 4.1 (continued)

Date	Land Reform	Government-Provided Mortgages for Homeowners	Universal Government Subsidies for Homeowners	Direct/Indirect Government Provision of Homeowner Dwellings
1966				Housing Act enabled local authorities provide low-cost sites for self-builders and extended right to buy to urban local authority tenants. Dwellings will be sold at a max discount of 30 per cent in urban areas and 45 per cent in rural areas.
1968		Raised max SDA loan to £2,700 outside cities and £3000 in cities.		

Source: Department of Local Government and Public Health and Department of Local Government (various years); Dooley (2004b); O'Connell (2004).

whose land was compulsorily acquired had to repay the commission the balance of the advance received to purchase the holding initially (Jones, 2001).

Blowick's reforms increased the level of land redistribution from the lows of the wartime period. Only 10,893 acres were acquired and redistributed by the Land Commission 1947/1948 (the last year of the Fianna Fáil administration), whereas this rose to 21,699 acres in 1949/1950 (the year following the election of the first inter-party government) (see Fig. 4.1). Neither Thomas Derrig, who was Blowick's successor as Minister for Lands in the Fianna Fáil administration of 1951–1954, nor Blowick himself, who was reappointed as lands minister in the second inter-party government of 1954–1957, managed to increase the budget available for land redistribution. This constraint and the shortage of land still eligible (or more correctly considered suitable) for compulsory purchase meant that the rate of land redistribution did now grow further during this period; it fluctuated between low and mid-20,000s between 1948 and the late 1950s (see Fig. 4.1). This issue and growing concerns about the efficiency of farming practices by formerly landless allotees and that small farms were not generating an acceptable standard of living for their owners also meant that for the remainder of its existence the Land Commission focused on the enlargement of existing holdings and very little land was allocated to landless applicants after World War II (Dooley, 2004b).

The re-election of Fianna Fáil in 1957 was initially marked by a significant shift in the tone of official discourse on land policy at least during Erskine Childers' short tenure as Minister for Lands between 1957 and 1958 (see Dooley, 2004b, for a detailed discussion). He used the opportunity of his fist ministerial address to parliament on the Lands Department budget to question the fundamental principles underpinning his party's land reform policy and its achievements. This landmark speech merits quotation at length:

> The people who live on the small western farms no longer accept the Land Commission ideas about what constitutes an economic holding. The population is reducing rapidly and leaving the same income for the fewer to enjoy...In fact, emigration has been making farms economic without enlargement. We tend to linger in the nineteenth century and to excuse our present state by references to history.

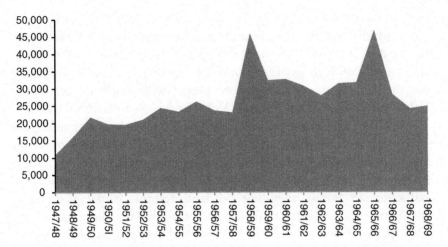

Fig. 4.1   Acres of land redistributed under the Land Acts, 1947/1948–1968/1969. *Source*: Dooley (2004b).

Note: Data refer to the financial year ending in March and exclude lands allocated in accommodation plots, turbary plots, forestry plots or for sportsfields

The facts available show that the farmers with large capital resources and modern machinery, close to the larger markets, have shown the major production since 1931 . . . the smaller farmers here are losing ground . . .

What are the conclusions to be derived from these studies? The Departments of Lands and Agriculture must concentrate their efforts on assisting the medium sized family farmer to progress, particularly in the West and North . . . We must face up to reality and recognise that a small farmer who receives a holding gets the equivalent of £1,000 to £2,000. This is a privilege accorded to only about 14 uneconomic land holders per thousand per year. It is too valuable a gift in our present state unless the result is to stimulate high grade commercial farming.

No one could occupy my position without questioning previous policy. We are beginning a new age and we can forget a great deal of what we thought in 1921 . . . At this stage, I can only say this: the system must change. It is outdated and the movements of our people in the last ten years afford complete justification for this statement.

(Childers, 1957, in Dáil Éireann, Vol. 161 No. 3, Cols 161–167)

He summed up his analysis in a bold plea for the reform of the Land Commission's key objective of settling as many families on the land as is practicable. In his view, "'Practicable' means that the policy will result in the growth of high grade commercial farming, enabling families to remain in Ireland, providing more people with work in our towns" (Childers, 1957, in Dáil Éireann, Vol. 161 No. 3, Cols 160–161).

Childers' radical rhetoric was accompanied by rather more moderate policy change as evidenced by the fact that the rate of land acquisition and redistribution did not fall during his tenure (see Fig. 4.1). However, Childers did preside over (and notably failed to bemoan) a reduction in public spending on land reform, issued a directive instructing the Land Commission to vet potentially allotees carefully for experience and aptitude in farming and changed the definition of "economic holdings" (from below a rateable value of £15 to below a rateable value of £10) to ensure that fewer farms were eligible for enlargement (Dooley, 2004b).

These modest changes inspired vociferous criticism from small farmers' representatives and Fianna Fáil backbenchers and the opposition. The Fine Gael TD James Dillon's response to Childers' 1957 speech reminded him that "there was a lot of blood spilt in this country in order to get the three Fs, fair rent, fixity of tenure, and free sale" (Dillon, 1957, in Dáil Éireann, Vol. 161 No. 3, Col. 184). As a result, despite his indubitable credentials as a moderniser and architect of Ireland's industrialisation, when Séan Lemass became Taoiseach in 1959, he felt the need to remove Childers from the post of Minister for Lands.

Childers was replaced with Michael Moran whose attitude to land reform was far more traditional and, because of his particularly long tenure in the Department of Lands, had the opportunity to comprehensively shape land policy to reflect his values (Dooley, 2004b). As Fig. 4.1 reveals, between Moran's appointment in 1959 and in 1968 the acreage acquired and redistributed by the Land Commission averaged at around 30,000 per annum – some 10,000 acres per annum more than the redistribution rates which pertained for most of the 1950s. Rebooting the Land Commission's programme of compulsory land acquisition was the main tool used to achieve this increase. To this end, in 1959 Moran instructed the Land Commission to undertake a survey of the remaining "substantial holdings" (the meaning of which was not defined but probably around 200 acres) which identified a total of 7,152 farms in this category (Dooley, 2004b). Dooley (2004b: 177) suggests that "these holdings had escaped possibly because of the loopholes in legislation that had allowed their owners to appeal continually against their acquisition and, just as likely, because of the changing post-Emergency [World War II] attitudes towards the importance of large-scale commercial farming". During Moran's time as lands minister, this situation changed. Between the late 1950s and late 1960s, the Land Commission targeted as many holdings for acquisition as it had during its previous peak in redistribution activity in the early 1930s. But because most of the large landlord's estates had been redistributed by the 1950s, this phase of acquisition focused on medium-to-large farms and took fewer acres from each holding targeted (Dooley, 2004b). Moran also encouraged the Land Commission to take a similarly energetic approach to compulsorily acquiring lands which had been let without the commission's permission but the parliamentary debates of the time reveal that this provoked significant controversy. His third and most significant initiative to increase the level of land redistribution was legislated for in the 1965 Land Act. This, the last significant Land Act introduced after Irish independence, removed restrictions on purchase of holdings for cash by the Land Commission, thereby enabling it to use cash purchases to implement all aspects of the Land Acts and also to offer elderly farmers a life annuity which would pay them a pension in return for making their holdings available for redistribution. In anticipation of growing levels of expenditure on these measures, Moran increased the relevant budget allocation by £95,000 to £365,000 in 1965, which accounted for 17.8 per cent of the total Department of Lands budget (Ó Móráin, 1965, in Dáil Éireann, Vol. 215 No. 5, Col. 517).

The increase in land redistribution activity from 1948 had significant knock-on implications of land bond issues which increased steadily through the 1950s and somewhat more strongly during the 1960s (see Fig. 4.2), but it had much greater implications for the direct public expenditure on land reform which rose dramatically from £1.68 million in the 1948/1949 fiscal year to £3 million in 1963/1964 (see Fig. 4.3). Rising land prices contributed to both of these developments, but the increased purchase of land for cash on the open market by the Land

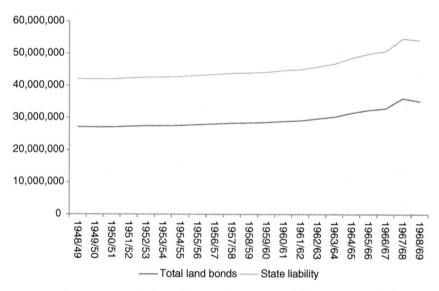

Fig. 4.2 Land bonds outstanding at the end of each fiscal year and the component of which were a direct state liability, 1948/1949–1968/1969. *Source:* Generated from the annual finance accounts as collated in Duanaire economic history database held by the National University of Ireland, Galway.

Commission and reforms to arrangements compensating those whose land had been compulsorily acquired also played a significant role. Due to the land redistribution financing reforms introduced in the 1950 and 1953 Land Acts, coupled with additional reforms in the 1965 Land Act which removed the upper limit of 4 per cent interest on land bonds and linked their interest rates to market rates, the cost per acre of land acquired in the early 1960s was significantly higher than that in the early 1930s. However, despite concerted pressure from a number of ministers for finance and senior civil servants in that ministry, the price at which the land was sold on to allotees was not increased commensurately; instead, the exchequer subsidy for acre redistributed rose. According to Jones (2001), between 1936 and 1944 the average loss to the state on the resale of land to allotees was 37 per cent of land acquisition and improvement costs, but this increased to 50 per cent between 1944 and 1952 and 87 per cent between 1952 and 1972.

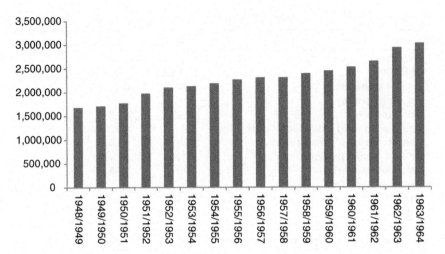

Fig. 4.3 Direct government expenditure on land reform, 1949/1949–1963/ 1964. *Source*: Generated from the annual finance accounts as collated in Duanaire economic history database held by the National University of Ireland, Galway.

Note: Data on the period between 1965/1966 and 1968/1969 are not available

Homeownership Subsidies

In the owner-occupied sector, the saturation period in the development of the property-based welfare state was distinguished by the further expansion of the socialised homeownership regime as exchequer subsidisation of the sector and Small Dwellings Acquisition Act mortgage lending by local government grew and the proportion of households living in this tenure increased, particularly in cities (see Table 4.2). In 1946, 52.6 per cent of Irish households, 25.6 per cent of Dubliners and only 13.2 per cent of Corkonians were homeowners. These figures rose to 70.8, 48 and 49.2 per cent, respectively, by 1971 (Central Statistics Office, various years).

These developments were strongly interrelated because growing exchequer subsidies and particularly their increased availability in cities were the key drivers of rising homeownership. The tenure expanded because the greater availability of mortgage credit (principally SDA mortgages provided by local authorities) enabled more urban households

Table 4.2 Number, tenure and standard of dwellings, 1946, 1961 and 1971

	1946 (%)	1961 (%)	1971 (%)
Dwellings			
Total (N)	662,654	676,402	705,180
Dwellings per head (N)	0.2405	0.2518	0.246
Housing tenure			
Homeowner	52.6	53.61	60.73
Being purchased from a local authority		6.20	10.08
Rented from a local authority	16.5	18.42	15.93
Rented from a private landlord	26.1	17.19	10.87
Other/special terms	4.70	4.58	2.39
Housing standards			
Fixed bath/shower	15.40	33.20	55.40
Piped water	38.70	57.20	78.20
Flush toilet	38.50	53.50	70.00
Average number of persons per room	1.01	0.90	0.86

Note: Data on the percentage of households being purchased from a local authority in 1946 are not available.

Source: Central Statistics Office (various years) and Threshold (1981).

to buy homes and thereby take advantage of the other government supports for home purchasers such as grants and rates remission which had previously been employed mainly by farmers self-building without a mortgage (see Chap. 3) and also because the terms of these supports which discriminated against urban dwellers were removed.

This focus on expanding urban homeownership was quite deliberate on the part of government. It was initially flagged in the 1948 housing white paper which offered a twofold rationale for this redirection (Minister for Local Government, 1948). Firstly, it reviewed housing need which had expended significantly due to the wartime reduction in housebuilding and estimated that 100,000 additional dwellings should be constructed in the next decade. However, due to a combination of migration to cities and high rates of historic investment in rural areas, over two-thirds of these new dwellings were required in urban areas, mainly in Dublin. Although the white paper assumed that a local authority social housing would account for 60 per cent of these dwellings, it also aimed to stimulate more private housebuilding for homeowners. The white paper also argued that urban middle-income households were not accessing the owner occupier sector in sufficiently large numbers and were continuing to rent privately, sometimes in poor conditions due to the impact of rent control legislation dating from World War I, whereas their working-class counterparts were gradually being moved from the private rented slums to new social housing (Minister for Local Government, 1948). On this basis, the policy statement reported:

> The government decided that the foregoing scheme of grants [for home owners] was inadequate...Building costs have risen far above 1939 levels...and the consequence has been that the middle income group are finding it increasingly difficult to command a share of the resources of the building industry commensurate with their urgent housing needs.
>
> (Minister for Local Government, 1948: 20)

To operationalise these plans, a series of reforms to homeowner subsidies were introduced during the 1950s which increased their generosity and also removed terms and conditions which disadvantaged urban households (see Table 4.1). In relation to the latter, the Housing (Amendment Act) 1950 was particularly significant. It extended eligibility for reconstruction grants (previously available only to farmers and farm labourers) to all urban and rural households whose incomes would qualify them for social housing. Grants for homebuyers and public utility societies building for sale to homeowners were also increased in 1948 and 1958 and index linked by the 1956 Housing (Amendment) Act. As a result, Daly (1997: 359) points out that these "grants showed a substantial increase in real terms at a time when the value of subsidies for local authority housing had fallen". This suite of homeowner subsidies were further augmented by the 1950 Act which increased the maximum floor area of dwellings eligible for homebuyer grants, made new grant-aided dwellings eligible for remission of two-thirds of their rates for 7 years after purchase and from stamp duty and enabled householders who had received a home purchase/building or reconstruction grant to avail of a second State reconstruction grant 15 years later. The 1952 legislation also introduced grants for the provision of water and sewage to dwellings not on public mains and increased the size of dwellings eligible for reconstruction grants; the 1954 Housing Act reduced the waiting period for a second grant to 10 years for certain works and the Housing (Amendment Act) 1958 enabled local authorities to advance loans for the reconstruction, repair or improvement of dwellings. Although the 1960s saw few further changes to the homeowner subsidy regime, increases in subsidy rates and widening of eligibility introduced in the 1950s were not rolled back.

These increases in generosity of homeowner subsidies substantially increased their value to aspirant purchasers. O'Connell (2004: 26) reports that:

> By the early 1960's...almost 30 per cent of the cost of a standard suburban house could be recouped [from government] by the purchaser. For example a house costing £3,000 would benefit from a state grant of £275, supplementary grant of £275, rates remission of £281, stamp duty reduction of £50 resulting in a total subsidy of £891.

However, this increased generosity and also the increased take-up of these grants substantially increased their cost for government. Figure 4.4 demonstrates that take-up of central government house purchase and reconstruction grants increased from 2,157 in 1948/1949 to 17,544 in 1963/1964. This reflects the fact that, contrary to the 1948 white paper's expectations, 70 per cent of dwellings constructed during the 1960s were provided by the private sector primarily for owner occupation (Department of Local Government, various years). In addition, the particularly strong growth in take-up of central government grants for the reconstruction of owner-occupied dwellings – only 732 of these grants were paid out in 1948/1949 compared to 12,439 in 1963/1964 – reflects the introduction of grants for the provision of water and sewage in 1952 which grew rapidly in popularity after their introduction and accounted for close to half of reconstruction grants paid in the 1960s. Figure 4.5 reveals that central spending on all categories of central government grants for homeowners increased from £356,697 to £5.6 million between 1948/1949 and 1963/1964.

These graphs significantly underestimate the total level of public subsidisation of homeownership, however, because they exclude both the

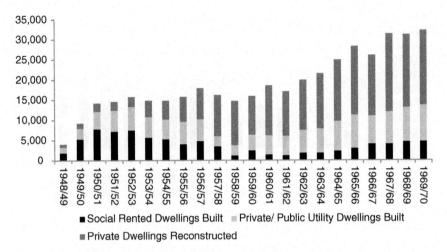

Fig. 4.4 Social rented, private and public utility dwellings built and private dwellings reconstructed with state aid, 1948/1949–1968/1969. *Source:* Department of Local Government (various years)

means tested supplementary grants provided by local government to home-owners and indirect government subsidies via remission of domestic rates and stamp duty. No national data on either of these subsidy types are available, but O'Connell's (2004) estimates of their value to individual households suggest that the cost to the exchequer was not significantly less than the direct central government subsidies detailed in Fig. 4.3. While Daly (1997) reports that supplementary grants accounted for at least £500,000 of local authority borrowings by 1953/1954.

In addition to providing ever higher levels of subsidy, government further increased its support for homeownership between the late 1940s and the late 1960s by expanding SDA mortgage lending. As Fig. 4.6 reveals, the total value of SDA lending was just £276,608 in 1948/1949, but by 1963/1964 it had reached £4.95 million. This growth was the result of both an increase in both the number of loans (638 SDA mortgages were issued in 1948/1949 compared to 2458 in 1964/1965) and also the average size of loans issued (which grew by 426 per cent between these years in part because the maximum loan available was increased on three occasions between the late 1940s

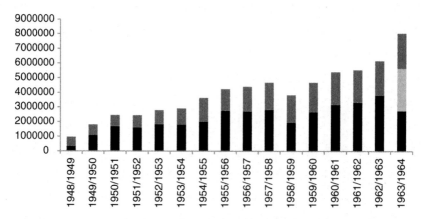

■ Housing grants   ■ Housing grants (Gaeltacht) ■ Subsidy to local authorities for housing

Fig. 4.5 Direct central government subsidies for housebuilding and recon-struction by tenure, 1948/1949–1963/1964. *Source:* Generated from the annual finance accounts as collated in Duanaire economic history database held by the National University of Ireland, Galway.

Note: Data refer to the fiscal year ended in March. The category "subsidy to local authorities for housing" relates primarily to central government sub-sidies towards interest payments on social housing development loans. Data for the period 1965/1966 to 1967/1968 are not available

and the late 1960s) (Department of Local Government, various years and see Table 4.1).

Daly's (1997) history of the local government ministry describes the significant pressure which this growth in SDA lending placed on public finances, particularly as the budgetary situation deteriorated in line with the health of the economy during the 1950s. These pressures were ampli-fied by the widespread practice among local authorities of granting approval for SDA mortgages to aspirant home buyers first and then seeking the money required to finance the loans afterwards. Irish social norms at this time created immense pressure to translate loan approvals into loans provided because couples got engaged and set wedding dates on the understanding that would have a marital home to move into after their wedding. As explained in Chap. 3, central government borrowing financed the local loans fund – which in turn provided the revenue for SDA

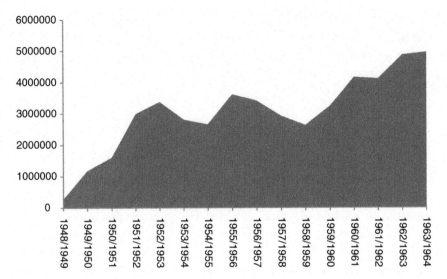

Fig. 4.6 Value of Small Dwellings Acquisition Act Mortgages drawn down, 1948/1949–1963/1964. *Source*: Generated from the annual finance accounts as collated in Duanaire economic history database held by the National University of Ireland, Galway

mortgages in most was local authorities, so their persistent breaches of local loans fund borrowing limits throughout the 1950s placed significant demands on the central exchequer. However, Dublin and Cork City Council's continuing need to finance SDA lending by issuing bonds on the market was even more problematic because, on several occasions in the late 1940s and 1950s, this finance was not forthcoming. Consequently, these authorities were forced to fund their activities from overdraft facilities or central government had to step in and guarantee their lending or "encourage" the banks to buy local government bonds (Daly, 1997). A particularly acute funding crisis emerged in the summer of 1954 when a Dublin City Council stock issue of £5 million attracted applications totalling only £840 and the council failed to negotiate a bank overdraft sufficient to cover its capital spending. Despite the fact that the national finances had deteriorated to the extent that three separate budgets were introduced in 1956, in the face of repeated threats and then action from Dublin City Council to suspend all SDA lending, central government granted the Dublin and Cork municipalities access to the local loans fund for housing purposes in 1956. Thus, despite concerted efforts from officials and ministers in the Department of Finance to control SDA mortgage lending, it continued to rise during the remainder of the 1950s and 1960s (Daly, 1997).

Social Housing as Property-Based Welfare

The growth of Ireland's property-based welfare system was further enhanced during the period under examination here by sales of social housing to tenants. As was explained in Chap. 3, the foundations of these developments were laid in the 1930s. Although the 1919 Housing Act empowered (but not required) local authorities to sell their dwellings to tenants (at a price which would cover the dwelling's development costs and therefore at no subsidy to tenants), they rarely did so prior to the introduction of the 1936 Labourer's Act which obliged rural local authorities to sell dwellings to tenants at a discount (just 75 per cent of the pre-purchase rents). No comprehensive data on the use of this provision are available until the mid-1950s, but the information which is available indicates that take-up was initially low – only 8,209 labourers' cottages were purchased prior to 1949/1950 (Department of Local Government, various years). Soon after, take-up increased drama-tically – 15,396 cottages were sold by 1953/1954 and the annual rate of sales increased significantly during the decade which followed to the extent that 68,444 labourers' cottages had been purchased by 1966/1967, which accounted for 76.8 per cent of all the rural social housing built (see Fig. 4.7). The increase in sales coincided with the raising of the discount available to tenants to just 50 per cent of pre-purchase rents in 1951 (Department of Local Government, various years). Sales patterns during the decades followed closely tracked subsidy rates, indicating that prospective tenant purchasers were highly sensitive to the generosity of the subsidies available from government.

Urban local authorities were also empowered (but not required) by the 1919 Act to sell dwellings to tenants, but only 13 dwellings in this category were sold prior to 1953 when urban local authorities were

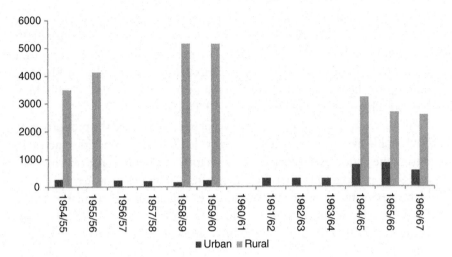

Fig. 4.7 Local authority social housing sold to tenants, 1954/1955–1966/1967. *Source*: Department of Local Government (various years).

Note: Comprehensive data are not available for 1956/1957, 1957/1958 and 1960/1961–1963/1964

instructed by the minister to adopt schemes to sell their dwellings on these terms (Department of Local Government, various years). Despite regular circulars from local government ministers urging local authorities to prepare sales schemes and promote them more vigorously, sales remained stubbornly low (around 200 dwellings per annum) until the late 1960s (see Fig. 4.6). However, the legislative and administrative basis for mass tenant purchase of urban social housing was laid down during the saturation period. The 1966 Housing Act consolidated all previous social housing legislation and thereby abolished the legal distinction between dwellings provided for rural labourers (previously governed by the Labourers' Acts) and the urban working class (the Housing of the Working Classes Acts). As a result, the right to "tenant purchase" afforded to rural tenants in the 1930s was extended to all local authority tenants in 1966. The terms of the new sales scheme were not announced until 1967; they provided substantial inducements to purchase but notably these inducements were higher in rural areas. The urban tenant purchase scheme specified that houses could be sold at their market or replacement value (whichever was lower) subject to a discount of 2 per cent for each year of tenancy rising to a maximum discount of 30 per cent in urban areas and 3 per cent per year of tenancy rising to a maximum discount of 45 per cent in rural areas. As detailed in Fig. 4.7, take-up of the tenant purchase scheme in urban areas was initially low, but this changed by the start of the 1970s.

Surprisingly, in view of the high level of sales to tenants, the proportion of households living in social housing provided by local authorities increased during the period under review in this chapter – from 16.5 per cent in 1946 to 18.42 per cent in 1961 (see Table 4.2). This was the result of very high rates of building of new dwellings in this tenure, particularly during the 1950s. Figure 4.4 reveals that local authorities built 52,741 dwellings between 1949/1950 and 1959/1960 compared to the 45,113 dwellings built by the private sector and public utility societies concurrently.

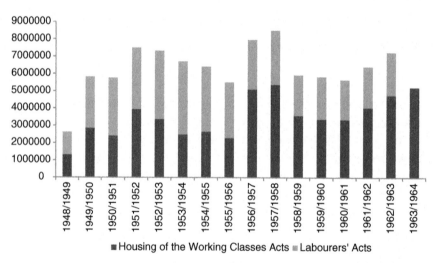

■Housing of the Working Classes Acts ■Labourers' Acts

Fig. 4.8 Government borrowing for social housing development under the Labourers' Acts and the Housing of the Working Classes Acts, 1948/1949–1963–1964. *Source*: Generated from the annual finance accounts as collated in Duanaire economic history database held by the National University of Ireland, Galway.

Note: Data refer to the fiscal year ended in March. Data for the period 1965/1966 to 1967/1968 are not available

Daly (1997) reports that, due to this rate of social housing output, by the middle of this decade most local authorities met the local output targets linked to the national output targets set in the 1948 white paper on housing. In contrast, during the 1960s local authorities completed 28,097 social rented dwellings, while the private sector built 67,047 dwellings and this was the first decade in the history of the independent Irish State in which output by the latter exceeded the former. This pattern of public/private housing output reflected first of all the weakness of the private housebuilding industry and the severe difficulties they experienced in raising capital during the first half of the twentieth century which eased from the 1960s and secondly variations in the rate of exchequer subsidisation of local authority social housebuilding. Figure 4.8 demonstrates that these subsidies expanded significantly during the 1950s, but, as explained later in this chapter, this rate of spending proved difficult to maintain during the decade which followed.

Drivers of the Saturation of the Property-Based Welfare System

As mentioned in the introduction to this chapter, the period from 1948 to 1968 was characterised by contradictory trends in the history of Ireland's property-based welfare system. These decades saw both the high watermark of this regime in terms of exchequer spending and household eligibility for subsidies and the emergence of significant levels of public criticism of this regime for the first time. This criticism proved unable to halt the growth of property-based welfare and the key reason for this was the distribution of power in the country at the time.

Figure 4.9 demonstrates that the rural population declined significantly during this period while the proportion of households living in urban areas expanded to the extent that, for the first time in the history of the State, the majority of the population lived in towns and cities of 1,500 people or more by the mid-1950s (53.1 per cent in 1956) (Central Statistics Office, various years). This change in the spatial distribution of the population had a clear impact on the political system, on politicians' agendas and agendas and also on public policy. For instance, during the late 1920s and early 1930s, Fianna Fáil's vote had a noticeable Western

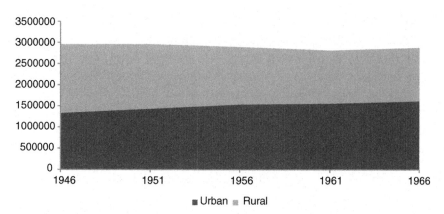

Fig. 4.9 Population of urban and rural districts, 1946–1966. *Source*: Central Statistics Office (various years).

Note: "Urban areas" refers to towns and cities with a population of 1,500 or more. "Rural areas" include everywhere else

and therefore rural bias which reflected both their higher levels of support in this part of the country and the concentration of the population in rural areas. However, due to Clann na Talmhan's success in mobilising the small farmer vote and population decline in rural areas, after the 1938 general election Fianna Fáil's Western support declined and its Dublin vote exceeded the national average for the first time in 1943 (Garvin, 1981). Garvin (1981: 180) argues that this development ultimately benefitted Fianna Fáil because it enabled the party to

> . . . to dissociate itself from the rather sterile small-farm protest politics of the 1930s and move into a central position in Irish society, benefiting from the mood of national solidarity that World War II encouraged and accommodating itself to more clearly modern political interests such as those of the business and working classes of the towns, the new and growing public sector and the protected industries set up under the new tariff regime in the 1930s.

Fianna Fáil's industry and commerce minister and later Taoiseach Seán Lemass had clearly learned this lesson well because he realised that the party's election losses in the 1950s and very narrow election victories in the early 1960s were strongly related to fluctuating support in urban areas, particularly Dublin, and responded with further efforts to increase the party's appeal to urban voters (Lee, 1989; Roche, 2009). These efforts centred on increased social spending particularly on housing. Local authority social housing provision was a key weapon in Fianna Fáil's electoral war with the Labour Party (on its left flank) and homeowner grants were useful aid in the battle for votes with Fine Gael (on the right) (Lee, 1989). Thus, despite strong practical pressures to reduce public spending on housing during the balance of payments crises of the 1950s and strong intellectual arguments from economic modernisers such as the head of the Department of Finance, T. K Whitaker, that exchequer housing expenditure should be redirected towards "productive investment" (i.e. to support industrial development), for most of Lemass's time as Taoiseach housing expenditure continued to rise (Barry, 2009). As discussed later, Lemass strongly concurred with Whitaker's views on the economic policy changes necessary to promote growth and implemented many of these, most notably the removal of protectionist tariffs from the late 1950s, but for electoral reasons cutting housing or land reform expenditure proved impossible (Barry, 2009).

The power of housebuilding industry also increased during the period under review in this chapter and was employed to push for new public subsidies for housing, particularly homeownership and also to protect the existing subsidy regime. This power was exercised directly through political lobbying and also indirectly by virtue of the employment-intensive nature of this housebuilding, which was a key consideration for government particularly in the context of the severe recession and unemployment crisis during the 1950s. The influence of the latter issue was evidenced by the diligent recording of the numbers employed on local authority housebuilding schemes in the Department of Local Government annual reports of this period. Furthermore, concurrent with the Department of Finance's efforts to roll back SDA mortgage lending in the midst of Dublin City Council's funding crisis during the mid-1950s, the cabinet committee on unemployment was exploring opportunities to provide additional homebuyer grants and SDA mortgages to encourage more private housebuilding (Daly, 1997).

Daly's (1997) history of the local government ministry identifies lobbying by homebuilding industry representatives as one of the key reasons
why the finance ministry was unsuccessful:

> Press headlines on 26 January 1956, reporting that Dublin Corporation
> [City Council] had ceased to provide SDA loans, prompted protests the
> building industry. The joint negotiating committee of the Dublin build-
> ing industry recalled the "unqualified assurance given by each successive
> Government that housing activities of the Corporation would not be
> retarded, delayed or diminished by lack of finance".
>
> (Daly, 1997: 369)

Lee (1989: 193), among many others, has highlighted the particularly
strong links between the building industry and Fianna Fáil which emerged
during this period to the extent that "the building industry soon came to
be widely regarded as an extension of the Fianna Fáil patronage system".

Although the power of the urban population increased in tandem
with their growing numbers, the influence of the agrarian lobby did not
decline in tandem with their falling numbers and, as the opening
sections of this chapter revealed, certainly not enough to effect any
radical redirection in land redistribution policy. This is because farmers'
political and economic import still significantly exceeded their numbers.
In economic terms, agriculture was still the dominant sector in the 1950s
and 1960s – in 1960, live animals accounted for 30 per cent of Irish
exports while manufactured goods made up only 19 per cent of exports
(Barry, 2000). In political terms, the 1950s and 1960s were also distinguished by growing militancy among farmers' representatives, supported
by new and more effective representative structures (Murphy, 1997).
These new structures were non-party political pressure groups such as the
Irish Creamery Milk Suppliers Association and the National Farmers'
Union (NFU) which were founded in 1950 and 1951, respectively. As
the 1950s and 1960s progressed, the latter gradually came to represent
the majority of farmers and replaced the multitude of smaller, largely
ineffective groups which had previously represented different producer
categories and the farmers' parties which had failed to unite big and
small farmers. Although the NFU's work focused primarily on lobbying

for increases in farm incomes to match rising industrial wages, cuts in rates (local property taxes) on agriculture and also promoting Ireland's entry to the European Economic Community, the land hunger which had inspired previous decades of land redistribution activity showed no sign of abating during the 1950s and 1960s so neither did agitation for further redistribution. Indeed, two lobby groups dedicated specifically to this cause also emerged during this period – Lia Fáil (established in 1957) and the Farmers' Rights Campaign (1966) (Jones, 2001). Jones (2001) describes how this Fianna Fáil backbenchers and the party's rank and file remained particularly susceptible to this lobbying and therefore supportive of land reform, while the presence of Clann na Talmhan in both inter-party governments meant that maintaining the land redistribution programme was crucial to keep these coalitions together.

Farm labourers' numbers contracted even faster than farmers during the 1950s and 1960s, but they remained influential in the Labour Party. This party's early failure to thrive is often attributed to the tiny industrial workforce on which it could rely for votes, but even as Ireland urbanised Labour failed to establish itself as a significant electoral force in cities (O'Connor, 2011). It won only a single Dáil seat in Dublin in both the 1957 and 1961 general elections and until the late 1960s remained heavily dependent on the farm labourer/rural working-class vote in the southern and eastern counties for the majority of its parliamentary seats (Gallagher, 1982). Chapter 3 explained how Labour tried unsuccessfully in opposition to increase the discounts available to tenant purchasers of labourers' cottages during the 1930s and 1940s. Not surprisingly then, after acceding to the post of Minister for Local Government in the first inter-party government, Labour's Michael Keyes was quick to implement his long-standing plans to bolster rural tenant purchase and decreased the purchase costs to 50 per cent of previous rents in 1951 (Hayden, 2013).

Both the Labour Party and Fianna Fáil, which was the former's main competitor for votes among the urban working class, also strongly promoted the need for more local authority social housing output to meet the needs of their voters. However, while Labour lobbied for the extension of the right to buy to urban local authority tenants, primarily on the grounds of equity of treatment between the urban and rural working classes, this was opposed by Fianna Fáil until the mid-1960s on the basis that no dwellings should be sold until urban social housing needs were fully satisfied (Hayden, 2013).

The factors which had underpinned the legitimacy of the property-based welfare system period during the construction phase (see Chap. 4) remained influential during its saturation phase and were employed to justify the extension of government subsidies for asset acquisition to previously excluded groups. Their continuing influence is illustrated by the parliamentary debate on the extension of the tenant purchase scheme of urban local authority tenants during the 1950s and 1960s. Fine Gael introduced a private members' bill to the Dáil with this intention in 1966. The arguments offered in support of the bill by its proposer Mark Clinton strongly echoed the arguments made in support of the right to buy labourers' cottages three decades earlier:

> Wherever houses have been vested [tenant purchased], it is quite apparent that a new interest is being taken in property. Small repairs are attended to at the right time. Windows and doors are painted before deterioration sets in. . . . The tenants who become owners of their own houses willingly accept responsibility and pride of ownership is demonstrated in many ways. Ownership gives them roots and they become interested not only in their houses but in the area the house is built. They become a community.
>
> (Clinton, 1966, in Dáil Éireann, 1966, Vol. 220, No. 7, Col 1031)

While his party colleague Richie Ryan raised distributist arguments in favour of selling urban social housing to tenants:

> May I direct attention once again in this House to the words of the late Pope John in his most significant and valuable encyclical, *Mater et Magistra*? He spells out here the principle of the right to private property in words that I should like again to put on the record . . . in the hope that they may yet bear fruit in the minds of the Minister and his advisers. In his encyclical at paragraph 113, Pope John said: "But it is not enough to assert that the right to own private property and the means of production is inherent in human nature. We must also insist on the extension of this right in practice to all classes of citizens". There is a social philosophy which I think must be accepted by all . . . The right to own property is

apparently accepted for certain sections of the community, but it will not be accepted by the Minister's fiat for the benefit of the less well-off classes of people in Dublin and other urban centres.

(Ryan, 1966, in Dáil Éireann, 1966, Vol. 220, No. 7, Cols 1043–1044)

However, most speakers' comments did not focus on the merits or demerits of the extending discounted sales to urban tenants, rather they supported the policy on the grounds of equity of treatment between town and country and these views echoed the arguments regarding equity of treatment between farmers and farm labourers made in support of the 1936 Labourers' Act. As mentioned earlier, this analysis was strongly promoted by the Labour Party. In this vein, for instance, its TD for Meath Jim Tully supported the bill on the grounds that it gives urban tenants "the same right of ownership, at a reasonable cost, as is given to their brethren in rural Ireland" and not just their local authority tenant brethren but their farmer brethren too:

It amuses me to hear people talk about the "three Fs'" which, apparently, apply to people who own farms but are not supposed to apply to people who own houses only. Apparently there is an idea that there are two different sets of people in the country; those who have land and a house, and those who have a house only. I should like to see the same thing applied to the people who own houses only as applies to those who have farms and houses.

(Tully, 1966, in Dáil Éireann, 1966, Vol. 220, No. 7, Col 1054)

Dooley (2004a) reports that familist arguments were also commonly cited in support of the continuation of land reform and other supports for small farmers during the 1950s and 1960s, and Daly (1997) suggests that this philosophy was also employed to legitimise increases in public spending on local authority social housebuilding during this period. Rather than conforming to the traditional practice of prioritising those living in overcrowded conditions or suffering from tuberculous in decisions regarding the allocation of social housing, Dublin City Council proposed in 1944 that some dwellings should be reserved for allocation to newlyweds. This approach was strongly supported by Minister Seán

MacEntee, who proposed a complex set of arrangements for prioritising newlyweds and also families with children in the allocation of local authority housing. These proposals were deemed too onerous by Dublin City Council officials, so they were never implemented to the letter but Daly (1997) argues that they were followed in spirit. Furthermore, their broad thrust was legalised by the 1950 Housing (Amendment) Act which afforded all urban local authorities the power to prioritise newlyweds.

Concurrent with campaigns to legitimise property-based welfare, the late 1940s, 1950s and 1960s were also distinguished by the emergence of unprecedented public criticism of this system by politicians, in contrast with the critiques raised in previous decades which had been voiced in private and mainly by civil servants. These criticisms did not affect significant policy change during the period under review in this chapter, but the fact that politicians felt able to voice them in public was significant. It reflected not only an emerging crisis in the legitimacy of property-based welfare but also in the wider socio-economic system in which it was grounded, which did not bode well for the long-term future of either regime.

The economic depression Ireland experienced during the 1950s and its coincidence with a "golden age" of economic growth and welfare state building across much of Western Europe created a crisis of confidence about the country's ability to survive as a viable economic and social entity (Rothman and O'Connell, 2003). Irish GNP increased by 8 per cent between 1949 and 1956, while concurrently GNP increased by 21 per cent in Britain and by 42 per cent among members of the Organisation for European Economic Cooperation (Department of Finance, 1958a). Between 1951 and 1961, Ireland's labour force shrank by 13 per cent, mainly due to falling employment in agriculture and emigration reached highs not seen since the late nineteenth century which raised the spectre of the *Vanishing Irish* (the name of a widely discussed book on the subject published in 1954 by J.A. O'Brien) (Daly, 2006).

Although the dismantling of protectionism and promotion of free trade were the key reasons for the end of this existential crisis, the same modernising politicians and civil servants who were the architects of the trade liberalisation project identified a link between Ireland's economic underdevelopment and the property-based welfare system (Bradley, 2004). T.K. Whitaker initially flagged his views in this regard in an address given to the Statistical and Social Inquiry Society in Dublin on the eve of his appointment as secretary general of the Department of Finance in 1956. Here he highlighted the trade-off between extensive state investment in housing and underspending on productive investment:

> In most European countries these basic productive activities have been receiving a higher proportion of the available capital than in Ireland. Here for many years dwellings have been the greatest single claimant on capital resources ... over the six years 1949–54 dwellings alone formed as high a proportion of gross domestic capital formation as agriculture, mining, manufacturing and other construction combined ... In Britain, Germany, and Belgium housing had to take a lower place in the early post-war years than the rehabilitation of industry and trade and it is only in the past few years that special efforts have been made to overtake arrears. ...
>
> (Whitaker, 1956: 193)

This line of thinking clearly influenced the landmark 1958 Department of Finance white paper – the *First Programme for Economic Expansion* (based on Whitaker's policy paper *Economic Development* which was published earlier the same year) because the policy statement argued that "the social capital investment of past years has given us an 'infrastructure', of housing, hospitals, communications etc., which is equal (in some respects, perhaps, superior) to that of comparable countries" and suggested that social investment (particularly on housing) should be reduced to support increased state productive investment to enable industrial development (Department of Finance, 1958b: 8).

The *First Programme for Economic Expansion* did not highlight a similar trade-off between land reform spending and productive investment; indeed, it proposed increased exchequer investment in agriculture because it envisaged that the sector would be a key engine of economic development. However, a debate on the economic costs of land reform raged in cabinet at this time and, on occasions, spilled out into parliament (see Jones, 2001). Thus in addition to Erskine Childers' aforementioned 1957 parliamentary address which raised concerns about the role of land redistribution in undermining the efficiency of agriculture, during a Dáil debate on land reform spending in 1956 the former minister for lands Seán Moylan (in Dáil Éireann, 1956, Vol. 158 No. 1, Col 77) complained:

> The Land Commission has been for many years in operation and it has spent many millions of pounds; yet, by the test of agricultural production, no improvement has been achieved. It may be that a relatively small number of families have had their economic position improved, but that does not justify the Department. The general situation agriculturally has not been bettered by the activities of the Land Commission. There has been no general improvement in the nation's economic position as a result of its efforts. Social welfare, in Mayo or elsewhere, like patriotism, is not enough.

Furthermore, a cabinet subcommittee which was established in 1958 to review land policy broadly agreed that scaling down of land redistribution was necessary and one member, Minister for Finance James Ryan, expressed support for "the termination of Land Commission activities over a wide area" (cited in Jones, 2001: 94).

As the preceding discussion reveals, as well as the increasing regularity with which they were raised, the critiques of the property-based welfare system proposed during the 1960s were also significant because they were attractive to a larger section of the population than those voiced by opponents of public investment in this policy field in earlier decades. During the 1930s and 1940s, the opponents of spending on property-based welfare generally shared a deflationist mentality and proposed further fiscal rectitude as a rather unattractive alternative to public spending on land reform or homeownership subsidies (Fanning, 1978). Whereas in the 1960s the property-based welfare system's critics such as T.K. Whitaker highlighted the trade-off between property-based welfare spending and the very attractive (and for large sections of Irish society desperately needed) increase in industrial development, living standards and jobs.

However, the property-based welfare system persisted in part because some strong efficiency arguments could be offered in its support. For instance, the parliamentary debate on the extension of subsidised tenant purchase to urban areas via the 1966 Housing Act emphasised the potential for sales to release capital to local authorities which could be spent on building replacement social housing or cutting rates and also the "substantial" savings in local authorities' housing maintenance expenditure which would be enabled by sales (Hayden, 2013). The parliamentary debates indicate that the members of Dáil Éireann did not consider the possibility that this capital might be insufficient to repay the development loans which were outstanding on most of these dwellings. Although Daly's (1997) history of the Department of the Environment points out that this was a major concern among senior officials and ministers in that department and was a key reason why the introduction of tenant purchase in urban areas lagged rural tenant purchase by such a long period.

A more convincing and therefore more significant efficiency argument for expanding property-based welfare relates to the relatively low level of housing standards and the consequent necessity for state investment to rectify this situation. Table 4.2 demonstrates that Irish housing standards were certainly poor at the start of the period under review in this chapter. In 1946, 38.7 per cent of occupied dwellings in Ireland had a piped water supply, while only 15.4 per cent had a bath or shower. In contrast, the 1947 social survey of Great Britain revealed that 97 per cent of households there had piped water and 55 per cent had a bath or shower (cited in Holmans, 2005). Irish housing standards had improved dramatically by the early 1970s (78.2 per cent of occupied dwellings had piped water and 55.4 per cent had a bath or shower by 1971), but they still lagged behind Britain (where 88 per cent of households had a bath or shower by 1971) (see Table 4.2 and Holmans, 2005). Therefore, government investment in new housebuilding and renovation in Ireland could certainly be justified on efficiency grounds. The extent to which this investment was focused on homeowners is more difficult to justify however because, particularly in towns and cities, substandard housing was largely concentrated in the cheaper end of the private rented sector particularly in rent-controlled dwellings. For instance, the 1946 census revealed that 32.6 per cent of dwellings in Dublin City Council's operational area (which accommodated 36,170 households) were tenement flats with toilets shared among several families (Central Statistics Office, various years). The occupants of these dwellings were unlikely to be able to afford homeownership, so improving their housing conditions would have required increased spending on social housing.

A further efficiency-related consideration which helped to promote the expansion of government subsidisation of homeownership was market failure among private mortgage lenders, specifically their failure to provide sufficient credit to satisfy the growing appetite for home purchase. Lack of lending to industry and agriculture by Irish commercial banks was the subject of vociferous complaints by politicians in the decades after independence and was a key factor behind the establishment of two commissions of inquiry into banking which reported in 1926 and 1938 (Girvin, 1989). However, neither commission raised significant concerns about the fact that, in common with their UK counterparts, Irish banks rarely advanced residential mortgages. In both countries, mortgage lending was dominated by mutually owned building societies which had been established especially for this purpose but, unlike the UK, Irish building societies failed to grow significantly during the first half of the twentieth century. In 1961, Irish building societies advanced £2.9 million in mortgages, while SDA lending totalled £3 million in 1961/1962 (see Fig. 4.6 and Dowling, 1974). In contrast, British local authorities provided only 14.5 per cent of mortgages (by volume rather than value) for new housing in 1961 and building societies provided the vast majority of the remainder (Holmans, 2005). Low levels of mortgage lending by Irish building societies were primarily related to their deposit base which remained weak until the 1960s, but it was also influenced by government intervention, most notably more attractive SDA loan conditions (e.g. lower down payments) and also legal restrictions on the proportion of deposits which could be advanced in mortgages (O'Connell, 2007; Carey, 1974).

These legal restrictions were eased incrementally from the early 1940s, with little impact on levels of lending from this sector initially. However, the marked expansion in SDA mortgage lending during the 1950s and the related strains on public finances which were described earlier prompted policymakers to take more radical action to increase non-governmental mortgage lending. In a Dáil debate on the 1956 Housing (Amendment) Act, the Minister for Local Government complained:

> It is not the function of the State or of local authorities to provide loan facilities for persons in a position to finance their houses from these or other sources. It is intended that local authorities should continue to operate the Small Dwellings (Acquisition) Acts for persons willing to provide their own houses and who are unable to provide the necessary finances otherwise but many persons have been availing of the facilities provided under the Acts who either did not need to do so or who would not have needed to do so if commercial agencies would advance a higher percentage of the purchase price and would allow a longer repayment period.
>
> (O'Donnell, 1956, in Dáil Éireann, 1956, Vol. 159 No.4, Col 150).

This legislation introduced government guarantees for building society mortgages to lower income households in order to encourage building societies to lend more and at higher rates of interest. Although this measure had a limited impact in the short term, building society mortgage lending did expand slowly during the decade which followed as their deposits grew and also restrictions were introduced on the availability of SDA mortgages. The 1956 Act limited SDA mortgages to 95 per cent of estimated market value of dwellings exclusive of grants, which effected a sizeable reduction in the maximum loan available and pushed higher-earning households to apply for building society mortgages (Daly, 1997; Dowling, 1974; see Table 4.1). Therefore, as this private mortgage market failure was slowly remedied during the late 1950s and 1960s the rationale for extensive government provision of mortgages also weakened.

Between the late 1940s and the late 1960s, the hand of critics of the property-based welfare state was strengthened by a number of other efficiency considerations. The first of these was flagged in the opening sections of this chapter (and are detailed in Figs. 4.2–4.6). It relates to the affordability of the increase in public spending on property-based welfare provision. These challenges were amplified by declining revenue available to meet these costs, particularly to service the loans taken out for social housing provision and also by the increased visibility of these loans on the state balance sheets.

Since the emergence of the social housing sector in the late nineteenth century, local government rates and tenants' rents had provided the main source of revenue for servicing housing development loans. Rates income declined throughout the twentieth century, however, because of the exclusion of more and more categories of homeowners from the property tax under the rates remission provisions of the Housing Acts and also because farmers campaigned successfully for similar concessions (Daly, 1997). Rents income declined because, in an effort to make their dwellings affordable to the poorest families, the municipality responsible for Cork decoupled its tenants' rents from the cost of housing provision in the 1930s and linked them to tenants' incomes instead. Due to campaigning from tenants' representatives (often via rent strikes), this system, which is known colloquially as "differential rents", slowly spread nationwide and all local authorities were required to use it by the 1966 Housing Act (National Economic and Social Council, 1977) (see Table 4.1). The architect of this system, Philip Monahan – the long-serving, formidable and innovative head of Cork City Council – envisaged that higher-income tenants would subsidise the low rents paid by their poorer counterparts, but this calculation proved wildly overoptimistic in practice (see Monahan, 1947). This pattern of declining revenue to service social housing development loans, coupled with increasing costs because these dwellings were sold for less than the cost of the outstanding development loan, created severe difficulties for financing social housebuilding. Rather than reducing output, central government initially reacted to these difficulties by incrementally raising its contribution to the costs of servicing the interest on social housing development loans until it finally reached 100 per cent in the late 1960s (Blackwell, 1988) (see Fig. 4.5 in which the cost of these interest subsidies is included in the category of "subsidies to local authorities for housing"). However, funding this arrangement proved challenging for the exchequer which is likely to have contributed to the marked decline in social housebuilding in the 1960s compared to the previous decade (see Fig. 4.4). Over the longer term, this development would undermine the property-based welfare system by reducing the potential for expanding homeownership by selling local authority social housing to tenants.

The increase in SDA lending in the 1950s also had a substantial impact on central government borrowing. This is because after 1956 all SDA mortgages were financed by the local loans fund which was sourced from exchequer borrowing, whereas previously they were funded in part by local authority bond issues which were not formally considered part of the national debt at that time. Developments in land reform financing during the 1950s, most notably the introduction and then the increased use of cash purchases of land for redistribution on the open market (rather than using land bonds), further reduced the potential "off balance sheet funding" of property-based welfare and increased the potential direct costs to exchequer. These direct costs were further increased by the expanding scale of land reform during the 1950s and 1960s and by other changes to arrangements for financing this activity such as the 1950 Land Act which obliged the Land Commission to pay market value for land compulsorily acquired rather than (generally lower) "fair value" and the removal of the 4 per cent limit on land bond interest by the 1953 Act (see Table 4.1).

Conclusions

This chapter has described the saturation phase of Ireland's property-based welfare system between the late 1940s and the late 1960s. During this period, the land reform project was extended to its furthest practicable limits and public subsidisation of homeownership was extended from the rural population to the urban middle class (via subsidies such as grants and rates remission and local government loans) and also to the working class in cities (via the extension of tenant purchase of social housing to this group). As a result of the latter development, Irish homeownership rates increased from 52.2 per cent of households in 1946 to 70.8 per cent in 1971 (see Table 4.2). These rates were among the highest in the developed world at the time – only 49 per cent of UK households, 35 per cent of Swedes and 60 per cent of Canadian households were homeowners in 1970 (Angel, 2000).

The saturation of the property-based welfare state required very marked increases in public spending on the associated policies, particularly on homeownership subsidies and government-provided mortgages for this sector and to a lesser extent on social housing. Although the number, complexity and variety of these subsidies mean that measuring their full scale is impossible, it is reasonable to conclude that the proportion of housing capital for housing derived from government was even higher during the saturation period than it had been in the 1930s and the early 1940s. The 1964 housing white paper *Housing Progress and Prospects* estimated that the total capital expenditure on housing between 1948 and 1964 came to £225 million. Central and local governments contributed £192 million of this, whereas banks, building societies, life assurance companies and savings made up the balance of just 15 per cent. According to the white paper, only a handful of new dwellings were constructed without state aid during this period. As a result, a United Nations (1958) study of 15 European countries in the mid-1950s calculated that Irish State housing subsidies were the highest among this group both in terms of the proportion of housing capital derived from the exchequer (75 per cent) and of new dwellings which received public subsidies (97 per cent). Thus the combination of high public spending on housing and on land reform meant that total Irish government spending on capital redistribution was unusually high by the standards of the times and also was atypical in its purpose as a social policy rather than as a means to support "productive investment" as T.K. Whitaker envisaged.

This chapter has explained that the scale of this spending became increasingly difficult for governments to afford during the 1950s, particularly in the context of falling revenue to service associated debts and the increased visibility of these debts on the state balance sheet. These affordability difficulties, together with opportunity costs of investment in property-based welfare, which impeded productive investment and concerns about the role of land reform in undermining commercially viable agriculture, all inspired increased public criticism of this welfare regime during the period under review in this chapter. However, the significant political power still enjoyed by small farmers, despite their declining numbers, and the growing political and economic power of the building industry and politician's strategy to attract urban votes by subsidising home purchase and social housing provision drove the consistent expansion of almost all categories of property-based welfare provision throughout the 1950s and 1960s.

Concurrent with this growth in property-based welfare, it is notable that Ireland's mainstream welfare state expanded only modestly, certainly in comparison with the dramatic growth in social services and benefits provision which occurred in most other Western European countries after World War II (Powell, 1992). William Beveridge's landmark 1942 report on *Social Security and Allied Services* which set out a road map for the post-war expansion of the UK welfare state inspired widespread comment among policymakers in Ireland and strongly influenced the Irish government's 1949 white paper on social security policy but ultimately the Irish policy reforms introduced on foot of this debate were modest (Carey, 2007). As recommended by Beveridge (1942) in the late 1940s, the post-war UK Labour Party government introduced a universal system of means tested and social insurance-based social security benefits which replaced almost all vestiges of the previous Poor Law system. The 1944 Education Act also introduced free secondary schooling in the UK and a comprehensive, free at the point of use the National Health Service was established in 1948 (Glennerster, 1995). By contrast in Ireland, the 1952 Social Welfare act extended access to social security benefits but still excluded substantial sections of the population from cover; the 1953 Health Act formally established a mixed public/private model of health care in which most of the population still had to pay for services and free second-level education was not introduced until 1967 (McCashin, 2004). Public spending on old age pensions in Ireland was very high by European standards during the period under review in this chapter due to the large proportion of older people in the Irish population. However, Tomka's (2013) analysis indicates that Ireland is the only one of nine Western European countries for which data are available where social spending as a proportion of GDP contracted between 1950 and 1960 (from 14.7 per cent to 14.0 per cent). Measured in these terms, spending in Ireland was lower than that in the UK, the Netherlands, Belgium, Germany, Austria, Sweden, Denmark and Italy in the latter year.

References

Angel, S. (2000). *Housing policy matters: A global analysis*, Oxford: Oxford University Press.

Barry, F. (2000). Convergence is not automatic: Lessons from Ireland for central and eastern Europe. *The World Economy, 23*(10), 1379–1394.

Barry, F. (2009). Politics and fiscal policy under Lemass: A theoretical appraisal. *Economic and Social Review, 40*(1), 393–406.

Beveridge, W. (1942). *Social security and allied services*. London: HMSO.

Blackwell, J. (1988). *A review of housing policy*. Dublin: National Economic and Social Council.

Bradley, J. (2004). Changing the rules: How the failures of the 1950s forced a transition in economic policy making. *Administration, 52*(1), 92–107.

Carey, E. (1974). *Building societies in Ireland*. Dublin: Stationery Office.

Carey, S. (2007). *Social security in Ireland, 1939–1952: The limits to solidarity*. Dublin: Irish Academic Press.

Central Statistics Office (various years). *Census of population of Ireland*. Dublin: Stationery Office.

Daly, M. (1997). *The buffer state: The historical origins of the Department of the Environment*. Dublin: Institute of Public Administration.

Daly, M. (2006). *The slow failure: Population decline and independent Ireland, 1922–1973*. London: University of Wisconsin Press.

Department of Finance (1958a). *Economic development*. Dublin: Department of Finance.

Department of Finance (1958b). *First programme for economic expansion*. Dublin: Department of Finance.

Department of Local Government (various years). *Tuarascáil/Report*. Dublin, Department of Local Government.

Dooley, T. (2004a). Land and politics in independent Ireland, 1923–48: The case for reappraisal. *Irish Historical Studies, 34*(134), 175–195.

Dooley, T. (2004b). *The land for the people: The land question in independent Ireland*. Dublin: UCD Press.

Dowling, B. (1974). The development of the financial sector in Ireland, 1949–72". *Journal of the Social and Statistical Inquiry Society of Ireland, XXIII*(I), 57–107.

Fanning, R. (1978). *The Irish Department of Finance, 1922–58*. Dublin: Institute of Public Administration.

Gallagher, M. (1982). *The Irish Labour Party in transition: 1957–82.* Manchester: Manchester University Press.

Garvin, T. (1981). *The evolution of nationalist politics.* Dublin: Gill and McMillan.

Girvin, B. (1989). *Between two worlds: Politics and economy in independent Ireland.* Dublin: Gill and Macmillan.

Glennerster, H. (1995). *British social policy since 1945.* Oxford: Blackwell.

Hayden, A. (2013). *Tenant purchase in Ireland: A study of path dependency.* Dublin: unpublished PhD thesis submitted to University College Dublin.

Holmans, A. (2005). *Historical statistics of housing in Britain.* Cambridge: Department of Land Economy, University of Cambridge.

Jones, D.S. (2001). Divisions within the Irish Government over Land Distribution Policy, 1940–70. *Eire-Ireland, 36*(3–4), 87–92.

Lee, J. (1989). *Ireland, 1912–1985: Politics and society.* Cambridge: Cambridge University Press.

McCashin, T. (2004). *Social security in Ireland.* Dublin: Gill and Macmillan.

Minister for Local Government (1948). *A review of past operations and immediate requirements, housing white paper.* Dublin: Stationery Office.

Minister for Local Government (1964). *Housing progress and prospects.* Dublin: Stationery Office.

Monahan, P. (1947). Housing. *Christus Rex, 3*(3), 46–62.

Murphy, G. (1997). Towards a corporate state? Sean Lemass and the realignment of interest groups in the policy process 1948–1964. *Administration, 47*(1), 86–102.

National Economic and Social Council (1977). *Report on housing subsidies.* Dublin: NESC.

O'Brien, J. (1953). *The vanishing Irish: The enigma of the modern world.* New York: McGraw-Hill.

O'Connell, C. (2007). *The state and housing in Ireland: Ideology, policy and practice.* London: Nova Science.

O'Connor, E. (2011). *A labour history of Ireland 1824–2000.* Dublin: UCD Press.

O'Connell C. (2004). The housing market and owner occupation in Ireland. In: M. Norris, & D. Redmond (Eds.), *Housing contemporary Ireland: Policy, society and shelter* (pp. 21–44). Dublin: Institute of Public Administration.

Powell, F. (1992). *The politics of Irish Social Policy 1600–1990.* New York: Edwin Mellen Press.

Roche, W. (2009). Social partnership: From Lemass to Cowen. *Economic and Social Review, 40*(2), 183–205.

Rothman, D. & O'Connell, P. (2003). The changing social structure. In B. Fanning, & T. McNamara (Eds.), *Ireland develops: Administration and social policy, 1953–2003* (pp. 68–88). Dublin: Institute of Public Administration.

Threshold (1981). *Private rented: The forgotten sector.* Dublin: Threshold.

Tomka, B. (2013). *A social history of twentieth-century Europe.* London: Routledge.

United Nations (1958). *Financing of housing in Europe.* Geneva: UN.

Whitaker, T.K. (1956). Capital formation, saving and economic progress. *Journal of the Statistical and Social Inquiry Society of Ireland, XVIX*(1955/1956), 184–209.

5

Retrenchment: 1969–1989

Introduction

Between 1969 and 1989, the property-based welfare system initially destabilised and subsequently collapsed and was largely dismantled during a period of wider public spending retrenchment. The first of these developments was halting, uneven and protracted – it was spread across the 1970s and early 1980s – the second was short and sharp and concentrated on the final three of the years under review here. The destabilisation of the property-based welfare system first became evident during the 1970s as escalating costs, particularly of homeownership supports and social housing provision, became increasingly difficult for government to bear in the context of the increasing challenging world economic context and strengthening competing claims on state investment associated with the expansion of "mainstream" welfare services such as education, health and social security. By the end of the 1970s, the economic and fiscal crisis became more acute. Initially, this crisis generated a period of policy instability as the Land Commission's migration schemes were ceased but its land redistribution work continued and some homeownership subsidies were cut back while others were

© The Author(s) 2016
M. Norris, *Property, Family and the Irish Welfare State*,
DOI 10.1007/978-3-319-44567-0_5

extended. However, in the mid-1980s, an unambiguous and radical policy redirection emerged and between 1986 and 1989 the property-based welfare system, which had been slowly and incrementally constructed over the course of the preceding century, was largely abolished. Most homeowner subsidies were abolished in 1987; in the same year, the century-old system of borrowing to fund social housing development was abolished and, as a result, output rates decreased radically; SDA lending also fell dramatically in 1988 and a bill to abolish the Land Commission was published in 1989 and finally enacted in 1992. This chapter describes the dismantling of the property-based welfare state, the period of policy instability which preceded it and the power, legitimacy and efficiency drivers which shaped these developments.

In economic terms, the period under examination here started well enough. The late 1960s and early 1970s saw strong economic growth of more than 4 per cent per annum, but the remainder of the 1970s was very mixed in economic terms and the first half of the 1980s was truly dismal. During the 1970s, Ireland, like other developed economies, was buffeted by two oil price shocks in 1973–1974 and 1979–1980. As a result, unemployment, which had averaged at around 5 per cent during the 1960s, increased to 9 per cent by 1978 and, after a short period of decline, grew strongly again to a peak of 17 per cent in 1987. In its 1972 budget, the Fianna Fáil government breeched the principle of balancing the current budget and borrowing only for capital spending which had been adhered to since the foundation of the State and planned a small current budget deficit for the following year (Lee, 1989). However, due to electoral considerations and the oil crises, the trickle through this small breech in the dam of fiscal prudence turned into a deluge. Despite very marked increases in taxation, particularly on earned income in the 1970s, and cuts in public spending during the first half of the 1980s, the national debt increased from 54.5 per cent of GNP in 1973 to 81.0 in 1980 and to 142.2 in 1986 and debt servicing costs accounted for 27 per cent of public spending by the mid-1980s (Kennedy et al., 1988).

The deteriorating economic situation in the 1980s had a significant political impact. Although the 1970s saw repeated changes of government (Fianna Fáil completed two terms, interrupted by a Fine Gael/ Labour coalition government), all administrations served out their full term and enjoyed clear parliamentary majorities. Whereas the early 1980s were distinguished by marked political instability. Four governments fell between December 1979 and December 1982, and although the Fine Gael/Labour coalition, which was elected on the latter date, managed to serve until 1987, its efforts to get a grip on the fiscal crisis were hamstrung by continuous internal conflict (Lee, 1989). In contrast, despite its lack of a majority in the Dáil, the Fianna Fáil government elected in 1987 managed to provide both administrative stability and radical policy change. This was the administration which dismantled most of the property-based welfare system.

Retrenchment of the Property-Based Welfare System

Land Reform

Land reform was the first element of the property-based welfare system to emerge in the 1880s and also the first to recede a century later. From 1980, the amount of land acquired and redistributed by the Land Commission fell significantly and its land reform activities were ended in 1983 (O'Kenny, 1989, in Dáil Éireann, Vol. 389, No. 4, Cols 944–945). This development was first officially signalled by the closure of Department of Lands in 1977 and the transfer of its activities into the agriculture ministry and was officially sanctioned by an Inter-Department Committee on Land Structure Reform which reported in 1978. However, the Irish political system, particularly Fianna Fáil, which had championed the land reform cause since its foundation, took much longer to come to terms with the end of this remarkable social and economic project. As a result, the political rhetoric took a long time to catch-up with the changed reality of land policy. A bill to close the Land Commission was not passed until 1992 and was not signed into law until 1999 (Dooley, 2004).

The Inter-Department Committee on Land Structure Reform was established in 1976 by the Fine Gael/ Labour coalition to "review the existing policy and programme of land structural reform and to formulate proposals and options (with associated costs) which would best achieve the government's social and economic policy objectives" (Inter-Department Committee on Land Structure Reform, 1978: 5) (see Table 5.1). The report dismissed the aims of the preceding 50 years of land reform policy by linking Ireland's agricultural problems and rural population decline not to the lack of small farms but to their overabundance and also raised questions about the cost and value of state investment in land redistribution. On this basis, it recommended that land migration schemes should be abandoned on the grounds that the very high level of associated investment "could be more effectively applied to alternative measures to improve the land structure" (Inter-Department Committee on Land Structure Reform, 1978: 32). This recommendation was immediately implemented and migration schemes officially ceased in 1978 (Dooley, 2004). Even more controversially, the committee condemned the Land Commission as "an anachronism" and the policy of relieving congestion as "archaic" because rising standard of living and income expectations and mechanisation of agriculture were pushing up the economic size of holdings to an extent that made it impossible for land redistribution to keep pace (Inter-Department Committee on Land Structure Reform, 1978: 80–81). On these grounds and also due to the cost to the exchequer, the committee recommended that the Land Commission should be closed and its land acquisition and redistribution activities be discontinued and "in the future the land market should be conducted, as far as possible, without the state becoming involved in land acquisition and allocation" (Inter-Department Committee on Land Structure Reform, 1978: 56–57).

The 1977 general election was held during the Inter-Departmental Committee's lifetime, and Fianna Fáil, which secured a landslide victory in this election, indicated that it would not support the termination of land reform. Its manifesto declared that it was opposed to a *laissez-faire* attitude to land sales and promised that land reform would be continued but under the direction of a new Land Development Authority which would combine responsibility for land reform with management of the farm development services which had emerged since the 1960s (Commins, 1982). Rather than accept the recommendations of the Inter-Department Committee on Land Structure Reform, the Fianna

Table 5.1 Key public policy milestones in the retrenchment of Ireland's property-based welfare system, 1969–1989

Date	Land Reform	Government Provision of Homeowner Mortgages and Enabling Mortgage Provision by Others	Government Subsidies for Homeowners	Direct/indirect Government Provision of Homeowner Dwellings
1970		Building societies' tax subsidies was linked to their allocation of 90 per cent of their lending to mortgages or housebuilding.	Housing Act restricts the size of dwellings eligible for home purchase grants but increases the maximum grant available and the income limits for access.	
1972		Maximum SDA mortgage was increased as was the income limit for access to SDA mortgages. Central government empowered local authorities to introduce schemes to guarantee mortgages provided by building societies.	House reconstruction grants increased from a maximum of £140 to a maximum of £200 per house. Qualifying income limit for local authority supplementary house purchase grants was increased.	Discount on sales of local authority dwellings to tenants increased as was the subsidy for government provision of private housing sites. New local authority tenants enabled to buy or rent their homes.

(continued)

Table 5.1 (continued)

Date	Land Reform	Government Provision of Homeowner Mortgages and Enabling Mortgage Provision by Others	Government Subsidies for Homeowners	Direct/indirect Government Provision of Homeowner Dwellings
1973		Qualifying income limits for SDA mortgages increased. Building societies' tax subsidies linked to agreeing mortgage interest rates with government. Societies given a short-term interest rates subsidy. Central Bank instructs banks not to increase property lending.	Qualifying income limits for local authority supplementary new house grants were increased.	Method of calculating the sale price of local authority housing was changed to reflect construction costs not market value.
1974		Building Societies' Act introduces government guarantees for the sector's borrowings and facilitates mergers of societies.	Qualifying income limits for local authority supplementary new house grants increased and tax deductibility of mortgage interest capped.	

Table 5.1 (continued)

Date	Land Reform	Government Provision of Homeowner Mortgages and Enabling Mortgage Provision by Others	Government Subsidies for Homeowners	Direct/indirect Government Provision of Homeowner Dwellings
1975			Profits from sale of owner-occupied homes are exempted from Capital Gains Tax which is introduced this year.	
1976		A "low rise" SDA mortgage was set-up for local authority tenants/social housing applicants. Building society interest rates subsidies reintroduced.		
1977	Lands ministry is shut down and its responsibilities taken up by the Department of Agriculture.	Government requires building societies to allocate 60 per cent of funds to mortgages of <£13,000 and 20 per cent to mortgages of £13,000–£16,000.	Multiplicity of grants available to all types of homebuyers replaced with one grant for first-time buyers only and an extra grant paid over the first 3 years of the mortgage.	

(continued)

Table 5.1 (continued)

Date	Land Reform	Government Provision of Homeowner Mortgages and Enabling Mortgage Provision by Others	Government Subsidies for Homeowners	Direct/indirect Government Provision of Homeowner Dwellings
1978	Inter-Department Committee proposes ending Land Commission's migration, land acquisition and redistribution work. Migration schemes end.	Stricter credit guidelines applied to banks.	Local Government (Financial Provisions) Act abolishes domestic rates.	The subsidy for government provision of sites for private housebuilding was increased.
1979		Government required building societies to allocate 70 per cent+ of funds to mortgages of <20,000 and 40 per cent + to new houses. Income limit for access to SDA mortgages and house improvement loans was increased.	A new scheme of house improvement grants to reduce dependence on oil and tax relief for the spending on the maintenance of owner-occupied dwellings was introduced.	Subsidy for public provision of sites for private housebuilding was increased. Additional once-off discounts for local authority tenant purchasers introduced.

Table 5.1 (continued)

Date	Land Reform	Government Provision of Homeowner Mortgages and Enabling Mortgage Provision by Others	Government Subsidies for Homeowners	Direct/indirect Government Provision of Homeowner Dwellings
1980		Short-term subsidies of building society interest rates introduced. Maximum SDA "low-rise" mortgage, standard SDA mortgage and house improvement loan increased as were quali-fying income limits.	The vast majority of house improvement grants are terminated.	

(continued)

Table 5.1 (continued)

Date	Land Reform	Government Provision of Homeowner Mortgages and Enabling Mortgage Provision by Others	Government Subsidies for Homeowners	Direct/indirect Government Provision of Homeowner Dwellings
1981		Housing Finance Agency set-up to issue state guaranteed bonds to fund social housing and mortgages for low earners. It initially provides mortgages directly. Maximum SDA mortgage and qualifying income limits increased. Low-rise mortgage scheme abolished. Short-term subsidy of building society interest rates introduced. Central Bank removes explicit bank credit guidelines.	A new scheme of home improvement grants is introduced. The maximum grant for water provision in rural areas is increased. A new mortgage subsidy payable over three years to first-time buyers is introduced.	

Table 5.1 (continued)

Date	Land Reform	Government Provision of Homeowner Mortgages and Enabling Mortgage Provision by Others	Government Subsidies for Homeowners	Direct/indirect Government Provision of Homeowner Dwellings
1982		The maximum amount of SDA loans and the income limits for eligible borrowers are increased. Building societies' tax subsidies are increased to enable them lend at lower rates. Explicit bank credit guidelines introduced.	Subsidy of £3,000 payable over three years to first-time homebuyers is made payable over five years. A new scheme to provide emergency repairs grants to elderly homeowners is established.	
1983	Land Commission's land acquisition and redistribution activities were ended.	Tax subsidies provided to building societies in 1980 are withdrawn and their tax rate is increased. Qualifying income for Housing Finance Agency mortgages is increased. Explicit bank credit guidelines ended by the Central Bank and replaced with indicative guidelines.		The maximum discount available to all local authority tenant purchasers is standardised at 30 per cent.
1984			Grant of £5,000 is introduced for social housing tenants who surrender their tenancy and buy a home.	

(continued)

Table 5.1 (continued)

Date	Land Reform	Government Provision of Homeowner Mortgages and Enabling Mortgage Provision by Others	Government Subsidies for Homeowners	Direct/indirect Government Provision of Homeowner Dwellings
1985		Bank interest rate "cartel" is ended and greater competition encouraged.	Grant for first-time buyers of new houses is doubled.	
1986		Housing Finance Agency's power to issue mortgages directly was ended. Qualifying income limit for SDA loans increased. Building societies' tax subsidies are withdrawn but they are empowered to offer bridging and refurbishment loans.	Subsidy of £3,000 is replaced with a builders' grant of £2,250 for new dwellings only.	Sale price of local authority dwellings to tenants is once again pegged to the market value rather than the original construction costs.

Table 5.1 (continued)

Date	Land Reform	Government Provision of Homeowner Mortgages and Enabling Mortgage Provision by Others	Government Subsidies for Homeowners	Direct/indirect Government Provision of Homeowner Dwellings
1987		Fixed interest SDA loans abolished. All SDA mortgages were variable rate from then on.	Ceiling on mortgage interest tax relief cut by 10 per cent. Grant for local authority tenants who surrender their dwelling and buy a home was abolished. Builders' grant and most home improvement grants were abolished.	

(continued)

Table 5.1 (continued)

Date	Land Reform	Government Provision of Homeowner Mortgages and Enabling Mortgage Provision by Others	Government Subsidies for Homeowners	Direct/indirect Government Provision of Homeowner Dwellings
1988		Local Loans Fund abolished. SDA mortgages will now be financed by the Housing Finance Agency and access limited to low-income earners who could not get a mortgage from a bank or building society. Government agreed that banks and building societies will provide most mortgages in future.		Additional once-off discounts were introduced for local authority tenants who applied to purchase their homes this year.

Table 5.1 (continued)

Date	Land Reform	Government Provision of Homeowner Mortgages and Enabling Mortgage Provision by Others	Government Subsidies for Homeowners	Direct/indirect Government Provision of Homeowner Dwellings
1989		Building Society Act enables societies to access inter-bank lending, ends their reliance on deposits to fund lending and removes most distinctions between societies and banks.		
1990			Ceiling on mortgage interest tax relief cut by 25 per cent.	

Source: Department of Local Government (various years); Dooley (2004); O'Connell (2007).

Fáil government promised to produce its own white paper on land reform which it did in 1980. However, the resultant white paper on *Land Policy* stated that the government was "in broad agreement" with the Inter-Departmental Committee's recommendations regarding the need for the land market to develop independent of government (Department of Agriculture, 1980: 16). Although the white paper did not support the proposal that the Land Commission be abolished, it highlighted the practical barriers to continuing with land redistribution and its arguments in this regard focused rather cleverly on the challenges for farmers rather than just those posed for the exchequer. Thus the policy statement highlighted the radical increases in land prices since the 1970s (due primarily to the availability of Common Agricultural Policy subsidies for farmers following Ireland's accession to EU membership in 1972) and suggested this meant that smallholders granted additional land would find it difficult, if not impossible, to meet the additional annuity payments required (Dooley, 2004).

The Fine Gael/ Labour government of 1982–1987 instructed the Land Commission to cease its land redistribution activities in 1983 and considered closing the organisation, but its loss of the 1987 general election prevented it from taking action in this regard. Thus ironically, it was left to Fianna Fáil government to finally bring an end to the project which it, more than any other party, had championed. The 1987–1992 Fianna Fáil government introduced a bill to abolish the Land Commission in 1989, but it was not enacted when the government fell. In 1992, a later Fianna Fáil administration finally enacted the Irish Land Commission (Dissolution) Act which shut down the commission and transferred its function to the agriculture ministry (Dooley, 2004).

Homeownership Subsidies

The process of cutting back government supports for homeownership was more halting and uneven than the withdrawal of land reform subsidies described earlier. Some efforts were made to control public spending on direct and indirect subsidies for homeowners in the 1970s and 1980s, but

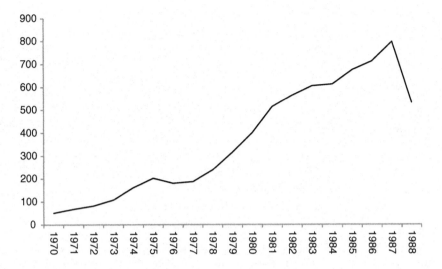

Fig. 5.1 Direct public spending on housing (€ million), 1970–1989. *Source:* Department of Local Government (various years).

the associated bill continued to climb for most of this period. In contrast, government involvement in the provision of mortgages flatlined concurrently, at least in relative terms. However, in 1987 and 1988 government subsidies and mortgage provision for homeowners were scaled back radically to the extent that this period saw the end of most elements of the socialised homeownership system with the exception of sales of social housing to tenants which are discussed in the next section.

Figure 5.1 outlines trends in direct government spending on housing during the period under review in this chapter. It highlights a marked growth during the 1970s which, a more detailed analysis reveals, was driven by a marked growth in spending on central government grants for homeowners (the main direct subsidy to the sector) which increased from £13.48 million in 1972/1973 to £72.8 million in 1980. This development reflected a sharp rise in the rate of housebuilding during this period (from 8,438 private dwellings in 1969 to 21,801 in 1980) which drove rising take-up of homebuyer grants (because the vast majority of these new dwellings were bought by homeowners) (see Fig. 5.2). Figure 5.2 reveals that during the

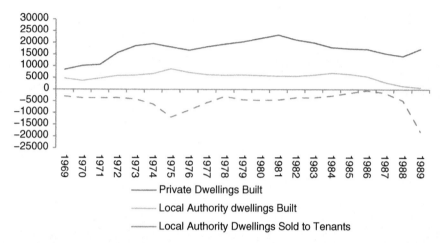

Fig. 5.2   Private and local authority social house building and sales of local authority social housing to tenants, 1969–1989. *Source*: Department of Local Government (various years)

1970s and, to a lesser extent, the early 1980s, rising spending also reflected the increasing generosity of the grants regime in terms of rates payable and the income limits for access which grew in aggregate over this period despite some efforts to cut them back at the margins. In 1970, restrictions on the size of dwellings eligible for home purchase grants were introduced, for instance, and in 1977, the plethora of grants available to all categories of homebuyers were replaced with a single grant for first-time buyers only. These developments reflected the commitment made in the white paper *Housing in the Seventies* which was published in 1979 and committed government to ensuring that supports for homeowners were better targeted on those who need them most (Department of Local Government, 1969). However, the significance of these reforms was more symbolic than practical at least initially. Due to rising take-up, the targeting of these subsidies had a limited impact on spending in the 1970s, but these reforms marked the first breech of the principle of universal subsidisation of all homeowners irrespective of income which underpinned the socialised homeownership regime.

No comprehensive data are available on the cost of indirect subsidies to homeowners during the period under review in this chapter, but the evidence which is available indicates that this also escalated dramatically during the 1970s despite some efforts to control spending by policy-makers. The principal subsidy of this type, mortgage interest tax relief (MITR), has existed since the income tax system was first established, but for decades its cost was limited by the small number of homeowners and low interest rates and offset by the taxation of imputed rent (i.e. of the amount which homeowners would have to pay to rent their homes) (Baker and O'Brien, 1979). This changed as homeownership expanded, tax on imputed rent was abolished in 1969 and interest rates dramatically rose during the 1970s. As a result, the cost of MITR to government increased from £5.4 million in 1971/1972 to £12.9 million in 1975 (National Economic and Social Council, 1977). In response, in 1974 government introduced a ceiling on the amount of interest which was tax deductible, but this ceiling was high initially and MITR still covered up to 22.6 per cent of the total costs of servicing the average building society mortgage in 1975 (National Economic and Social Council, 1977). Between the 1920s and 1970s, first-time buyers received a further tax subsidy in the form of remission from domestic rates for a number of years after purchase. The level of this subsidy varied over the years, but by the mid-1970s it provided 100 per cent relief from the payment of rates during the first year of homeownership, falling by 10 per cent for each subsequent year down to zero in year 10 (National Economic and Social Council, 1977). The abolition of domestic rates in 1978 (on foot of a commitment made by Fianna Fáil in the 1977 general election but reflecting similar commitments made by the other main parties) therefore extended this tax subsidy to all homeowners (and residential landlords) and greatly increased its cost to the exchequer in terms of potential income forgone. First-time buyers were also exempted from payment of stamp duty on their house purchase during the 1970s and, due to the increase in new housebuilding, the associated cost to government in terms of revenue forgone increased from £0.7 million in 1971/1972 to £4.3 million in 1975. Furthermore, profits made on the sale of owner-occupied dwellings were exempted from capital gains tax following the introduction of this new duty in 1975 which provided homeowners with an estimated additional public subsidy of £3 million in that year (National Economic and Social Council, 1977, and Table 5.1).

As mentioned earlier, during the 1970s the government had more success in arresting the marked growth in local government mortgage provision seen in the preceding decades. SDA mortgage lending declined from 31.6 per cent of total mortgage lending (by value) in 1966/1967 to 17.7 per cent in 1976 and remained around 20 per cent of all lending between the latter date and the mid-1980s (Carey, 1974, and see Fig. 5.3). Due to the radical concurrent expansion in total mortgage lending, SDA lending increased markedly in absolute terms however (from £25.8 million in 1976 to £164.3 million in 1986) and it remained a very important source of mortgages for low-income households. However, the bulk of the total rise in mortgage lending for housing came from non-governmental sources, principally the building society

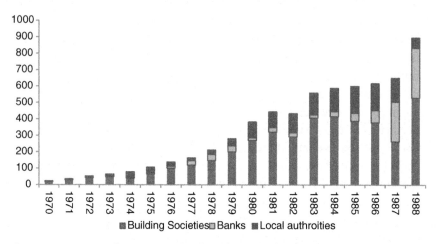

Fig. 5.3 Sources of mortgage lending (by value), 1970–1990. *Source*: Baker and O'Brien (1979) and Department of Local Government (various years).

Note: Data on local authority mortgages include mortgages issues by the Housing Finance Agency between 1982 and 1985. This graph excludes lending by life assurance companies which was high in the mid-1970s (they lent £1.45 million worth of mortgages in 1974) but very small outside this short period

sector which provided 41 per cent of mortgages by value in 1966/1967 and 68.5 per cent in 1976.

These changes in mortgage lending patterns were heavily influenced by government intervention. Improving the flow of capital to housing by increasing private sector mortgage lending was identified as a central policy objective in *Housing in the Seventies* and to achieve this objective a mixture of carrot and stick was employed (Department of Local Government, 1969). The stick was wielded by changing the terms of tax subsidies building societies had enjoyed for decades (Carey, 1974). Under these subsidy arrangements, interest on building society deposits below a ceiling was tax free to savers and the societies themselves paid tax at a special "composite" rate set below the standard rate of tax (Department of the Environment, 1986). From 1970, the continued availability of these subsidies was linked to societies allocating 90 per cent of their lending to mortgages or housebuilding and the government issued further requirements in this regard in 1973, 1977 and 1979. Also in 1973, the societies were debarred from lending for non-housing purposes. The inducements used to encourage more building society mortgage lending included enabling local authorities to guarantee these mortgages in certain cases from 1972, and the provision of additional short-term government subsidies to enable building societies offer higher interest rates to savers and lower rates to borrowers and government guaranteed borrowings at a number of points in the 1970s and the early 1980s (see Table 5.1). Some efforts were made to increase mortgage lending by the banks during the 1970s but with limited success. Following negotiations with government in 1974 and 1975, the banks did commence mortgage lending for the first time, but they provided a low proportion of mortgages (between 8 and 17 per cent) until the mid-1980s (see Fig. 5.3; Department of Local Government, various years).

In the mid-1980s, however, the long-standing, albeit uneven, pattern of growing and universally available public subsidies for home-ownership came to an abrupt halt, and over the course of just a couple of years, most elements of the socialised homeownership regime were dismantled. There first signs that this development was looming came in 1980 when several home improvement grants were abolished.

Although these were reinstituted at lower rates of payment in 1981, further minor cuts to home purchase grants were introduced the following year. However, the pace of cuts to homeowner subsidies quickened radically in 1987 (see Table 5.1). In this year, the builders' grant for first-time homebuyers and the vast majority of home improvement grants were all abolished and the ceiling on mortgage interest tax relief was cut by 10 per cent. In 1987 and 1988, the SDA mortgage programme was also radically rolled back significantly. In the former year, fixed interest SDA loans were abolished, in the latter the government announced that access to these mortgages would in future be limited to low-income earners who could not secure a bank or building society loan. In 1988, the government also announced that it had reached an agreement with the banks and building societies that they would service the bulk of the segment of the population previously reliant on SDA loans and that these non-governmental lenders had committed up to £70 million for that purpose. In the same year, the Local Loans Fund was abolished and the government announced that in future all finance for SDA loans (and for some elements of social housing finance) would be borrowed by a new semi-state organisation called the Housing Finance Agency (Department of Housing, Planning and Local Government, various years).

Following these reforms to SDA, mortgages lending by local authorities fell from €164.3 million (26.5 per cent of total mortgage lending by value) in 1986 to €62.72 million (7.0 per cent of total mortgage lending) in 1988 and has remained below this level ever since. Miraculously, despite this development, total mortgage lending expanded by just under one-third concurrently, but unlike in the 1970s the additional lending was not provided mainly by building societies. Rather, banks' mortgage lending almost trebled between 1986 and 1988, while building societies' lending declined by 2 per cent by value (see Fig. 5.3).

This development was primarily the result of the deregulation of the banking and building society sector during the early mid-1980s in a process which reflected, but lagged, developments elsewhere in the developed world, particularly in English-speaking countries and the Eurozone (Kelly and Everett, 2004). The elements of this process which are most relevant to mortgage lending are summarised in Table 5.1, which include:

- the removal of most government controls on credit in terms of the ratio of deposits to loans and the sectors of the economy targeted for lending;
- the ending of the interest rate "cartel" which had existed since the 1920s, the removal of government controls on interest rates and the promotion of greater competition among banks at retail level;
- the abolition of building societies' tax subsidies in 1986 which eliminated their competitive advantage over banks as a source of mortgage lending; and
- the 1989 Building Societies' Act which enabled societies to access inter-bank lending which thereby reduced their dependence on deposits to fund lending and eliminated the key remaining difference between mutual and commercial lenders.

These measures facilitated not only an increase in mortgage lending by existing banks but also the transfer of several building societies and therefore the associated mortgage lending into the banking sector. One building society was bought by Bank of Ireland in the mid-1980s and two others demutualised in the early 1990s (Murphy, 2004).

Social Housing as Property-Based Welfare

Sales of local authority social housing to tenants proved to be the most resilient part of the property-based welfare during the retrenchment phase. While the exchequer supports for land redistribution and home-ownership were being rolled back, the tenant purchase scheme increased in generosity during the 1970s and 1980s and a new variant of the scheme called the £5,000 surrender grant was introduced between 1984 and 1987. As a result, 103,119 dwellings were sold to tenants between 1969 and 1989, which almost cancelled out 114,533 additional dwellings built or bought by local authorities for letting as social housing during the same period. However, reforms of arrangements for financing social housing instituted as part of the austerity programme in the mid-1980s resulted in a very dramatic decline in public investment and consequently in housing output (see Fig. 5.2). Over the longer term, this development would undermine social housing's role as a form of property-based welfare by reducing the number of social rented dwellings available for sale and (because social housing is allocated on the basis of need, so only the poorest households can gain new tenancies if fewer dwellings are available for letting) reducing the capacity of tenants is sector to buy their homes (Norris et al., 2007).

The first increase to the subsidies for local authority tenant purchasers during the period under review in this chapter was introduced in 1972 when the discount of the price at which dwellings were available to them was increased from 2 per cent to 3 per cent of market value per year of tenancy (subject to a ceiling), and this discount was calculated from the first year of tenancy rather than after the fifth year as was previously the case. In the same year, households granted a local authority tenancy were given the option of buying the dwelling immediately rather than renting it. In 1973, the method for calculating the sale price to tenants was also changed. It was no longer based on the market value but on the original cost of construction updated by the consumer price index to which the discounts introduced in 1972 were applied (see Table 5.1). According to O'Connell (2007: 108), these new arrangements "resulted in very modest sales prices as the consumer price index was increasing over time at a rate less than the rate of increase of house prices" to the extent that he estimates "after discounts and allowances were factored in the actual cost of acquiring a dwelling was often 50 per cent or more below its market value" during this period. However, this situation changed as the 1980s dawned and the onset of a housing market depression meant that the current market value of many local authority dwellings was less than their updated construction costs. To address this problem, the tenant purchase scheme was revised again in 1986 to enable sale prices to be pegged to market values where these were lower than the updated construction costs. In addition, in 1983 the long-standing discrimination in favour of rural local authority which dated back to the birth of the tenant purchase scheme in the 1930s was at last ended. Prior to the discount on the sale price available to rural tenant purchasers was capped at 45 per cent, while their urban counterparts could avail of a maximum discount of just 30 per cent, but from 1983 the discount available was standardised at 30 per cent for all regions (see Table 5.1).

In October 1984, the Fine Gael/ Labour coalition expanded the property-based welfare role of local authority social housing in a new direction by introducing the £5,000 surrender grant scheme. As its name implies, this scheme provided £5,000 to local authority tenants and tenant purchasers who were prepared to surrender their dwelling and to buy a home in the private sector. It was intended to free up social rented dwellings for letting without incurring the cost of new building while at the same time supporting the building industry which was very depressed at this time (O'Connell, 2007). Blackwell (1988) reports that by the time the scheme was abolished in March 1987 a total of 7,700 surrender grants were paid out – accounting for just 6.5 per cent of the entire local authority renting population at the time. However, the uneven spatial take-up of the grant meant that it made a significant contribution towards increasing the residualisation (i.e. concentration of disadvantaged households) of a number of urban local authority estates and thereby undermining their social sustainability in the longer term. A study of the effects of the grant in the Dublin area carried out by the housing advice charity Threshold (1987) found that 75 per cent of take-up in Dublin was in Darndale, Ballymun and Tallaght/Clondalkin – three disadvantaged neighbourhoods all located on the edge of the city. This study confirms that practically 100 per cent of the households which took advantage of the scheme were in employment, and the residualising effects associated with the departure of these households from public-sector estates were compounded by the fact that many of those who moved into the dwellings vacated as a result of the grant and were at high risk of poverty such as lone parents or single unemployed men. Concerns about these perverse outcomes of the £5,000 grant led to its abolition less than three years after its introduction.

Figure 5.2 reveals that the generosity of the subsidies available to tenant purchasers of local authority social housing proved insufficient to maintain the rate of sales during the latter part of the 1980s, however, as high unemployment and falling house prices (in real terms) reduced the number of tenants willing or able to buy their homes. In response, in February

1988 the government announced that the most generous discounts ever provided would be made available to tenants who applied to buy their home before 1 September in that year. Under the terms of this scheme – dubbed "the sale of the century" by the media after a popular television game show of the time – all sale prices were pegged to the market value, to which a discount of 40 per cent and an additional discount of £2,000 in view of the first-time buyers' grant was applied to all cases. In addition, a further discount of 10 per cent was applied to dwellings built prior to 1960 and local authorities were enabled to discount the price further in the case of dwellings in poor repair (rather than repairing the dwelling prior to sale as they were previously required to do) (Department of the Environment, various years). The 1988 Department of the Environment (1988: 42) annual report reported an "unprecedented response to the scheme and 45% of the 91,000 eligible tenants applied to purchase their homes", and Fig. 5.2 reveals that a record 18,166 local authority dwellings were sold to tenants in 1989 (when most applications under the 1988 scheme would have been processed).

During the 1970s and early 1980s, social housing output contracted slightly in relative terms, compared to previous decades, because private housing output raced ahead during this period. Social housing accounted for 27 per cent of all housebuilding in the 1970s compared to 31 per cent in the 1960s. However, social housebuilding rose significantly in absolute terms during this period – 93,959 social housing units were built in the 1960s while 229,183 were constructed in the 1970s. This level of social housing output was remarkable in view of the significant challenges associated with raising loans for this purpose of funding their repayment particularly as the economic crisis escalated from the late 1970s, and it is testament to the strong ideological support for this tenure among policymakers (Daly, 1997; Norris, 2014). This commitment to social housing was in large part linked to the fact that high social housing output in the 1960s and 1970s provided an amble stream of new dwellings for sale and was available to support social housing's role as the property-based welfare system.

However, this changed in 1987 when the Fianna Fáil Finance Minister Ray MacSharry announced the termination of the century-old system of borrowing to fund social housebuilding, the abolition of the local loans fund and that in future the capital costs of social housing provision would be met in full by central government grants (MacSharry, Dáil Éireann, 1987, Vol. 374, No. 2, Cols. 344–346). Although this new funding arrangement ensured that no additional social housing development loans were accumulated, funding the costs of building social rented dwellings "upfront" in a lump sum grant proved difficult to afford particularly in the context of fiscal crisis which was still ongoing in the late 1980s. As a result, social housing output declined significantly during this period – from 6,523 units in 1985 to just 768 units in 1989 (see Fig. 5.1). As mentioned earlier, this development ultimately undermined the potential for selling social housing to tenants and by extension this element of the property-based welfare system.

Drivers of the Retrenchment of the Property-Based Welfare System

Preceding chapters have identified the concentration of power among the farming community and, to a lesser extent, the construction industry and the relative lack of power of the urban working class as the key drivers of the emergence, growth and endurance of Ireland's property-based welfare system. The changing distribution of power also influenced the decline of this policy regime, but power-related issues played a less central in shaping this retrenchment phase than they had in the preceding stages in the development of property-based welfare.

There is no doubt that the declining influence of agriculture by the 1980s was one of the factors which enabled government to think what had been previously unthinkable and put an end to the land redistribution project. The number of males working in agriculture, forestry and fishing fell by 29.3 per cent between 1971 and 1981, and this sector accounted for just 15.6 per cent of the workforce by the latter year (Central Statistics Office, various years). Moreover, Garvin (1982) reports that in 1958, 28.2 per cent of the parliamentary questions tabled in Dáil Éireann related to "Agriculture, Fisheries, Land and Agriculture related trade", but this fell to 11.9 per cent in 1966 and 4.3 per cent in 1979 and a quarter of TDs were farmers in 1957 compared to just 11 per cent in 1981.

However, farmers retained significant political influence in the 1970s and 1980s, certainly in excess of declining numbers; therefore, the end of the land redistribution project was not related just to weakening agrarian influence but rather to the redirection of the famers' lobbying efforts. This new target was agricultural price supports: government cash subsidies intended to provide farmers with guaranteed prices for certain agricultural produces which were first introduced in tandem with the protectionism in the early 1930s. Their significance, and therefore their cost to the exchequer, was initially small – they cost the Irish government £4.6 million in 1956/1958 and accounted for 4.3 per cent of agricultural incomes in that year – but they expanded significantly over the decades to the extent that they cost the government £32.9 million and accounted for 11.9 per cent of agricultural incomes by 1972/1923 (Mathews, 1982). Therefore, these supports, not land redistribution, became the principal target of the National Farmers' Union's lobbying to ensure that farmers' incomes kept pace with the growth in employees' incomes. Following Ireland's accession to EU membership in 1973, the cost of agricultural price subsidies increased further to £245 million in 1977; however (much to the relief of Irish policymakers), the bulk of this bill now fell to taxpayers in other European countries (Mathews, 1982). Thus, the focus of Irish farmers' lobbying shifted again to Brussels and the EU bureaucracy. Although Irish Farmers' Association (IFA), which replaced the NFU in the 1960s as the main representative of the sector, continued to dutifully campaign for land redistribution throughout the 1970s, the EU's Common Agricultural Policy was the main focus of its lobbying activities (Daly, 2002).

Employment in the building industry was greatly diminished by the economic crisis of the late 1970s and 1980s to the extent that one in four building workers was unemployed in 1981 (*Irish Times*, 1981, November 24). However, there is no evidence that the political and economic power of the sector was diminished as a result; rather, the opposite appears to have been the case. The autobiographies of ministers who served during the late 1970s and the early 1980s indicate that the impact on construction employment was a major consideration in decisions regarding the rolling back of subsides for homeowners and spending on social housebuilding (e.g. Quinn, 2005). This was particularly the case for Labour due to its strong links with the trade union movement and ideological commitment to statist solutions to socio-economic problems at this time and for Fianna Fáil due to its strong construction industry links. Furthermore, representatives of the construction industry and construction workers' trade unions lobbied furiously throughout the 1970s and 1980s for government intervention to shore up employment in the sector, although, like their counterparts in agriculture, there is evidence that the focus of the builders' lobbying efforts changed during this period. Newspaper reporting indicates that throughout the 1970s and 1980s these organisations lobbied for additional public capital spending on construction (for instance, *Irish Times*, 1981, November 24; 1984, July 16). From the early 1980s, however, construction industry representatives in particular also began to demand government support for private investment in construction. This was inspired initially by the provision of a limited number of tax incentives for residential construction which were commonly known as Section 23 incentives of the 1980 Finance Act which introduced them. Builders lobbied for the extension of these measures both in terms of time and geographical focus (for instance, *Irish Times*, 1981, October 1; 1984, January 26; 1985, January 25). Their efforts were rewarded when the 1985 Urban Renewal Act made these incentives available in a limited number of run-down, inner areas of Ireland's five cities. Take-up was very high, and they proved much more successful at regenerating these neighbourhoods than the grants and free lands transfer schemes used previously (Norris and Gkartzios, 2011).

The sequencing of the steps in the process of fiscal retrenchment in Ireland during the 1980s also indicates that proponents of the property-based welfare regime still wielded significant power. When efforts to deal with the fiscal crisis commenced in the late 1970s, they initially focused on raising revenue rather than cutting spending. Tax as a percentage of GDP remained static at around 30 per cent between 1977 and 1979 but grew steadily to over 41 per cent by 1984, principally as a result of rising taxes on the incomes of employees (Honohan, 1992). O'Connor (2011: 235) reports that 87 per cent of income tax in 1987 came from employees and "there was particular resentment at the fact that farmers paid little tax, although real per capita income in agriculture had risen by 72 per cent between 1970 and 1978". The rising tax burden and in particular a government decision to yield pressure from the IFA to drop a 2 per cent levy on farmers' incomes, which was announced in the 1979 budget but never implemented, prompted large-scale protests about inequity between the levels of tax paid by employees compared to the self-employed/ farmers. A total of 50,000 people marched in Dublin on 11 March 1979 and 9 days later 150,000 people attended a second protest, while a national strike took place on 22 January 1980 and 700,000 people took part in associated street rallies (O'Connor, 2011). These protests, which were organised by trade unions' local committees, at least partially inspired a commitment to freeze the tax/GDP ratio in Fine Gael and Labour coalition's economic plan for the 1985–1987 period – *Building on Reality* (Government of Ireland, 1984).

Thus, in the early 1980s the government turned to cuts in current and capital spending expenditure in an attempt to improve its financial position. Developments in this regard are set out in Tables 5.2 and 5.3 which respectively examine macro-level trends in social spending in Ireland during the entire period under examination in this chapter and micro trends in cuts made in the 1980s. They reveal that between 1980 and 1985 total social spending in Ireland fell only marginally from 29.78 to 29.69 per cent of GDP, despite reductions in healthcare spending, the imposition of an embargo on public service recruitment, the abolition of the income-related element of most insurance-based social security benefits and the "postponement" of most large-scale infrastructure projects (Honohan, 1992). The early 1980s austerity programme failed to eliminate the budget deficit and therefore stabilised the national debt because the cuts were deflationary and also their impact was counterbalanced by rising debt servicing and social security costs, which jointly accounted for 85.7 per cent of the increase in the real value of exchequer spending between 1981 and 1984 (Honohan, 1992). Therefore, it was only when the government had exhausted most or all other possible revenue raising or expenditure reducing

Table 5.2 Social expenditure as a percentage of GDP, 1970/1971–1990

Date	Social Expenditure	Income Maintenance	Education	Health	Housing
1970/1971	19.10	7.31	5.03	4.38	4.13
1975	27.50	10.72	6.12	6.53	3.64
1980	29.78	10.99	6.54	8.61	2.98
1985	29.69	13.57	6.12	7.02	1.32
1990	23.90	11.40	5.27	5.91	1.44

Note: These data refer to direct public spending only; therefore, this substantially underestimates the true level of spending on housing particularly prior to 1985.

Source: Pellion (2001).

Table 5.3 Changes in real government expenditure, 1981–1991 (in 1991£)

	1981–1985	1985–1989	1989–1991	1981–1991
Social security benefits	687	−7	195	876
Interest	832	−234	143	741
Health	−33	−73	137	31
Education	68	121	54	243
Other current	198	−455	453	196
Total current	1,753	−648	982	2,087
Pubic capital programme	−1,143	−658	374	−1,426
EBR for capital	−767	−667	312	−1,122
Total[a]	986	−1,314	1,293	965

Note: [a]Current plus EBR for capital. Data were brought to real terms by GNP deflator.

Source: Honohan (1992).

options, or at least run out of the political capital necessary to implement them, that it finally turned to the option of rolling back the property-based welfare system.

Ultimately, though, the bulk of property-based welfare provisions was rolled back which demonstrates that the power of the supporters of this regime was not without limit. Furthermore, the fact that cuts to this and other non-social categories of capital spending accounted for most of the public expenditure cuts made during the 1980s while other mainstream welfare services expanded concurrently points to a definite shift in the balance of power in Irish society. As mentioned earlier, the income-related element of most social insurance benefits was abolished during the fiscal crisis, but the real value of means tested benefits increased between 1980 and 1991 – by 10.2 per cent in the case of short-term benefits for a married couple with two children and by 17.7 per cent for an identical household on long-term benefits between 1980 and 1991 (Honohan, 1992). Honohan (1992: 304–305) singles out this determination to maintain or even increase benefit payment rates as a remarkable feature of the Irish fiscal crisis of the 1980s in view of the fact that it was pursued during " . . . a time of falling or static per capita income generally, and when a considerable tightening of welfare entitlements was happening in Britain". He points out that this strategy was subject to considerable criticism at the time for discouraging re-entry to the workforce and return migration from abroad, but it probably reaped significant benefits in terms of mitigation of poverty.

The declining legitimacy of the land reform project was also an important factor in enabling the government to rollback this element of the property-based welfare state. The previous chapter recounted increasing criticism of land reform in the late 1950s and 1960s but expressed mainly in the privacy of cabinet meetings or less commonly in public by particularly forthright politicians. By the 1970s, these criticisms began to permeate media and academic debates and policy documents.

The first academic instalment in this "revisionist" academic debate on Irish land tenure slightly pre-dates the period examined in this chapter – it is Raymond Crotty's landmark study *Irish Agricultural Production* which was published in 1966. This remarkably original and ambitious book contracted the overwhelming consensus that land reform made both ethical and economic sense. Instead, Crotty (1966) argued that the agricultural landlord system was more productive than peasant proprietorship because rent-maximising landlords forced tenants to be more efficient. Following land reform, there was no longer an active market for land holdings in Ireland which would force inefficient farmers to cede their holdings to the better qualified therefore inefficiency inherent in this system. Although Crotty's (1966) analysis was flawed in some key respects, it inspired other critics of land reform to enter the debate (Ó Gráda, 2004). The American academic Solow (1971) was next out of the traps. Her 1971 book *The Land Question and the Irish Economy*,

1870–1903 supports the view that agricultural landlordism was more efficient and argues that state interference such as tenancy regulation had destroyed agricultural landlords' entrepreneurship. Similarly, Vaughan (1984) argues that Irish agricultural landlords had not sought to maximise their returns in the post-famine period and in this regard were unfairly characterised by the land reform movement. The most energetic journalistic critic of the land reform was Des Maguire, who significantly was deputy editor of the IFA's newspaper the *Irish Farmers' Journal*. In addition to newspaper articles criticising land reform, he published two short books in 1976 and 1983 which argued that the Land Commission's objective of relieving congestion was outmoded and resulted in the inefficient use of resources. Instead, he suggests that agricultural policy should aim to distribute land among the most resourceful farmers to "assure the country of a farm structure capable of utilising all agricultural resources" (Maguire, 1976: 8).

The declining support for land reform also reflected the demise of the other ideologies which had helped to legitimate this project – the distinctive Irish variant of familism which Fahey (2002) has called the "family economy" and the Catholic social philosophy of distributism (see Chap. 3). Although Ireland was a late adopter of the global trend of falling fertility rates, shrinking family size and the replacement of the extended family with nuclear and non-marital families which demographers call the "second demographic transition", Irish family structures had finally come to match the Western European norm by the 1980s. Thus the policy of subsidising land redistribution to strengthen the economic foundations of the extended family model no longer reflected the dominant family structures, and this approach was replaced with new family policies which reflected contemporary needs. A plethora of "modernising" family policies were introduced during the period under review in this chapter including the provision of social security benefits of different categories of lone parents (between 1970 and 1974) and mothers on maternity leave (1981); the legalisation of contraception (1979 for married couples only and 1986 for the rest of the population) and the prohibition of pay discrimination against women (1976) (Fahey and Nixon, 2014). These developments were also facilitated by changing Catholic social and moral teaching after Vatican II. The anti-statism, which had inspired the Catholic social philosophy of distributism and helped to legitimise land reform during the first half of the twentieth century, was replaced by support for social justice on the part of Church leaders which (probably in tandem with a concern that Irish women would avail of abortion in the UK which was legalised in the late 1960s) led them to support the introduction of lone parents' benefits in the early 1970s (McLoughlin and Rodgers, 1997).

Notably, in marked contrast to their changing views on land reform, policymakers' ideological commitment to homeownership did not weaken during the 1970s or 1980s at least ostensibly. Government confirmed its commitment to promoting this tenure as the one preferred by the majority of the population in the housing policy white paper published at the start of the period under review in this chapter (*Housing in the Seventies* published in 1979) and in the housing policy statement published at the end of this period (*A Plan for Social Housing* published in 1991) (Department of the Environment, 1991; Department of Local Government, 1969). This commitment was regularly repeated by politicians in the intervening period despite their concurrent efforts to rollback public spending on the subsidisation of the tenure. For instance, when announcing the virtual abolition of SDA lending and plans to rely more on non-governmental mortgage lending in his statement on the 1987 budget, the Fianna Fáil Environment Minister Padráig Flynn (1987 in Dáil Éireann, Vol. 374, No. 5, Cols 291–293) affirmed his commitment to ensure that "any new arrangements do not reduce the capacity of any potential house purchasers to secure home ownership".

Policymakers' continued commitment to supporting this element of the property-based welfare system – at least in words if not in deeds – may have reflected the fact that homeownership complemented modern social structures such as the nuclear family and urban living. The marketised (rather than socialised) homeownership enabled by the deregulation of mortgage markets also complemented the increased faith in market (rather than government) solutions to social and economic problems which emerged as a strong theme in Irish political discourse at this time. Although the extent to which this development was influenced by the neo-liberal ideological and political movements which were influential in other English-speaking countries in the 1980s is often overstated by commentators on Ireland, there is no doubt that the fiscal crisis Ireland experienced at this time did inspire qualms about the efficiency of government solutions among voters and policymakers and increased support for marketisation of services which were previously publicly provided and for deregulation of markets (Ó Rian, 2014). The emergence of a new political party, the Progressive Democrats, in 1985 and their success in securing almost 12 per cent of the vote in the 1987 general election on an economically and socially liberal policy platform is testament to this. In addition, Lee (1989) highlights growing criticism of the efficiency of public services in parliamentary debates and policy documents in the early 1980s. For instance, despite the strong links between Labour and the public-sector trade unions, the *Building on Reality* plan which this party produced with Fine Gael acknowledged that the perception of "pubic employment . . . as a drain on the economy and a burden on the taxpayer . . . has become more widespread in recent years" (Government of Ireland, 1984: 33).

In contrast to the norm during the periods of expansion of property-based welfare, efficiency considerations had a much greater influence on the policy decisions taken during the retrenchment phase. Part of the reason for this was flagged in the preceding discussion: the long duration and acute nature of the fiscal crisis which stretched from the late 1970s to the late 1980s meant that by the latter date government had exhausted most other options available to balance the books and they decided that rolling back property-based welfare was less controversial than cutting benefits or raising taxes further (Honohan, 1992). However, as explained in Chap. 4, the fiscal crisis of the 1950s was also acute and protracted, but the property-based welfare system expanded during this period. Therefore, efficiency-related drivers of this collapse of the property-based welfare system are more complex and multifaceted than solely lack of funds. They also relate to the context in which the 1980s fiscal crisis occurred, the particular nature of the public spending challenges which arose at this time and the availability of alternatives to publicly subsidised capital asset redistribution. In these three crucial respects, the fiscal crisis of the late 1970s and

1980s differed from its counterpart of the 1950s and these differences explain why property-based welfare flourished in the latter crisis and collapsed in the former.

For instance, by the mid-1980s municipal borrowing for SDA mortgage lending and social house building had ceased and these activities were funded entirely by central government borrowing via the local loans fund. International public accounting rules were standardised incrementally from the 1960s, and Ireland was obliged to adhere strictly to these rules as a condition of its accession to EU membership in 1973. Thus, key financial supports for property-based welfare such as SDA mortgages and land bonds, which were not formally included in the national debt in the 1950s, were firmly "on balance sheet" in the 1980s. Furthermore, even taking account of municipal and Land Commission borrowing, total public debt in Ireland in the 1950s was modest. Whereas, by the mid-1980s, Ireland's government debt to GDP ratio reached 142.2 per cent and debt servicing costs accounted for 27 per cent of public spending, so the prospect that this level of borrowing could not be serviced was a very real one (Kennedy et al., 1988). The risk that Ireland would require an International Monetary Federation (IMF) emergency loan or support from the EU was regularly mentioned in parliamentary debates and discussed in the media at this time (e.g. O'Brien, 1982; Walsh, 1981).

The preceding chapter described how the ongoing challenges associated with financing the construction of local authority social housing (and by extension its discounted sale to tenants) increased during the middle of the twentieth century because the linking of tenants' rents to their incomes rather than the cost of housing provision and the erosion of revenue from domestic rates reduced the income available to local authorities to service their social housing development loans. This forced central government to increase its contribution to the interest payments on these loans to 100 per cent in the 1960s while income from domestic rates covered the capital repayments and rents barely covered maintenance costs (National Economic and Social Council, 1985). However, this financing system was placed under further strain when the Fianna Fáil government abolished domestic rates in 1978. Domestic and business rates provided 41 of local government revenue in 1976, but (following the abolition of the latter) this fell to 12 per cent by 1984 (National Economic and Social Council, 1985). Central government filled the resulting revenue gap, and therefore, covered both the interest and capital repayments on social housing development loans which resulted in a very large increase in spending in the early 1980s. Spending on interest subsidies alone increased from £80 million in 1980 to £152 million in 1983 (National Economic and Social Council, 1985). In 1987, Finance Minister Ray MacSharry (in Dáil Éireann, 1987, Vol. 374, No. 2, Col. 344) told the Dáil that as a result of these reforms "the Exchequer meets the entire cost of funding local authority capital programmes by means of an elaborate, expensive and needless circle of payments" and he undertook to "break this circle" by abolishing the local loans fund, writing off most outstanding social housing loans and funding the future capital costs of social housing provision in full from the central exchequer. Although the minister claimed that this reform would have "no adverse effect on the amount of funds available" for social housing provision, as explained earlier in this chapter, this did not prove correct and output declined radically in the late 1980s (in Dáil Éireann, 1987, Vol. 374, No. 2, Col. 344) (see Fig. 5.2).

Another important efficiency-related reason for the contraction of the property-based welfare system in the 1980s relates to the availability of alternatives to government subsidised capital redistribution which did not exist in previous decades. As mentioned earlier, EU-funded agricultural price subsidies eliminated the need for the Irish government to finance land redistribution in order to ensure that farms could generate an adequate living. However, in many cases, market alternatives to government supports for asset-based welfare became available during the period under review in this chapter and these had the efficiency benefit of reducing the burden on the exchequer as well as the ideological advantage of complementing the growing faith in market solutions to socio-economic problems highlighted in the preceding section.

For instance, by the 1980s the market failure which SDA mortgages had long endeavoured to fix had finally disappeared, thereby eliminating the need for continued need for large-scale government involvement in mortgage provision. Consequently, as well as citing its impact on reducing the national debt, the housing minister Padráig Flynn justified reducing SDA mortgage lending on the grounds that:

> I believe that both banks and building societies have considerable scope for providing loans to many applicants who would otherwise consider they had no alternative but to approach their local authority for a house purchase loan. In recent years there has been a marked trend in other European countries towards greater reliance on private sector funding of the mortgage market, and we must recognise the scope that now exists for positive developments in this direction in this country.
>
> (Flynn in Dáil Éireann, 1987, Vol. 374, No. 5, Col. 982)

This call proved correct – new mortgages increased from 27,632 in 1986 to 38,580 in 1989 and, as mentioned earlier, banks provided the vast majority of this additional lending (Department of Housing, Planning and Local Government, various years). These developments reflected banks' eagerness to grow their involvement in mortgage lending to compensate for the increasing unprofitability of the traditional lending markets such as agriculture and industry and the removal of building societies' tax subsidies in 1980, and the legal distinctions between banks and building societies by the Building Societies Act, 1989, would further accentuate this trend (see Table 5.1). These tax reforms eliminated what the banks regarded as "unfair competition" from building societies and encouraged banks to become heavily involved in mortgage lending. These legal reforms granted building societies access to wholesale money markets (i.e. borrowing from and lending to other financial instructions and governments in Ireland and internationally) for the first time, and they used these new funds to increase their mortgage lending. Furthermore, in the years following the 1989 Act a majority of Irish building societies either converted into banks or were taken over by banks and subsequently banks provided the vast majority of mortgages in Ireland (Murphy, 2004).

The Fianna Fáil government, which was largely responsible for rolling back property-based welfare in 1987–1988, and key decision makers in civil society and industry also expressed confidence in the ability of private builders and developers to meet housing needs with lower levels of *direct* public subvention that they had traditionally enjoyed. This view was evident in *The Programme for National Recovery* for instance – the corporatist pay agreement and socio-economic plan negotiated between the government, employers, trade unions and farmers in 1987 which many credit with laying the foundations for Ireland's economic recovery (Government of Ireland, 1987). This, the first in a long series of "social partnership" pay and public policy agreements, included a rather minimalist pledge regarding the future role of government in housing provision: "The Government will ensure that, within the Public Capital Programme special emphasis will continue to be given to the housing needs of disadvantaged groups" (Government of Ireland, 1987: 23). Whereas it sounded a much more optimistic note about the potential for commercial construction to provide jobs and houses and, to facilitate this, pledged to "improve the climate for private sector investment which will support the construction industry" (ibid.). This view that commercial building and lending would dominate in future and the appropriate role of government should be to facilitate, rather than bankroll, this investment was restated by Minister Padráig Flynn during a parliamentary debate on cuts to public spending on housing in 1987. In this vein, he argued:

> ... new [public capital] projects should be started only where there is a genuine need and not just for their own sake. Any reduction in employment which may follow the reduced allocations for public expenditure programmes should be off-set by employment created by increased private investment arising from the Government's success in reducing interest and mortgage rates.... As stated in the *Programme for National Recovery*, the Government's fiscal and monetary policies should encourage extra private investment, through the creation of a climate which will stimulate investment, increase confidence and generate economic activity.
> (Flynn in Dáil Debates, 1987, Vol. 374, No. 4, Cols. 817–881).

The final and probably the most significant efficiency-related reasons for the rolling back of the property-based welfare state relate to trade-off between investment in this area and spending on the mainstream welfare state. As explained earlier, mainstream welfare was cut back during the 1980s, but it came through this retrenchment period far more unscathed than the asset-based welfare state which was largely dismantled during this period. Furthermore, in a pattern which significantly lagged the post-war expansion of other European welfare states, its strongest period of enlargement of public services and social security benefits in Ireland took place in the late 1960s and 1970s. For instance, free second-level education was introduced in 1967 and participation in third-level education expanded as a nationwide network of Regional Technical Colleges (polytechnics) opened from 1970; the 1970 Health Act modernised the public health system and introduced free GP care for benefit claimants and soon after free hospital care was granted to all. In addition, social security benefit coverage was radically extended in 1973 when the income ceiling for social insurance contributions was removed and all employees were granted eligibility for these benefits and benefits for different categories of lone parents were introduced between 1970 and 1974 (Pellion, 2001). As argued earlier, the growth of mainstream welfare in part reflected shifting power distribution as the Labour Party in particular pushed successfully for increased social security spending in the 1970s. However, spending on education also had a practical purpose in that it enabled badly needed industrial development and increased investment in this was supported by developmentally minded politicians on this basis; for instance, this argument is proffered in the autobiography of the architect of the 1987–1988 retrenchment programme Ray MacSharry (MacSharry and White, 2000). A similar rationale inspired developmentalist opposition to land reform for the reasons identified by Raymond Crotty and Des Maguire – by the 1970s and 1980s, a combination of high land prices and an unwillingness of elderly farmers to part with their holdings (despite government inducements) had radically increased the cost of land acquisition by the Land Commission and reduced the amount of land changing hands on the open market to almost zero, thereby undermining the potential for entrepreneurialism in agriculture (Commins, 1982). In the context of pressures to increase spending on mainstream welfare and a concern about facilitating industrial and agricultural development, the level of public spending on the property-based welfare system became unsustainable. Thus, from the perspective of the new political elite, "diminishing returns" had emerged as the disadvantages of adhering to this policy path now outweighed the benefits (Malpass, 2011).

Conclusions

This chapter has described the retrenchment phase of Ireland's property-based welfare system between the late 1960s and late 1980s. During this opening decade of this period, this regime destabilised as escalating costs, particularly of homeownership supports and social housing provision, became increasingly difficult for government to bear in the context of the increasing challenging world economic context and strengthening competing claims on state investment due to the expansion of mainstream welfare services. These pressures generated marked policy instability as contradictory policy initiatives were introduced and reforms were initiated and then quickly reversed. For instance, the Land Commission's migration schemes were ceased but its land redistribution work continued and some homeownership subsidies were cut back while others were extended. However, an unambiguous and radical policy redirection emerged between 1986 and 1989 and, as a result, the property-based welfare system which has been slowly and incrementally constructed over the course of the preceding century was largely abolished during this time. Most homeowner subsidies were abolished in 1987; in the same year, the century-old system of borrowing to fund social housing development was abolished and, as a result, output rates decreased radically; SDA lending also fell dramatically in 1988, and the Land Commission's activities were stalled in 1983 and it was finally closed in 1992.

This development reflected very marked socio-economic changes which resulted in a shift in the balance of power in Irish society as the influence of small farmers decreased because the Irish population had urbanised, the majority of workers were employed in industry and services rather than agriculture and the nuclear family replaced extended family living. In addition, the ideological bulwarks of familism, peasantism and distributism which had supported the property-based welfare system weakened concurrently, while competing ideologies which were inimical to this welfare regime strengthened. For instance, from the 1980s policymakers and voters were more likely to support free-market solutions to social and economic problems or the focusing of public on mainstream welfare services such as social security or productive investment such as education. This change in attitude enabled government to think what had previously been unthinkable and rollback the very substantial public expenditure required to support the property-based welfare system. Their willingness to do this was also inspired by efficiency considerations which had a much greater influence on the policy decisions taken during the retrenchment phase than in previous phases in the development of the property-based welfare system. This reflected in part the long duration and acute nature of the late 1970s–early 1980s fiscal crisis which meant that by the latter date government had exhausted most other options available to balance the books and they decided that rolling back property-based welfare was less controversial than cutting benefits or raising taxes further (Honohan, 1992). The national debt had also reached unprecedented heights by the 1980s, standardisation of national accounting rules and pressures from international markets limited the opportunity for accumulating further borrowing and due to the radical expansion of the mainstream welfare system during the 1980s which created a clear trade-off between spending on this area and spending on the property-based welfare system to an extent which had not been the case when public services and benefits were less developed. Furthermore, in contrast to previous decades, alternatives to publicly subsidised capital asset redistribution were more widely available by the 1980s including EU Common Agricultural Policy price subsidies for farmers, large-scale private housing construction and non-governmental mortgage provision.

As explained in the next chapter, the availability of these alternatives to the traditional property-based welfare system had two very significant implications in the longer term. Firstly, their availability meant that policymakers did not have to completely abandon their long-standing support for small farming and homeownership or their habits of using construction as an economic and employment stimulus and deferring to the power of farmers and the building industry. Policymakers still worked to achieve these goals in the 1990s and

2000s but operationalised this goal *indirectly* by enabling the private sector to support housebuilding and homeownership rather than by means of direct public spending. The second long-term implication of the availability of alternatives to the property-based welfare system was that the socio-economic impact of this collapse of this regime was disguised, at least until the mid-1990s. Thus the proportion of the Irish population employed in agriculture and living outside cities remained high by Western European standards. Furthermore, home-ownership continued to expand, from 70.8 per cent of households in 1971 to 80 per cent of households in 1991, and by the latter date the Irish homeownership rate remained among the highest in Western Europe (Central Statistics Office, various years).

References

Baker, T. & O'Brien, L. (1979). *The Irish housing system: A critical overview.* Dublin: ESRI.

Blackwell, J. (1988). *A review of housing policy.* Dublin: National Economic and Social Housing.

Carey, E. (1974). *Building societies in Ireland.* Dublin: Stationery Office.

Central Statistics Office (various years). *Census of population of Ireland.* Dublin: Stationery Office.

Commins, P. (1982). Land policies and agricultural development. In P. J. Drudy (Ed.), *Ireland: Land, politics and people* (pp. 127–140). Cambridge: Cambridge University Press.

Crotty, R. (1966). *Irish agricultural production: Its volume and structure.* Cork: Cork University Press.

Daly, M. (1997). *The buffer state: The historical origins of the department of the environment.* Dublin: Institute of Public Administration.

Daly, M. (2002). *The first department: A history of the department of agriculture.* Dublin: Institute of Public Administration.

Department of Agriculture (1980). *Land policy.* Dublin: Stationery Office.

Department of Local Government (various years). *Report/Tuarascáil.* Dublin: Department of Local Government.

Department of Local Government, (1969). *Housing in the seventies.* Dublin: Department of Local Government.

Department of the Environment (1986). *Financing of housing in Ireland –
1985*. Dublin: Department of the Environment.
Department of the Environment (1991). *A plan for social housing.* Dublin:
Department of the Environment.
Department of the Environment (various years). *Report/Tuarascáil.* Dublin:
Department of the Environment.
Department of Housing, Planning and Local Government (various years). *Annual
housing statistics bulletin.* Dublin: Department of the Environment.
Dooley, T. (2004). *The land for the people: The land question in independent
Ireland.* Dublin: UCD Press.
Fahey, T. (2002), The family economy in the development of welfare regimes:
A case study. *European Sociological Review, 18*(1), 51–64.
Fahey, T. and Nixon, E. (2014). Family policy in Ireland. In M. Robilia (Ed.),
Handbook of family policies across the globe (pp. 125–136). New York: Springer.
Garvin, T. (1982) Change and the political system. In F. Litton (Ed.), *Unequal
achievement: The Irish experience 1957–1982* (pp. 21–40). Dublin: Institute
of Public Administration.
Government of Ireland (1984). *Building on reality: 1985–1987.* Dublin:
Stationery Office.
Government of Ireland (1987). *The programme for national recovery.* Dublin:
Stationery Office.
Honohan, P. (1992). Fiscal adjustment in Ireland in the 1980s. *Economic and
Social Review, 23*(3), 258–314.
Inter-Department Committee on Land Structure Reform (1978). *Final report.*
Dublin: Stationery Office.
Irish Times (1981, October 1). Noonan calls for new tax incentive deal for
renewal schemes. *Irish Times,* p. 20.
Irish Times (1981, November 24). Jobs crisis in the building industry". *Irish
Times,* p. 12.
Irish Times (1984, January 26). Builders criticise lack of incentive. *Irish Times,* p. 13.
Irish Times (1984, July 16,), Boost for building urged to create jobs. Irish
Times, p. 8.
Irish Times (1985, January 25) Pre-Budget appeal on tax incentives made by
auctioneer. *Irish Times,* p. 20.
Kelly, J., & Everett, M. (2004), Financial liberalisation and economic growth
in Ireland. *Central Bank Quarterly Bulletin, 04*(03), 91–112.
Kennedy, K., Giblin, T., & McHugh, D. (1988). *The economic development of
Ireland in the twentieth century.* London: Routledge.

Lee, J. (1989). *Ireland, 1912–1985: Politics and society*. Cambridge: Cambridge University Press.

MacSharry, R., & White, P. (2000). *The making of the Celtic Tiger: The inside story of Ireland's boom economy*. Cork: Mercier Press.

Maguire, D. (1976). *The land commission*. Dublin: Irish Farmers' Journal.

Maguire, D. (1983). *The land problem*. Dublin: Agri-books.

Malpass, P. (2011). Path dependence and the measurement of change in housing policy. *Housing, Theory and Society, 28*(4), 305–319.

Mathews, A. (1982). The state and Irish agriculture, 1950–1980 In P.J. Drudy (Ed.), *Ireland: Land, politics and people* (pp. 241–270). Cambridge: Cambridge University Press.

McLoughlin, E., & Rodgers, P. (1997). Single mothers in the Republic of Ireland: Mothers not workers. In S. Duncan and R. Edwards (Eds.), *Single mothers in an international context: Mothers or workers?* (pp. 9–44). London: Routledge.

Murphy, L. (2004). Mortgage finance and housing provision in Ireland, 1970–90. *Urban Studies, 32*(1), 135–154.

National Economic and Social Council (1977). *Report on housing subsidies*. Dublin: NESC.

National Economic and Social Council (1985). *A strategy for development 1986–1990*. Dublin: NESC.

Norris, M., Coates, D., & Kane, F. (2007). Breeching the limits of owner occupation? Supporting low-income buyers in the inflated Irish housing market. *European Journal of Housing Policy, 7*(3), 337–356.

Norris, M., & Gkartzios, M. (2011). Twenty years of property-led urban regeneration in Ireland: Outputs, impacts, implications. *Public Money & Management, 31*(4), 257–264.

O'Brien, K. (1982, February 1). Ireland in danger of turning into west European banana republic. *Irish Times*, p. 5.

O'Connor, E. (2011). *A labour history of Ireland 1824–2000*. Dublin: UCD Press.

O'Connell, C. (2007). *The state and housing in Ireland: Ideology, policy and practice*. London: Nova Science.

Ó Gráda, C. (2004). Irish agriculture after the Land War. In S. Engerman & S. Metzer (Eds.), *Land rights, ethno-nationality and sovereignty in history* (pp. 131–152). London: Routledge.

Ó Rian, S. (2014). *The rise and fall of Ireland's Celtic Tiger: Liberalism, boom and bust*. Cambridge: Cambridge University Press.

Pellion, M. (2001). *Welfare in Ireland: Actors, resources, strategies*. London: Praeger.

Quinn, R. (2005). *Straight left: A journey in politics.* Dublin, Ireland: Hodder Headline.

Solow, B.L. (1971). *The land question and the Irish economy, 1870–1903.* Harvard: Harvard University Press.

Threshold (1987). *Policy consequences: A study of the £5000 surrender grant in the Dublin housing area.* Dublin: Threshold.

Vaughan, W. (1984). *Landlord and tenants in Ireland, 1848–1904.* Dundalk: Dundalgam.

Walsh, S. (1981, September 11). More harsh measures predicted next year. *Irish Times,* p. 6.

6

Marketisation: 1990–2007

Introduction

This chapter examines the policy and socio-economic developments which followed the collapse of Ireland's state subsidised system of property redistribution in the 1980s. The primary insight offered here is that policymakers continued to pursue their long-cherished goal of promoting property acquisition and habit of using construction as an economic and employment stimulus during the 1990s and early 2000s, but they used different mechanisms to achieve these objectives. As explained in previous chapters, until the late 1980s property redistribution had been primarily a socialised activity which was dependent on an expensive and extensive variety of public subsidies including loans, grants, tax subsidies, compulsory government acquisition and redistribution of land, government construction of dwellings for sale and sale of social housing to tenants. This system enabled property distribution patterns which were more progressive than the distribution of income or other types of wealth (Norris, 2016). This chapter explains that from the 1990s construction and property redistribution was primarily a marketised activity supported by commercial bank lending and private property

© The Author(s) 2016   **203**
M. Norris, *Property, Family and the Irish Welfare State*,
DOI 10.1007/978-3-319-44567-0_6

developers and these developments provoked a marked growth in "financialisation" by radically increasing the availability of and necessity for commercial credit and thereby increasing the power of the finance industry over the economy, government and households (Ó Rian, 2012). As a result of these developments, the distribution of property ownership became more regressive and a much larger proportion of the population was excluded from homeownership than had been the case during the 1970s and 1980s.

Numerous authors have highlighted the growth in financialisation across most developed countries since the 1980s and linked this development to the widespread housing market boom and busts which took place in the late 1990s and 2000s (see van der Zwan, 2010, for a review of these arguments). A number of influential analyses also emphasise the extent to which financialisation and the attendant growth in asset prices were deliberately engineered by policymakers to support consumer demand and therefore economic growth. Brenner (2006) argues that this strategy, which he calls "asset price Keynesianism", was employed by the USA as a solution to the widespread decline in the profitability of industry from the late 1960s. His thesis is that the role of rising asset prices in supporting consumer spending, particularly housing which is the most widely held asset, explains why the USA boomed in the 1980s and 1990s despite stagnating wages. Homeowners were able to "cash in" the rising value of their home by selling it and keeping part of the profit or releasing equity by increasing the size of their mortgage or using one of the increasing varieties of equity release products. Crouch (2009, 2011) identifies a similar development in the English-speaking countries which had embraced mainstream Keynesian economics until the 1970s/1980s and consequently were heavily dependent on consumer spending to support demand. Similarly, Watson's (2010) analysis of the UK suggests that as well as supporting consumer demand this approach had a social function – it was intended to support the acquisition of dwellings such as dwellings which could be liquidated if required to meet costs such as eldercare and therefore would in part replace the mainstream welfare state.

The analysis which follows suggests that an asset price Keynesianist regime also emerged in Ireland after the collapse of the property-based welfare system but, in a number of fundamental respects, the Irish case remained distinctive in the international context during the 1990s and early 2000s. This distinctiveness is path dependency related. Unlike the USA and Britain, in Ireland asset price Keynesianism was not rooted primarily in the industrial restructuring of the 1970s and 1980s, but rather it was a response to the much longer process of the expansion and decline of the distinctive Irish property-based welfare system. Due to these historical factors, the Irish government continued to play a much stronger role in supporting property markets than was usual in Western Europe during this period both in terms of the scale and focus of policy interventions (Norris and Byrne, 2015, argue that Spain is the only other European country which followed a similar policy path). The Irish property market was supported by the "light touch" regulation of commercial mortgage lenders seen in many other countries which facilitated a radical expansion in credit volumes, but also by a typically Irish package of supports for construction such as permissive land use planning and tax subsidies (Norris and Shields, 2007). In addition, some minor vestiges of the property-based welfare system, such as sales of local authority social housing to tenants, remained in place in the 1990s and early 2000s which have helped to support the property market, as did some new supports for low-income homebuyers which were introduced during this period (Norris et al., 2007). Consequently, in contrast to the norm in most of the rest of Western Europe the Irish version of asset price Keynesianism supported both property market-related borrowing *and* construction and thereby facilitated an unusual two-dimensional boom in both house prices *and* in housebuilding (Norris and Coates, 2014). The two-dimensional nature of the Irish housing boom explains the acute nature of the bust which occurred when the boom ended in 2007–2008.

In part due to the housing credit and construction boom, in economic terms the period examined in this chapter was by far the most successful one in Ireland's history as an independent state. The arrival of the "Celtic tiger" economic boom in the mid-1990s marked the end of the long period of economic stagnation which had commenced in the late 1970s and the much longer pattern of economic underperformance compared to the rest of Western Europe (Kennedy et al., 1988). Ireland's economic fortunes improved radically as GDP per capita increased from 14.8 per cent below the average of the 15 Western European longest EU member states (EU15) in 1995, to 48 per cent above the EU15 average in 2006 and, concurrently, the Irish unemployment rate fell from 10 per cent above the EU15 average to 45 per cent below this average (Eurostat, various years), although, of course, it is clear in retrospect that over-reliance on credit expansion and construction-related employment and tax revenue to fuel this boom generated and also disguised critical risks in the macroeconomy and public finances, among mortgage lenders and in the finances of individual households (Norris and Coates, 2014). The extent of these risks was revealed when the Irish economy experienced a collapse of unprecedented scale in 2007–2008. In political terms, the 1990s and early 2000s were one of the most stable periods in modern Irish history. Apart from the period 1994 to 1997 when a coalition consisting of Fine Gael, Labour and a small and short-lived party called the Democratic Left was in power, all governments during the period under examination in this chapter were led by Fianna Fáil and its leader Bertie Aherne was Taoiseach for most of this period. All of these Fianna Fáil governments were coalitions with the small Progressive Democrats party and the PD leader held the position of Tánaiste (deputy prime minister) (Murphy, 2016).

The Emergence of Asset Price Keynesianism

Land Use Planning and Housing Supply

Figures 6.1 and 6.2 reveal that the house price and housebuilding booms, which were the defining features of the period under discussion in this chapter, did not occur concurrently. Nor did they occur evenly across different regions of the country or different elements of the housing stock.

House price growth commenced as the economy started to boom in the early 1990s. Nationwide second-hand house price inflation rose from 7.7 per cent per annum between 1990 and 1993 to 22 per cent per annum between 1996 and 2000, before slowing slightly to in the region

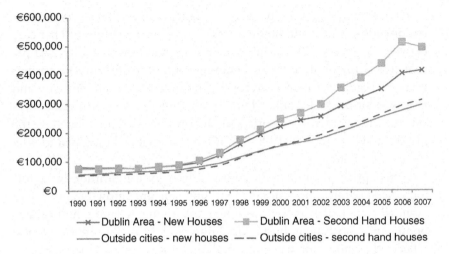

Fig. 6.1 House prices in Dublin and the rest of Ireland, 1990–2007. *Source*: Department of Housing, Planning and Local Government (various years a)

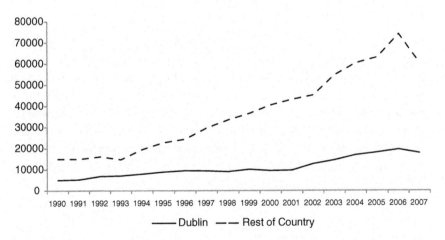

Fig. 6.2 New housing output in Dublin and the rest of Ireland, 1990–2007. *Source*: Department of Housing, Planning and Local Government (various years a)

of 10 per cent per annum between the latter date and 2007. As a result, nationwide second-hand house prices grew by a remarkable 340 per cent between 1996 and 2007 while new house prices increased by 270 per cent (Department of Housing, Planning and Local Government, various years a). Figure 6.1 demonstrates that house prices in Dublin City and largely suburbanised County Dublin grew much faster than prices outside the capital. New house prices in Dublin were 18.2 per cent above the prices outside Dublin in 1996, but the differential had increased to 40.8 per cent by 2007.

House price inflation is of course driven by a multitude of factors including population, employment and income growth and credit availability, all of which contributed to driving Ireland's house price boom and subsequent bust (McQuinn and O'Reilly, 2008). It also reflects the supply of dwellings and the context of Ireland's housing boom, in particular the uneven supply response over time and space and the disconnect between the number of dwellings constructed and occupied. Figure 6.2 demonstrates that in nationwide terms housing supply displayed a very elastic response to rising demand. The total number of dwellings built increased from 20,039 units in 1990 to a peak of 93,419 in 2006. To put these figures in context, in the latter year just over twice as many dwellings were built in the UK for a population of 60 million (compared to a population of 4.2 million in Ireland) and Spain was the only EU member state which built more dwellings per capita than Ireland (Norris and Byrne, 2015). However, many of the dwellings built during the Celtic tiger boom were not provided in areas where population growth and therefore housing demand was concentrated. Population growth during this time was strongest in cities, particularly Dublin, the Dublin commuter belt and Galway city in the West but the housing supply response was weaker in these areas particularly in the 1990s (Norris and Shields, 2007). The number of households in Dublin City and County increased by 26.4 per cent between 1991 and 2002, but only 23.6 per cent of the additional dwellings built during this period were located in this area. In contrast, 20.2 per cent of the dwellings built between 1991 and 2002 were located in the six rural countries which run along Ireland's western seaboard, but the number of households resident in these countries increased by just 14.9 per cent (Central Statistics Office, various years and see Fig. 6.2).

By the early 2000s, the scale of housebuilding in Ireland and the spatial mismatch between output and population growth had generated an over-supply problem in parts of the country as evidenced by growing numbers of vacant dwellings. FitzGerald (2005) found that one-third of dwellings built in Ireland between 2000 and 2003 were left vacant and the growth in such properties added up to 10 per cent to house prices in the period 2000–2003. These empty dwellings were heavily concentrated in rural areas. In 2006, 9.7 per cent of dwellings in Dublin were empty, which is not substantially higher than the 4–6 per cent of the housing stock which is usually vacant in most developed countries, whereas 23.4 per cent of dwellings in the six rural counties on the western seaboard were empty in this year (Central Statistics Office, various years). Following Ireland's property market collapse in 2007–2008, the extent of housing oversupply was further evidenced by the proliferation of empty, partially completed housing developments which were dubbed "ghost estates". The housing ministry identified 2,846 unfinished housing estates nationwide in 2010 and in 777 of these half or more of the dwellings were either vacant or under construction (Kitchin et al., 2012). Oversupply was also evident in the office and retail space markets. Also, 23 per cent of office space in Dublin was vacant by the end of 2010 and vacancy rates in suburban locations were even higher than this (45 per cent of office space in the northern suburbs was vacant in this time) as were vacancy rates in older buildings, and, as a result, average office rents contracted by around 45 per cent from peak to trough (MacLaran, 2014). At the same time, there was estimated to be over 2 million m^2 of shopping centre space and 1.32 million m^2 of retail park space nationwide – double the level available in 2005 and the second highest level of provision per capita in the EU (CBRE, 2010). Unsurprisingly, vacancy rates were also high in these sectors, particularly in peripheral or economically depressed locations (e.g. DTZ Sherry FitzGerald, 2013).

The reasons for this excess and inappropriately located supply of housing and other property in Ireland during the period under exam-ination in this chapter are at first glance difficult to relate to land use planning policy. Ireland's modern planning system was established by the Local Government (Planning and Development) Act 1963, which was very closely modelled on the UK Town and Country Planning Act 1947. Like its UK counterpart, the 1963 Act obliges local authorities to specify their spatial development proposals in development plans of at least 5 years duration and to control adherence to the terms of development plans using planning permissions (Bannon, 1989). In the UK, the regime has strictly constrained building in the countryside and expansion of urban areas and on this basis has been blamed for inadequate housebuilding rates since the 1960s and house price growth and volatility (Cheshire, 2004; Monk et al., 1996). Whereas, as explained earlier, an almost identical land use planning regime has achieved the opposite outcomes in Ireland – very high housing and other property output in nationwide terms to the extent that oversupply was evident in some rural areas, coupled with a degree of undersupply of housing (but not retail or office space) in large urban centres, particularly Dublin.

These radically different construction patterns in Ireland and the UK reflect different approaches to implementing the similar land use planning legislation which applies to both countries. Compared to the UK, development control procedures have traditionally been applied much more liberally in Ireland, as has the development planning process. Many rural local authorities did not regularly revise their development plans until the 1980s, and the 1963 Act did not require development plans to estimate and make provision for meeting future housing needs. In addition, in contrast to most of Western Europe, the Irish planning system was characterised by a very weak strategic regional or national planning. Although a national spatial plan was published in 1968, as were strategies for the Dublin and Eastern Regions in 1967 and 1985, respectively, the first two of these were implemented only in part and the third was not implemented at all (Bannon, 1989).

In the context of minimalist controls on housing and other types of property development in Ireland, new building naturally clustered in locations which were most convenient to develop rather than where supply was most urgently required. Building on urban, brownfield sites is inherently more challenging than developing greenfield rural or peri-urban sites because the urban sites are surrounded by more neighbours who may object to planning and may have to be painstakingly assembled by purchasing parcels of land from several landowners or decontaminated if formerly used for industry. In addition, urban development land is scarcer and therefore more expensive to buy and often requires high-density construction to ensure development is financially viable which requires high upfront investment from developers and government to pay for provision of sewage, road and water infrastructure (Williams et al., 2002). For these practical reasons, coupled with other socio-economic, financial and political factors which are examined later in this chapter, in the Irish context building on greenfield sites on the periphery of cities and in rural areas was most convenient; therefore, output was unduly concentrated in these areas. This is evident in rate of construction of single-family houses in the open countryside for occupants not engaged in farming. From the 1960s and 1970s, in Ireland output of these "one-off" houses increased significantly and they increased further during the Celtic tiger boom (Corcoran et al., 2007). Some 80,000 one-off dwellings were built in the open countryside between 1991 and 2002, which is more than the total number built in the Dublin City and County and all other Irish cities over the same period (Keaveney and Walsh, 2004).

By the late 1990s, the failure of rising housing supply to moderate house price inflation raised increasing concerns among policymakers. In response, the housing ministry commissioned three studies of the housing market from the economist Peter Bacon (Bacon and Associates, 1998, 1999, 2000) and published three policy statements which detailed the policy reforms which would be initiated in response to these reviews (Department of the Environment and Local Government, 1998, 1999, 2000) (see Table 6.1). These housing market analyses identified the limited supply of dwellings, particularly in Dublin, and other cities as the primary cause of increasing house prices and to resolve this problem recommended a large number of reforms which would increase urban housing output. They also highlighted the role of stamp duty (taxes charged on the purchase of housing) in impeding the effective operation of the market and the presence of large numbers of property investors buying dwellings in artificially inflating housing demand. However, not all of Bacon and Associates' recommendations were acted on by policymakers. Instead

Table 6.1 Key policy milestones in the emergence of the asset price keynesianist policy regime, 1990–2006

Date	Land Use Planning and Housing Supply	Credit for House Purchase and Construction	Tax Treatment of House Purchase and Construction	Supports for Low-Income Renters and Homebuyers
1991		Last remaining government controls on banks and building societies' interest rates were removed and banks' required primary liquidity ratio reduced from 10 to 8 per cent.		Mortgage allowance for tenants, low-income housing sites and shared ownership scheme introduced.
1992		Banks' primary liquidity ratio requirements reduced to 6 per cent.		The level of the mortgage allowance for tenants was increased.
1993		Banks' primary liquidity ratio requirements reduced to 4 per cent.		Discount for the local authority tenant purchase scheme was set at a minimum of €3,809 or 3 per cent for each year of tenancy to a maximum of 30 per cent.
1994		Banks' primary liquidity ratio requirements reduced to 3 per cent.	Section 23 tax incentives extended to include city suburbs as part of the Urban Renewal Scheme.	

Table 6.1 (continued)

Date	Land Use Planning and Housing Supply	Credit for House Purchase and Construction	Tax Treatment of House Purchase and Construction	Supports for Low-Income Renters and Homebuyers
1995				Local authority tenant purchasers could purchase their dwelling via the shared ownership scheme rather than buying it outright and could use commercial mortgages rather than only SDA mortgages. The mortgage allowance for tenants was increased and eligibility extended to housing association tenants. The minimum equity which shared ownership purchasers had to buy was reduced from 50 to 40 per cent.

(continued)

Table 6.1 (continued)

Date	Land Use Planning and Housing Supply	Credit for House Purchase and Construction	Tax Treatment of House Purchase and Construction	Supports for Low-Income Renters and Homebuyers
1998	Bacon and Associates' first housing market review was published. In response, additional funding for land servicing was provided and additional planning staff were employed to expedite housebuilding and new planning guidelines to encourage high-density urban developments were issued.		As recommended in Bacon and Associates' first housing market review, tax deductibility of landlords' mortgage interest was removed; stamp duty new homes purchases by property investors was increased and Capital Gains Tax on the sale of land zoned for development was reduced to 20 per cent.	

Table 6.1 (continued)

Date	Land Use Planning and Housing Supply	Credit for House Purchase and Construction	Tax Treatment of House Purchase and Construction	Supports for Low-Income Renters and Homebuyers
1999	The second housing market review by Peter Bacon and Associates is published. In response, additional funding for the serviced land initiative was provided.	Ireland's adopts the euro currency which facilitates a significant increase in mortgage lending because interest rates call and access to interbank lending to fund mortgage lending is easier. Banks' primary liquidity ratio reduced to 2 per cent.	Section 23 tax incentives were extended to include parts of 38 large towns (the Urban Renewal Scheme) and also to a sparsely populated region of the northwest (the Rural Renewal Scheme). As recommended in Bacon and Associates' second report, restrictions on the availability of the lower rate of Capital Gains Tax on sales of development land were removed.	All periods of tenancy in local authority dwellings were taken into account when calculating the discount received by tenant purchasers. The income limits for eligibility for the shared ownership scheme and the level of the rental subsidy were increased. The affordable housing scheme is introduced.

(continued)

Table 6.1 (continued)

Date	Land Use Planning and Housing Supply	Credit for House Purchase and Construction	Tax Treatment of House Purchase and Construction	Supports for Low-Income Renters and Homebuyers
2000	Planning and Development Act 2000 reforms require local authorities to include housing strategies in their development plan for meeting future housing needs. Third housing market review by Peter Bacon and Associates is published and a range of policy reforms are introduced in response.		Stamp duty payable by purchasers of dwellings for owner occupation was cut in 2000, while the rates payable by investors were not. Section 23 incentives extended again to include parts of 100 small towns, under the Town Renewal Scheme. MITR for private residential landlords in reintroduced.	The level of the mortgage allowance for tenants was increased. The income limits for eligibility for the affordable housing and shared ownership schemes were increased. The Planning and Development Act, 2000 enabled provision of affordable housing via the planning system.
2001				The income limits for eligibility for the shared ownership scheme and the level of the rental subsidy were increased. Income limits for eligibly for affordable housing were increased.

Table 6.1 (continued)

Date	Land Use Planning and Housing Supply	Credit for House Purchase and Construction	Tax Treatment of House Purchase and Construction	Supports for Low-Income Renters and Homebuyers
2001		UK-headquartered Bank of Scotland starts mortgage lending in Ireland. This is the first of a number of foreign mortgage lenders which enter the Irish market and the resultant increase in competition is associated with a decline in interest rates and lending standards.		
2002	A National Spatial Strategy covering the period 2002 to 2020 was published.		The first-time buyers' grant (the last universal homebuyers' grant) was abolished.	
2003		Central Bank was replaced with Central Bank and Financial Services Regulatory Authority of Ireland .		The rent payable by shared ownership purchasers was reduced.

(continued)

Table 6.1 (continued)

Date	Land Use Planning and Housing Supply	Credit for House Purchase and Construction	Tax Treatment of House Purchase and Construction	Supports for Low-Income Renters and Homebuyers
2004		Specialist "sub-prime" lenders enter the Irish mortgage market. 100 per cent mortgages and mortgage equity with-drawal products are made available for the first time.		

Source: Kelly and Everett (2004); Norris (2016).

of intervening to dampen demand, the policy action taken on foot of their recommendations focused overwhelmingly on increasing supply particularly in urban areas. Thus in response to Bacon and Associates' (1998, 1999, 2000) research, the government increased funding for the provision of water, sewerage and road infrastructure to enable more land to be developed in Dublin; changed planning guidelines to encourage higher-density housing in urban areas and increased the number of planners employed by local authorities to expedite processing of planning applications.

These reforms, together with the advent of a strongly "pro-development" ethos among senior management in Dublin City Council, were successful in increasing supply to the capital and in restraining house price inflation there which fell from 94 per cent between 1996 and 2000 to 54 per cent between 2001 and 2005 in the new house sector (MacLaran and McCrory, 2014) (see Fig. 6.1). However, house price inflation continued to significantly outpace wage inflation in the early 2000s, particularly in Dublin. Concurrently, rural housing output continued to climb during the late 1990s and early 2000s and little or no progress was made in controlling its scale despite clear evidence of emerging oversupply particularly in the midlands and west of Ireland (FitzGerald, 2005).

The lack of progress in balancing the spatial distribution of housing supply and demand certainly did not reflect lack of land use policy making activity. The Planning and Development Act 2000 reformed and consolidated all of the preceding land use planning legislation and also required local authorities to plan for adequate future housing supply for the first time (see Table 6.1). This was to be done by including "housing strategies" which would assess the likely scale and nature of future housing need in local authorities' development plans and linking decisions regarding the zoning of land for residential development to these strategies. A *National Spatial Strategy* was also published in 2002 with the objective of facilitating more balanced regional development between then and 2020 (see Table 6.1) (Department of the Environment and Local Government, 2002). Some commentators have characterised the Celtic tiger boom as a period when planning legislation was "neo-liberalised" on the grounds that some of the reforms introduced during this period were clearly inspired by Thatcherite-era policies in the UK (Murphy et al., 2016). However, in the context of the planning free for all which prevailed for much of the history of the Irish State, the opposite case could be convincingly made – the 2000s were a period when Irish planning rules and regulations were significantly tightened up.

These policy reforms had limited practical impact, however, because as is traditional in the Irish planning system a gaping implementation gap emerged between the objectives of policy and the outcomes achieved on the ground. For instance, both the *National Spatial Strategy* and the regional planning guidelines which were intended to enable its operationalisation were largely ignored in local authorities' development plans, particularly in rural areas, which often rezoned land for housing far in excess of the guidelines' recommendations (Williams and Shiels, 2002). According to Kitchin et al. (2015: 11), "In many parts of the country there was enough zoned land for dozens of years of supply, with the average being 16.8 years if the household growth with each local authority continued at the same pace as 1996–2006 (a period of rapid growth)." For instance, County Monaghan, a mostly rural local authority located on the border with Northern Ireland, had a housing stock of 21,658 units in 2006 but enough zoned land for an additional 18,147 dwellings, enough to last for over 50 years. A legal challenge to one of these development plans on the grounds of its failure to reflect the regional guidelines was unsuccessful because the law only requires the former document to "have regard to" rather than to adhere to the latter (Simons, 2003).

Credit Availability for House Purchase and Construction

In marked contrast to the decades when the property-based welfare system prevailed, the years under examination in this chapter saw very little policy action to address the availability of credit for house purchase and building. In fact, the 1990s and 2000s are distinguished by an almost entirely hands-off approach to credit provision and regulation on the part of the Irish government. Despite this, the period between 2000 and 2007 in particular saw unprecedented change in the extent of credit availability, in the institutional structure for credit provision and arrangements for raising finance for lending, but these developments were not facilitated by concurrent national policy reform. Rather, these changes in mortgage credit provision were primarily shaped by the policy and regulatory reforms initiated in the 1980s and described in the previous chapter and also by international developments, particularly in wholesale money markets; in the governance of the Eurozone following Ireland's adoption of the euro as its currency in 1999 and as part of the Basle II international accord on banking supervision and regulation (Kelly and Everett, 2004) (see Table 6.1).

The implications of these credit market developments did not become evident until the early 2000s because the weakness of the Irish economy and the high unemployment and interest rates constrained borrowing for house purchase and therefore house prices. Table 6.2 demonstrates that this changed when the economy began to boom. Mortgage lending began to expand from 1996, but the pace of growth quickened considerably as the decade progressed and was particularly strong after 2000. Between 2000 and 2007, mortgage credit outstanding in Ireland rose by over 300 per cent (from 31.1 to 75.3 per cent of GDP). This trend of course reflected similar concurrent developments in most other developed countries, but it was especially pronounced in Ireland (Doyle, 2009). The growth in total mortgage credit outstanding in Ireland between 2000 and 2007 was four times the rate of growth in the 27 current EU members (EU27). Consequently, in the latter year, the average Irish mortgage debt to GDP ratio was over one-third higher than the EU27 average (European Mortgage Federation, various years). Table 6.2 reveals that this credit expansion reflected a rise in both the number and size of mortgages granted. The number of mortgages granted per annum rose from 57,300 in 2000 to a peak of 111,300 in 2006, but residential mortgage debt per capita rose even faster concurrently – from €8,620 to €29,290.

This table also illuminates the factors which enabled this dramatic growth in lending – increased reliance on wholesale money markets to fund mortgage lending and proportionately less reliance on retail deposits by households and private institutions which traditionally were the

Table 6.2 Macro mortgage credit trends in Ireland, 1996–2006

	1996	1998	2000	2002	2004	2006
Mortgage credit outstanding (€ million)	NA	NA	29,474	43,416	73,120	110,602
Mortgage debt to GDP ratio (%)	NA	NA	31.1	36.3	55.2	70.1
New mortgages (N)	56,000	61,400	74,300	79,300	98,700	111,300
Mortgage debt per capita (€)	3,830	5,650	8,620	12,110	19,120	29,290
Interest rates on new mortgages	7.10	6.00	6.17	4.69	3.47	4.57
Percentage of MFI's funding generated from						
Private sector deposits	NA	NA	50.2	48.8	38.7	32.1
Inter-bank lending and debt securities	NA	NA	30.2	32.5	46.0	53.5
Real estate-related lending as a percentage of total	NA	NA	37.4	43.3	54.4	72.0

Notes: All monetary data are at current prices.
NA not available.

Source: Central Bank (various years).

principal source of funding for non-governmental mortgage lending in Ireland. Retail deposits provided 50.2 per cent of funding for mortgage lending in 2000. Although total retail deposits in Irish mortgage lenders grew by 76.2 per cent between 2003 and 2007, lending expanded faster. The resultant funding gap was filled by borrowing from wholesale money markets which provided 30.2 per cent of funding for mortgage lending in 2000 compared to 53.7 per cent in 2006 (see Table 6.2). Unlike the USA, in Ireland mortgage lenders accessed wholesale money market funding primarily via interbank lending and debt securitisation was not widely used in the Irish context (Norris and Coates, 2014).

This globalisation of finance for mortgage lending was made possible by the banking deregulation implemented during the collapse of the property-based welfare system in the 1980s. As explained in Chap. 5, the building societies which had provided most non-governmental mortgage finance prior to this were legally debarred from accessing wholesale money markets and thereby forced to rely entirely on deposits for lending. These arrangements naturally constrained credit availability (and often necessitated credit rationing) because building societies had to ensure they had sufficient deposits to finance new lending. Thus the removal of the legal distinctions between banks and building societies by the Building Societies Act, 1989, which gave building societies access to wholesale money markets and facilitated their transformation into banks, also eliminated these constraints on credit availability. This process was reinforced by further banking deregulation in the early 1990s. Regulatory restrictions on credit growth were removed entirely by 1992 and banks' reserve requirements (required liquidity ratios) were decreased from 10 per cent to 6 per cent in 1992 and to 2 per cent in 1999 (Kelly, 2014). In the late 1990s, Irish mortgage lenders' access to the wholesale markets was eased further by Ireland's adoption of the euro which eliminated the exchange rate risk previously associated with accessing this finance and, by extension, the need to cost this risk into the interest rates charged to customers (Conefrey and FitzGerald, 2010) (see Table 6.1).

Euro membership also enabled increased mortgage lending because interest rates fell sharply following the adoption of the currency to reflect the historic norm and economic requirements of Germany and France which jointly accounted for the vast majority of the Eurozone economy. This enabled borrowers to take on more debt and therefore further fuelled house price inflation (Norris and Coates, 2014). Table 6.3 reveals that falling interest rates reduced average mortgage servicing costs from 36 per cent to 31 per cent of income between 2000 and 2006, despite marked concurrent house price growth. The impact of this decline in interest rates was reinforced by wage and price inflation which further decreased loan-servicing costs for borrowers (real interest rates, taking account of inflation, averaged –0.9 per cent between 1999 and 2004) and also the history of high and volatile interest rates in Ireland (Honohan and Leddin, 2006).

The same factors also drove a marked increase in lending in many Eurozone and other developed countries, but in Ireland's case unusually intense competition in the mortgage market further intensified these pressures for credit growth (European Central Bank, 2009). Between 2000 and 2010, the number of major mortgage lenders operating in the Irish market increased from 12 to 17 (Central Bank, various years). This

Table 6.3 Micro-level mortgage credit trends in Ireland, 1996–2006

	1996	1998	2000	2002	2004	2006
Percentage of average income required to service a mortgage on an average priced dwelling[a]	23	35	36	34	25	31
Percentage of outstanding mortgages which are						
Fixed rate	NA	NA	31.1	23.7	17.2	18.3
For principal private residences	NA	NA	NA	NA	80.0	73.7
For buy-to-let dwellings	NA	NA	NA	NA	18.8	25.1
For holiday/second homes	NA	NA	NA	NA	1.1	1.2
Percentage of new mortgages which are						
>€250,000	NA	NA	2.3	5.9	18.0	37.0
100 per cent loans	NA	NA	NA	NA	4.0	14.0
>30-year term	NA	NA	NA	NA	10.0	31.0
Interest only	NA	NA	2.4	2.7	5.7	12.6

Notes: NA not available.
[a]Data refer to two earner, married households, whose income = average industrial wage + average non-industrial wage. Mortgage payments are on a 20-year mortgage for 90 per cent of the average new house price for that year, repaid at average mortgage rates for that year.

Source: Department of Housing, Planning and Local Government (various years a, b).

was due to the entry of some Irish banks into the mortgage market for the first time, the establishment of specialist mortgage lending subsidiaries by existing Irish mortgage lenders and the entry of a number of foreign lenders into the Irish market. In 2007, these foreign lenders accounted for approximately 30 per cent of mortgage loans advanced in Ireland (European Central Bank, 2009). This level of market penetration by foreign mortgage lenders is unusual in Europe – traditionally, these institutions have been reluctant to lend for mortgages in other countries because of national variations in property rights and therefore in lenders' ability to repossess dwellings in the case of delinquent loans (Stephens, 2003). Foreign lenders' fondness for entering the Irish mortgage market in the 2000s may reflect the fact that the UK and Ireland are both common law jurisdictions (large numbers of British lenders also commended lending in Malta and Cyprus concurrently which also employ the common law system) and also the lack of competition in the Irish mortgage market prior to 2000 and therefore its potential for growth (European Central Bank, 2009). This extreme competition forced Irish mortgage lenders to cut their interest rates further to maintain market share, a process which was sparked by the entry of UK-headquartered Bank of Scotland into the Irish market in 2002 (see Table 6.3) (Kelly, 2014).

Table 6.3 reveals these mortgage market developments were also associated with a step change in the nature and focus of mortgage lending in Ireland (Doyle, 2009). For instance, from 2004 the pace of "financial product innovation" in this market increased markedly. In this year, First Active (a former building society which had been bought by the Royal Bank of Scotland) introduced the "100 per cent mortgage" to the Irish market and the other banks soon followed suit and interest-only mortgages and mortgage equity withdrawal products also became available for the first time and take-up of these products and the size and duration of mortgages increased radically between 2004 and 2007 (see Table 6.2) (Doyle, 2009). Four specialist "sub-prime" mortgage lenders also entered the Irish market between 2004 and 2007, but they accounted for only 0.5 per cent of mortgage lending by value in the latter year (Coates, 2008). Thus unlike in the USA, in Ireland the credit boom was associated primarily with declining lending standards among mainstream lenders rather than with the growth of a specialist sub-prime sector. This period is also distinguished by a marked rise in lending to private landlords who would have found it difficult to access loan finance during the property-based welfare period when lending was dominated by local government and building societies which were both mandated to lend for homeownership. Homeowners held 80.0 per cent of outstanding mortgages in 2004 but only 73.3 per cent in 2006, whereas the proportion of outstanding mortgages held by buy-to-let landlords by this sector rose by 6.3 per cent between 2004 and 2006 (see Table 6.2).

Soon this hyper-competition in mortgage lending came to be matched by intense competition in the market for property development loans. Consequently, the diminution in lending standards and banks' margins evident in mortgage lending also became evident in property development lending. This development was in part inspired by the particularly aggressive lending strategy adopted by the small, niche property development lender Anglo Irish Bank and it was soon joined by the Irish Nationwide Building Society. Without a significant branch network, neither organisation could compete with the main high street banks in mortgage lending, so they focused instead on lending for property development and offering very quick decisions on loan applications and cultivating strong personal relationships with particular developers (Kelly, 2014). Consequently, a small number of developers came to dominate their loan book and the associated risks were accentuated by the fact that many of these loans were inadequately secured by paper equity and "personal guarantees" and the interest was often "rolled up" into the principal and not repaid (Joint Committee of Inquiry into the Banking Crisis, 2015a). However, these practices generated stratospheric growth in Anglo Irish Bank's profits and share price and management of the larger banks came under pressure from boards, shareholders and journalists to achieve a similar performance and therefore adopted the Anglo Irish business model.

Banks' exposure to the real estate sector obviously increased in tandem with rising lending for mortgages and construction. In 2000, real estate-related lending made up 37.4 per cent of the total lending by banks and building societies operating in the Irish market but this had increased to 72 per cent by 2006 and in 5 of these 13 credit institutions real estate accounted for over 80 per cent of the loan book in 2005 (Kearns and Woods, 2006). Despite this, the mortgage market was the subject of very few policy or regulatory interventions during the period under examination in this chapter. Irish policymakers failed to counter the loss of national control over interest rates following accession to the euro with the introduction of alternative mechanism to control demand for credit such as mortgage lending controls. Neither did they introduce non-credit market-related mechanisms to control housing demand such as property taxes (Honohan and Leddin 2006 and Conefrey and FitzGerald 2010, among many others, criticise these omissions). Instead, in addition to accelerating housing output, the other main response to the credit boom was institutional reform of banking regulation and there is evidence that this focus in part explains the lack of action to control credit availability.

In 2003, the Central Bank of Ireland was replaced with a non-supervising Central Bank responsible for ensuring the stability of the financial system as a whole and a separate financial regulator, but both organisations were combined within a single framework, overseen by one board. This new regulator called Irish Financial Services Regulatory Authority (IFSRA) was responsible for ensuring the stability of individual financial institutions, protecting consumers of banking services and encouraging the success of the financial services industry. Government-commissioned research on banking crash which Ireland suffered in the late 2000s concluded that the IFSRA focused on the second and third of these responsibility and neglected the first (Regling and Watson, 2010). Kelly (2014: 43) suggests that these responsibilities could not be achieved concurrently in any case because they were mutually contradictory: hyper competition in financial services and expansion of the sector delivered benefits for consumers such as easy credit terms and super-low interest rates but also undermined the stability of financial institutions. These problems were compounded by the complexity of the dual central bank/financial regulator structure and acute shortcomings in arrangements for implementation of banking regulation (Joint Committee of Inquiry into the Banking Crisis, 2015a). Kelly's (2014) analysis of this issue emphasises the problems associated with the adoption of a "principles-based" approach to banking regulation by the IFSRA which involved scrutinising banks and building societies' compliance with principles in relation to solvency, governance, consumer protection and disclosure. In her view, the key problem with this arrangement was that principles were "to be subject to consensus" between bankers and regulators (the IFSRA established an industry consultation group for this purpose) and crucially were therefore "flexible . . . aiming to promote innovation in compliance procedures, business models and financial product development" (Kelly, 2004: 43). Honohan's (2010: 8) shares these concerns about the use of principles-based regulation but highlights additional shortcomings in the implementation of this supervisory model:

By relying excessively on a regulatory philosophy emphasising process over outcomes, supervisory practice focused on verifying governance and risk management models rather than attempting an independent assessment of risk, whether on a line-by-line or whole-of-institution basis. This approach involved a degree of complacency about the likely performance of well-governed banks that proved unwarranted. It was not just a question of emphasising principles over rules, it was the degree of trust that well-governed banks could be relied upon to remain safe and sound.

Tax Treatment of Property Purchase and Construction

During the period under review in this chapter, the process of rolling back the universal subsidies for homeowners associated with the property-based welfare system which had commenced during the 1980s was completed. Mortgage interest tax relief – the last remaining universal tax subsidy for this sector – was radically reduced during the 1990s, and by 2002 it covered just 4.6 per cent of the gross repayments on an average, 20-year mortgage. In addition, the first-time buyers' grant (the last universal homebuyers' grant) was abolished in 2002 (see Table 6.1) (National Economic and Social Council, 2004). Bacon and Associates' (1998, 1999, 2000) reviews of the housing market recommended that no new universal homebuyer supports be introduced because they would be capitalised into house prices and this analysis was accepted by policymakers. However, on foot of the recommendations of Bacon and Associates' (1998) first report, the stamp duty payable by homeowners when purchasing their dwelling was cut in 2000 and entirely removed in the case of first-time homebuyers. This was an effort to enable first-time buyers enter the market and help existing homeowners trade up.

As mentioned earlier, Bacon and Associates' (1998) analysis of the housing markets also emphasised the role which speculative demand for housing from property investors played in driving house price inflation. They recommended a number of measures to control this demand which appear to have been far less attractive to policymakers than Bacon and Associates' ideas for increasing housebuilding rates. Thus Bacon and Associates' (1998, 1999, 2000) recommendation that the stamp duty payable by residential property investors be increased and tax deductibility of interest on buy-to-let mortgages be removed were implemented in 1998, but the latter measure was repealed in 2000. In 2015, the author of the housing market analyses Dr Peter Bacon told the parliamentary committee of enquiry into the banking crisis that the reintroduction of MITR for landlords was a mistake, its repeal had moderated house price inflation and its introduction was responsible for extending the duration of the house price boom by enabling speculators to re-enter the housing market (Joint Committee of Inquiry into the Banking Crisis, 2015b). Bacon and Associates (1998, 1999, 2000) also proposed that "anti-speculative tax" on the value of residential investment properties should be introduced from which landlords would be exempted if they could demonstrate that they planned to let out the dwelling long term and the abolition of the Section 23 tax incentives for property renovation and construction in selected inner-city neighbourhoods which had been introduced in the early 1980s (see Chap. 5). However, neither of these recommendations were taken up by policymakers. Instead, the availability of the Section 23 incentives was extended significantly during the housing boom and they played a significant role in driving the problems of excess and inappropriately located housing output outlined earlier.

As explained in the previous chapter, these tax incentives were intended to encourage the provision of additional dwellings and commercial premises in selected parts of the country. They enabled capital spending on the construction and refurbishment of these buildings to be offset against income or business tax for a 10-year period and they were initially applied to the inner areas of Ireland's five cities (Williams, 2006). Although the tax incentives enabled high levels of office building in inner Dublin in particular, dwelling accounted for the vast majority of property provided with the help of these incentives in most regions. Both homeowners and residential landlords could avail of the associated tax benefits, but they were more lucrative for landlords; consequently, the vast majority of Section 23 subsidised dwellings were purchased by this group. These incentives had been initially envisaged as short-term measures which would kick-start development in run-down inner-city neighbourhoods which commercial construction firms deemed too risky for investment. However, their duration and scope was repeatedly extended by successive governments with the result that they were abolished only in 2006 and by then had been extended to cover parts of every city and large town in the country, most small towns and a large swathe of the rural northwest of Ireland.

The geographical expansion of the Section 23 scheme began in 1994 when it was extended to include city suburbs (this phase was known as the Urban Renewal Scheme) and continued in 1999 when these incentives were expanded to include parts of 38 large towns and also to a sparsely populated region of the northwest (the Rural Renewal Scheme). Furthermore, in 2000 the Section 23 incentives were extended again to include parts of 100 small towns, under the Town Renewal Scheme (Goodbody Economic Consultants, 2005) (see Table 6.1). The cost (in terms of tax revenue foregone) to the exchequer of the Section 23 incentives was substantial – an average of €370 million per annum between 1999 and 2004 (Goodbody Economic Consultants, 2005). This high cost reflected the high take-up of the incentives, so in that sense they were successful. However, their record in terms of achieving their objectives and in particular in achieving unintended outcomes is more mixed.

A review of the early inner-city targeted phase of Section 23 found that it was successful in encouraging developers to build in parts of locations which they previously would not have considered viable and thereby in combatting dereliction (KPMG, 1996) In addition, in Dublin's inner city these incentives were successful in reversing the century-long pattern of population decline (Norris et al., 2013). The later phase of Section 23 was less successful in driving population growth but was associated with significant "dead weight" (developments which would have gone ahead in the absence of the subsidy) and therefore provided poor value for money (Goodbody Economic Consultants, 2005). More significantly, this later phase was associated with some negative unintended outcomes. The Rural Renewal Scheme iteration of the Section 23 programme has also been identified as one of the drivers of housing oversupply in the rural part of the northwest it targeted as evidenced by the particularly high rates of vacant dwellings and ghost estates in this part of Ireland in the late 2000s (Norris et al.,

2013; Kitchin et al., 2012). This unintended outcome is related to the fact that these incentives enabled buy-to-let landlords to shelter all their rental income not just the rent from the Section 23 designated dwelling they purchased. This encouraged landlords to buy Section 23 properties in parts of the country where rental demand was low and leave these dwellings empty but use the incentive to shelter revenue from the profit-making dwellings elsewhere from tax. FitzGerald (2005) argues that the impact of this oversupply was not solely a localised one – by drawing construction resources away from Dublin, the Section 23 tax incentives exacerbated the aforementioned problems of housing undersupply and price inflation in the capital.

The role of Section 23 in driving inappropriate, excessive or poorly located construction was amplified by a number of other similar construction tax incentives schemes introduced in Ireland which, although individually smaller in scale, were also numerous and therefore collectively significant in impact. Details of these measures are set out in Table 6.4, which reveals they focused a wide variety of construction projects ranging from private hospitals to childcare facilities. Take-up of these incentives varied – the sports injury clinics, park and ride facilities and multistorey car park tax incentives had low take-up, while take-up of the incentives for hotels and student accommodation was much higher. As in the case of the Section 23 incentives, the popularity of the hotels tax incentive in particular resulted in significant oversupply in this sector. This incentive resulted in the addition of 26,802 new hotel rooms between 1999 and 2008. However, a review of the industry concluded that a large proportion of the tax incentive-funded hotels were insolvent and this situation was especially common among hotels constructed between 2005 and 2008 (comprising an estimated 217 hotels and 15,600 rooms). This report concluded that investment in these hotels "was categorically not driven by the fundamentals of the hotel industry . . . the investments never made sense from the point of view of operating hotels and would have been insolvent if market conditions had stayed as they were at the time of the investment" (Bacon, 2009: ii–iii). The tax incentives for student accommodation and seaside resorts were also associated with very significant excessive supply in target districts to the extent that it was blamed for encouraging dereliction of existing dwellings in some of the target towns and cities (Department of Finance, 2011; Department of Tourism, Sport and Recreation, 1999).

Other concerns raised about the suite of tax allowances for capital investment which were introduced in the 1990s and early 2000 relate to their impact on property prices and tax progressivity. Indecon Economic Consultants' (2005) review of the non-Section 23 incentives (i.e. those

Table 6.4 Non-section 23 property-based tax incentives, 1990–2007

Tax Incentives	Date Introduced	Gross Tax Forgone to 2005 €000	Net Tax Foregone to 2005 €000
Childcare facilities	1998	9,000	6,000
Convalescent homes	1998	NA	NA
Enterprise areas	1994	NA	NA
Guest houses	2005	NA	NA
Hotels and holiday camps[a]	1994	169,000	125,000
Holiday cottages[b]	1997	38,000	27,000
Hostels	2005	NA	NA
Mental health centres	2007	NA	NA
Multistorey car parks	1995	23,000	17,000
Living over the shop scheme	2001	81,000	30,000
Nursing homes	1997	55,000	38,000
Park and ride facilities	1990	6,000	4,000
Private hospitals	2002	37,000	23,000
Seaside resort scheme	1995	320,000[c]	NA
Sports injury clinics	2002	0	0
Student accommodation	1999	214,000	159,000
Third-level educational buildings	1997	87,000	54,000

Notes: *NA* not available.
[a]Capital allowances for hotels had been available since the 1960s but from 1994 they were made available on an accelerated basis over a 7-year period.
[b] The same applies to incentives for holiday cottages which were initiated in 1968.
[c]This figure is an estimate.

Source: Department of Finance (2011), Indecon Economic Consultants (2005) and Goodbody Economic Consultants (2005).

listed in Table 6.4) found that all of the financial institutions and accountancy/tax professionals consulted believed that value of incentives was largely capitalised into property prices with the result that purchasers paid higher prices for tax incentive subsidised properties compared to their non-subsidised counterparts. The finance ministry also raised concerns that high earners were using the property tax incentives to shelter almost all of their income from tax. In response to the public outcry which this revelation promoted, the government too introduced a restriction on the use of these tax shelters by high earners in 2010 (Department of Finance, 2011).

Support for Low-Income Tenants and Homebuyers

Although the period examined in this chapter was characterised primarily by the marketisation of arrangements for the funding and provision of housing and other types of construction, government did remain involved in subsidising housing provision and providing some housing directly. However, the scale of its involvement was significantly less than in previous decades. This is because homeownership supports were no longer universally available but instead were targeted at low-income groups. Social housing accounted for a lower proportion of total housing output than it had during the mid-twentieth century and local authorities were no longer its sole provider because non-profit sector housing associations played a growing role in this regard. Furthermore, the private rented sector accommodated a larger proportion of low-income households supported by means-tested public subsidies for much longer than the norm in the past, to the extent that this sector operated as a form of "quasi-social housing". Thus the social housing sector was also partially marketised during the 1990s and early 2000s and public subsidisation of private landlordism also helped to fuel the buy-to-let boom enabled by the growth in mortgage lending to this sector as highlighted earlier (Norris and Coates, 2010).

The growth in housing association provided by social housing was enabled by the introduction of dedicated public funding schemes for this sector which, for most of the twentieth century, had relied on charitable donations and *ad hoc* grant aid from government (Brooke,

2001). The first of these funding schemes for housing associations – the Capital Assistance Scheme – was introduced in the early 1980s (and used primarily to provide supported housing for groups such as older people and people with a disability). In 1992, a second funding scheme for this sector called Capital Loan and Subsidy Scheme was introduced (see Table 6.1) to fund "general needs housing" for households with no additional support needs. With the help of these new funding programmes, output of housing association housing increased from 500 units in 1990 to 1,685 dwellings in 2007 (see Table 6.5). Output of local authority housing increased from 1,003 to 6,988 units concurrently, so in absolute terms total social housing output rates during the early 2000s exceeded the previous peak achieved during the high watermark of the property-based welfare system in the early 1950s (an average of 6,671 social housing units per annum were built between 1950 and 1955). However, when assessed in relative terms the rate of social housing output during the Celtic tiger boom appears less impressive. The Irish population expanded at an unpreceded rate during this time (from 3.53 million in 1991 to 4.24 million in 2006) and, as explained earlier, so did housebuilding rates (Central Statistics Office, various years). Therefore, social housing accommodated only 7.1 per cent of households in 2002 and 11 per cent in 2006 and accounted for 11 per cent of total housing output during the 1990s and 8.7 per cent between 2000 and 2007. In contrast, 16.5 per cent of Irish households lived in social housing in 1949 as did 18.4 per cent in 1961, and this sector accounted for 51.7 per cent of total housing output in the 1950s and 31 per cent in the 1960s (Central Statistics Office, various years; Department of Housing, Planning and Local Government, various years a).

Rather counterintuitively, the relative decline in the social rented sector during this period examined in this chapter was not due solely to declining public funding. Public spending on new social housing more than kept pace with population growth – it increased from €52.6 million in 1990 to €1.24 billion in 2007 and in the latter year social housing accounted for 15.9 per cent of total public capital spending (Department of Public Expenditure and Reform, various years) (see Table 6.5). Lower social housing output in relative terms during the 1990s and 2000s also

Table 6.5 Mainstream social housing capital expenditure and output, 1990–2007

	Local Authority Social Housing		Housing Association Social Housing		Total	
	Output	Expenditure (€000s)	Output	Expenditure (€000s)	Output	Expenditure (€000s)
1990	1,003	43,044	500	9,602	1,503	52,646
1991	1,180	43,450	500	10,570	1,680	54,020
1992	1,482	53,735	519	12,461	2,001	66,196
1993	1,569	84,195	890	20,657	2,459	104,852
1993	2,841	155,097	901	31,105	3,742	186,202
1995	3,842	191,085	1,011	40,951	4,853	232,036
1996	3,573	202,414	917	38,778	4,490	241,192
1997	3,217	222,136	756	38,909	3,973	261,045
1998	3,282	265,584	485	31,263	3,767	296,847
1999	3,713	298,994	579	49,054	4,292	348,048
2000	3,207	419,994	951	97,473	4,158	517,467
2001	5,022	670,799	1,253	153,164	6,275	823,963
2002	5,074	792,151	1,360	169,807	6,434	961,958
2003	4,972	659,475	1,617	230,917	6,589	890,392
2004	4,510	707,566	1,607	205,619	6,117	913,185
2005	5,127	804,976	1,350	194,482	6,477	999,458
2006	5,121	902,020	1,240	218,518	6,361	1,120,538
2007	6,988	941,273	1,685	301,548	8,673	1,242,821

Note: Data on local authority social housing include contributions from both local and central government.

Source: Department of Public Expenditure and Reform (various years).

reflected arrangements for the disbursement of this funding. As explained in previous chapters, until the 1980s social housing in Ireland was funded by very long-term loans which were repaid incrementally using tenant's rents and domestic and business rates (local property and business taxes). This funding model spread out the costs of social housing provision and also shared the repayment burden with tenants and local government and therefore ensured that providing these dwellings was affordable for central government even in very strained economic times such as the 1950s. In contrast, from the mid-1980s, loan financing of social housing was replaced with capital grants in the case of local authorities and non-repayable loans in the case of housing associations (i.e. *de facto* grants). This meant that the central exchequer had to meet the full costs of buying or building social housing upfront in a lump sum, which was not easily affordable even in the context of the Celtic tiger boom. Table 6.5 indicates that this model also affected pro-cyclical social housing investment patterns. Just 1,503 new social housing units were provided in 1990 when the construction industry was still in recession and social house building would have had positive economic impacts and provided good value for money in the context of a weak market. Conversely in 2007 at the peak of the housing boom, when construction and land prices were also at their peak and arguably generating additional demand for construction had fewer positive economic impacts, tax revenue was also buoyant and therefore the Irish government had the finance for capital grants to procure an additional 8,673 social rented dwellings.

In part because of these difficulties in financing adequate numbers of social rented dwellings, government came to rely increasing on the private rented sector to accommodate low-income households with the help of a means-tested allowance called Rent Supplement. This support was first introduced in 1977 and initially take-up was very low, to the extent that no data on claimant numbers prior to 1994 are available. As social housing output failed to keep up with the pace of population growth in the 1990s, take-up of Rent Supplement increased radically. Figure 6.3 outlines trends in the total number of tenant households living in Rent Supplement subsidised accommodation compared to social housing between 1994 and 2007. It reveals

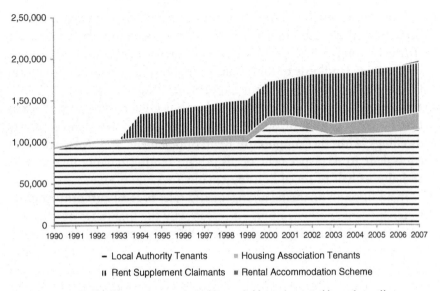

Fig. 6.3 Households accommodated in social housing and housing allowance subsidised private rented accommodation, 1990–2007. *Source*: Department of Housing, Planning and Local Government (various years a) and Department of Social Protection (various years)

that between 1994 and 2000 the number of Rent Supplement claimant households increased by 48.2 per cent (from 22,800 to 57,872 claimant households), whereas the number of social housing tenants increased by 23.3 per cent concurrently (from 94,813 to 129,915 households). This trend accelerated between 2001 and 2007 when Rent Supplement claimant numbers increased by 32.6 per cent and social housing tenant households expanded by just 2.7 per cent concurrently. Although Rent Supplement had been established as a short-term benefit, intended to support households during the transition from unemployment to employment and/or from private renting into social housing, during the early 2000s in particular the average duration of claims lengthened substantially (Norris and Coates, 2010). Therefore, this benefit came to act as a "quasi-social housing" – albeit without the security of tenure enjoyed by tenants of mainstream social housing because Rent Supplement is withdrawn entirely once recipients enter full-time employment.

Rent Supplement's status as a quasi-social housing sector was confirmed by the establishment of the Rental Accommodation Scheme (RAS) in 2004. RAS enabled local authorities to enter into agreements with private landlords to long-term lease accommodation for long-term (18 months +) receipts of Rent Supplement (Norris and Coates, 2010). Take-up of this new benefit started low but grew rapidly to the extent that by 2006 a total of 60,694 low-income households rented private dwellings with the support of Rent Supplement and RAS which is equivalent to 41.8 per cent of all private renting tenants in that year and almost half of social housing tenants (see Fig. 6.3).

In addition to financing arrangements, sales of local authority housing to tenants are another important reason why the high rates of spending on new social housing in the late 1990s and early 2000s failed to translate into substantial additional social housing supply. This policy, which was one of the last vestiges of the property-based welfare system left after the 1980s, was promoted with vigour by policymakers. The discounts available to tenant purchasers were increased on several occasions during the 1990s; they enabled 32,807 local authority tenant households to buy their homes between 1990 and 2007 which is close to half the number of additional local authority dwellings built during this period (see Figs. 6.3 and 6.4 and Table 6.1). Notably the tenant purchase scheme was never extended to housing associations which greatly helped the expansion of this sector.

Until 1995 all of the local authority tenants who bought their homes did so with the help of another remnant of property-based welfare – SDA mortgages – which provided approximately 2 per cent of mortgages during the period under examination in this chapter. Table 6.1 demonstrates that from 1995 tenant purchasers were also allowed to avail of commercial mortgages and during the 1990s and 2000s a number of additional supports for low-income homebuyers were introduced and their terms were made steadily more generous (Norris et al., 2007). Some of these reforms were recommended by Bacon and Associates' (1998, 1999, 2000) analyses of the housing market. For instance, 1991 saw the introduction of the shared ownership scheme, the low-cost housing sites scheme and the mortgage allowance scheme for tenants. The first of these schemes enabled households to buy dwellings in joint ownership with their local authority – the

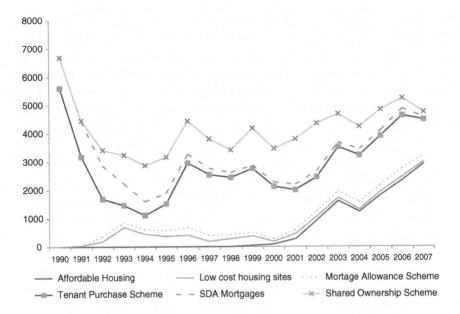

Fig. 6.4   Take-up supports for low-income homebuyers, 1990–2007. *Source*: Department of Housing, Planning and Local Government (various years a)

householder would purchase a proportion of the equity and rent the remainder from the authority with a view to buying the entire equity within 25 years; the second provided low-cost sites for self-building of dwellings and the third provided local authority tenants who surrendered their dwelling and bought a private sector home with a subsidy towards the cost of their mortgage. The terms of these supports for low-income home-buyers were reviewed and made more generous at the end on the recom-mendation of the reviews of the housing market carried out, and additional supports for this category of aspirant homeowner were introduced. In 1999, for instance, a new scheme called affordable housing was introduced which empowered local authorities to building dwellings and sell them at cost price to low-income households. The Planning and Development Act 2000 empowered local authorities to require that up to 20 per cent of new residential developments must be employed to meet the need for affordable housing and also for social housing provision.

At first glance, these low-income homebuyer supports appear reasonably successful – 29 per cent of the additional households which accessed homeownership between 1991 and 2002 used one of these schemes (Norris et al., 2007). However, despite regular changes to the terms of these schemes to increase their effectiveness in enabling low-income households to buy a home, take-up did not increase significantly in response and these schemes failed to contain the decline in homeownership highlighted earlier. In total, 4,456 households availed of these low-income homebuyer supports in 1991 compared to 4,356 in 2002 and owner occupation shank by 1.8 per cent between these years and by a further 2.8 per cent between 2002 and 2006 (Central Statistics Office, various years). Furthermore, concerns have been raised about the sustainability of the home purchases facilitated by these schemes. Norris et al.'s (2007) research on this issue found that one-third of participants on these schemes had 35 per cent of their gross incomes to housing (which indicates their housing costs are not affordable) and mortgage arrears were high particularly among participants on the shared ownership, tenant purchasers and affordable housing schemes (between 35 and 45 per cent of the participants in these schemes were in mortgage arrears of longer than 3 months duration).

Drivers of the Emergence of Asset Price Keynesianism

The preceding analysis has revealed that between 1990 and 2007 marked changes were made to long-standing arrangements for housing and property provision and distribution between 1990 and 2007 as these previously socialised activities were substantially marketised and the property-based welfare regime was replaced with asset price Keynesianism. In addition to change, this analysis has also highlighted some continuity as government continued to play a strong role in facilitating construction and property acquisition during the Celtic tiger boom, albeit by supporting the market during rather than by replacing it as was the norm in preceding decades. This suggests that substantial changes accompanied by some continuity were also evident in the power-, legitimacy- and efficiency-related factors which shaped these policy and property market developments.

A very significant new development which occurred during the 1990s and 2000s was that the power of the banks and the associated finance industries increased significantly in tandem with the growth in businesses and households' reliance on commercial borrowing and therefore the role of credit in driving economic growth. The strong correlation between economic booms and credit booms is well established in the comparative economic literature, and the Celtic tiger boom confirms this thesis (e.g. Ranciere et al., 2003). Although there is a consensus among economists that the early years of the Celtic tiger boom were propelled primarily by investment by foreign multinationals, Irish economic growth stalled following the US tech industry bust in the early 2000s and the marked expansion in private sector credit which followed almost entirely responsible for kick-starting growth again, and it was the key driver of economic growth between 2003 and 2007 (Kelly et al., 2011). It is reasonable to assume that policymakers' reluctance to strengthen banking regulation was at least in part inspired by a concern that this might stall economic growth again. The strength of the contribution of credit to economic growth reflected the concentration of lending in job-rich sectors of the economy such as construction, hospitality and retail. The economic power of the finance industry naturally engendered political power too because politicians were loath to challenge an industry which played such a strong role in economic growth. However, there is ample evidence that the strong links also developed between the banks and Irish politicians and other policymakers during the 1990s and 2000s which increased the political power of the former and that these links were particularly strong in the case of Fianna Fáil. Five per cent of donations to this party between 1997 and 2001 were from banks (Joint Committee of Inquiry into the Banking Crisis, 2015b). Furthermore, in 1998 the Fianna Fáil Environment Minister Noel Dempsey appointed Seán Fitzpatrick the Chair of Anglo Irish Bank to the board of the Dublin Docklands Development Authority (DDDA) which was responsible for regenerating the area surrounding Dublin Port and was the largest development landowner in the city. Directors of major accounting, public relations, engineering and architecture firms which subsequently secured DDDA contracts were also appointed by subsequent environment ministers to the agency's board, and the DDDA chair was also appointed to the board of Anglo Irish Bank, thus a web of relationships developed between the two which has been characterised as "rife with potential conflicts of interest" (Sunday Independent, September 26th, 2010, p 14).

Relationships between the construction and property industry and policymakers were even stronger during the period under review in this chapter. This is evident in the scale of donations from this sector to government parties – they accounted for 35 per cent of disclosed donations to Fianna Fáil and 34 per cent of disclosed donations to the Progressive Democrats – and the weight which the views of the sector's representatives were afforded by policymakers. Carswell (in Joint Committee of Inquiry into the Banking Crisis, 2015b) argues that lobbying from the construction industry was a key reason why the Section 23 tax incentives were extended and efforts to control housing demand such as removal of tax deductibility of interest on buy-to-let mortgages in 1998 were rolled back. Norris (2006) blames the same influence for the dilution of the requirements for builders to supply social and affordable housing which were introduced by the year 2000 by the Planning and Development Act but partially reversed in 2002.

More significantly, although building played a crucial employment generation role from the 1950s, its economic import increased even further during the early 2000s. Table 6.6 reveals that during the Celtic tiger boom construction constituted an increasingly large proportion of national wealth and employment. This sector accounted for 5.5 per cent of GNP in 1996, but this rose to 10.3 per cent by 2006. It accounted directly for 8.4 per cent of total employment in 1998 and 12.4 per cent in 2006 and indirectly generated a further 3 per cent of total employment in the former year and 5 per cent in the latter (DKM Economic Consultants, various years). In contrast, 8 per cent of the EU15 working-age population worked in construction in 2006 (Eurostat, various years).

Table 6.6 also reveals that the property market also achieved an increasingly important fiscal role during the early 2000s in particular.

Table 6.6 Indicators of the economic and fiscal importance of construction and property development, 1996–2006

Indicator	1996	1998	2000	2002	2004	2006
GNP(€ million)	51,906	68,531	89,530	106,768	126,465	154,078
Of which is gross value added from construc-tion (€ million)	2,875	4,270	7,008	8,966	11,813	15,924
Employment (N)	1,328,500	1,505,500	1,684,100	1,768,500	1,852,200	2,034,900
Of which is in construction (N)	NA	126,100	166,200	182,200	206,000	241,400
Total tax revenue (€ million)	18,187	23,381	30,947	34,346	41,805	53,787
Of which is from residential property related taxes (%)[a]	NA	NA	NA	8.0	10.9	15.1
Of which is from income taxes (%)	35.0	29.8	28.2	27.5	27.3	24.9

Note: All monetary data are at current prices.

NA not available.

[a]Calculated using Addison-Smyth and McQuinn's (2009) estimates.

Source: Central Bank (various years).

Receipts from property market-related taxes (stamp duties on house purchases, consumption tax on new houses, tax on the profits from house sales and property taxes) rose from €2.75 billion in 2002 to a peak of €8.1 billion in 2006. As has been extensively documented elsewhere, this windfall revenue facilitated a marked increase in public spending and also reductions in income taxes and therefore underpinned the very strong electoral record which Fianna Fáil enjoyed during the 1990s and 2000s (Leahy, 2010). These tax and spending developments in turn further increased reliance on property-related taxes. These accounted for 8.0 per cent of total tax revenue in 2002, but this grew to 15.1 per cent by 2006, while income taxes fell from 27.5 to 24.9 per cent of tax revenue concurrently (Addison-Smyth and McQuinn, 2009). Therefore, this combination of high rates of construction and strong property price appreciation facilitated a particularly effective form of asset price Keynesianism. In this context, most politicians were understandably loath to challenge the construction industry and were more than willing to facilitate its further expansion.

Significantly, from the perspective of the discussion at hand, the economic and fiscal importance of the construction industry was much greater in rural areas than in cities, which at least in part explains why overbuilding was most severe in the former regions while Dublin was undersupplied with new dwellings (but not offices or retail developments). In 2006, construction employed 10.1 per cent of the male workforce in Dublin City and County but it employed more than 19 per cent of men in many of the peripheral counties in the west, border and midlands regions (e.g. Galway, Mayo, Donegal , Kerry, Leitrim, Roscommon) (Central Statistics Office, various years). There is also evidence that rural local authorities had a stronger financial rationale for facilitating construction than their urban counterparts. Between 2000 and 2005, local government charges to builders and developers for the costs of providing the infrastructure required for construction (called development levies) rose from €0.11 billion to €0.55 billion. Although councils were legally obliged to spend this revenue on land servicing, these charges became an increasingly important part of the sector's total income. By 2005, they represented 13.6 per cent of the financial resources of local authorities nationwide, but reliance on this revenue was lower in five city municipalities (between 7.7 and 12.2 per cent) and much higher in many rural areas (over 20 per cent of revenue in Laois, Kilkenny, Wexford County Councils) (Kitchen et al., 2012). Local property taxes (called business rates) also provided particularly useful income for Irish local government because they are one of the few income sources which councils can spend as they wish, without central government restrictions. Large urban local authorities traditionally enjoyed large amounts of revenue from business rates but their rural counterparts did not because farmers are exempt. Therefore, rural local authorities had a strong incentive to grant planning permissions for commercial developments in order to generate business rates income – an activity which campaigners for stronger controls on construction referred to as "rates chasing" (An Taisce, 2012).

These economic and fiscal drivers of overbuilding in rural areas and undersupply in cities were reinforced by local political factors. Williams et al.'s (2002) research on planning in Dublin indicates that existing residents' views were a key consideration for the local government politicians who make planning decisions and these pressures often restricted construction because residents were concerned about associated disruption and loss of amenities. Whereas in rural areas landowners' interests were a bigger concern for local politicians and this facilitated development. Redmond et al.'s (2011) survey of rural local government politicians also reveals that facilitating one-off rural housing was a key concern for this group because they viewed such development as an effective mechanism for stemming population decline and providing affordable housing. These analyses are supported by data on spatial variations in the operation of the land use planning system. At the start of the Celtic tiger boom, in particular, refusal rates for planning applications were much higher in Dublin than in rural areas. In 1996, refusal rates were less than 5 per cent in 9 of the 24 local authorities with rural operational areas compared to 157 per cent in Dublin. Although urban and rural planning permission refusal rates equalised in the mid-2000s, rural local government politicians were consistently much more likely to overturn the decisions of professional land use planners (as they are empowered to do under the planning legislation) than their urban counterparts. Between 2003 and 2007, just one planners' decision was overturned by the elected members of Dublin City Council, whereas in four rural local authorities over 200 decisions were overturned between these years (these are South Tipperary, Westmeath, Cork and Kildare County Councils) (Department of Housing, Planning and Local Government, various years b). As mentioned earlier, problems of excessive zoning of land for residential development (also a decision which is also in the remit of local politicians) were also concentrated in rural areas (An Taisce, 2012).

In some parts of rural Ireland, the combination of these economic, financial and political pressures enabled the emergence of "growth coalitions" similar to those identified by Molotch (1976) in US cities. In the Irish context, the "place entrepreneurs" at the centre of these coalitions focused on villages and small towns, rather than cities, and they lobbied for increased building irrespective of the demand for the resultant dwellings and commercial developments. Gkartzios and Norris' (2011) study of the application of Section 23 tax incentives to five rural countries in the northwest under the Rural Renewal Scheme bears out this thesis. They point out that, unlike the Urban and Town Renewal iterations of these inventives, the geographical focus of the Renewal Scheme was not decided on the basis of Integrated Area Plans submitted by local government and examined by an expert advisory committee. Rather, one local government planner from the Rural Renewal Scheme target area told them that its geographical focus was decided on the basis of "a certain amount of pressure to do something. There was lobbying from the elected members of the Council, to put forward the idea of actually doing an RSS" (cited in Gkartzios and Norris, 2011: 489). They also report that the numbers employed in construction increased by 27.4 per cent in the Rural Renewal Scheme area between 2002 and 2006, while it contracted by 0.6 per cent nationally. Most of the local business owners, politicians and local government officials they interviewed viewed this additional employment as a key benefit of the scheme. One local government official suggested to them that the resultant pro-development pressures rendered over building inevitable:

Leitrim had not seen any development for 100 years. It has been said that if somebody wants to build a house on a white line in the middle of the Dublin Sligo road in Leitrim would get it! 'Cause there was nothing happening. It was very naive to think that the [local] politicians would take a long term overview as to what was appropriate. I am afraid that the attitude was that every house built in Leitrim is five jobs for a year. It didn't matter that there was nobody going to be able to buy it.

(Cited in Gkartzios and Norris, 2011: 489)

These power and efficiency drivers of the emergence of asset price Keynesianism were undoubtedly reinforced by ideological factors, but assessing their influence is complicated by the fact that, unlike their counterparts in the USA and the UK, Irish governments during the 1990s and early 2000s rarely offered explicitly ideological justifications for their policy decisions (Kirby, 2010). This has not stopped a large number of commentators on the Celtic tiger period from arguing that policy reforms during this time were inspired primarily by neo-liberal ideology (e.g. MacLaran and Kelly (Eds.) (2014) and Kirby (2010), amongst many others). Their analysis is supported by the fact that policy reforms in a number of fields clearly produced liberalised outcomes. As explained earlier, during the 1980s and 1990s the previously socialised system of mortgage and construction credit provision was almost entirely marketised and almost all regulation of this sector was removed. Furthermore, some Irish politicians, such as members of the Progressive Democrats party (particularly during the 1990s) and Charlie McCreevy, who was Fianna Fáil finance minister between 1997 and 2004, justified these reforms on explicitly neo-liberal grounds (Murphy, 2016). For instance, McCreevy justified rolling back the measures to control property investor measures introduced on the recommendation of Bacon and Associates' (1998) first review of the property market on the grounds that "I am a believer in the market, that is no secret" (in Dáil Éireann, 2000, Vol. 522 No. 2, col 203).

However, these politicians were very much the exception, and Kitchen et al. (2012: 1306) argue convincingly that the neo-liberal policy reforms initiated during the Celtic tiger period were not an explicitly "ideologically informed project". Rather, they were driven by a set of "deals" brokered by government with "various companies, individuals and representative bodies" and shaped by the power and efficiency concerns outlined earlier and inspired more by an unspoken consensus among politicians and senior civil servants that the market was the logical mechanism for providing credit, an overly optimistic assessment of the benefits of unfettered free credit markets and a lack of appreciation of associated risks, rather than an explicit ideological commitment to free market solutions in all cases (ibid.). Mercille (2014) demonstrates that the media played a key role in supporting this consensus and normalising the house price and credit boom. Their stance in this regard was inspired at least partially motivated by heavy reliance on property market advertising among the newspaper industry in particular (Joint Committee of Inquiry into the Banking Crisis, 2015a).

It is also important to acknowledge that Irish politicians were not all powerful in shaping policy decisions. As mentioned earlier, liberalisation of Irish credit markets was driven primarily by international developments in credit market regulation, most notably the Basle II international accord on banking supervision and regulation and the removal of barriers to financial national competition in the finance industry as part of the process of EU "Economic and Monetary Union" and preparation for the establishment of the euro (Kelly and Everett, 2004). Although Bieling and Jäger (2009) and many others argue that these international developments were themselves neo-liberal in motivation.

In addition, the policy reforms described in this chapter were not uniformly liberalising. Tax cuts and banking deregulation were accompanied by much more extensive government support for construction and property acquisition and also for industrial development than would be acceptable to neo-liberal purists and particularly after 2000 increases in social spending of a scale which would not be typical of a neo-liberal regime (Ó Rian, 2014). Government spending doubled in real terms between 1995 and 2007, and the real growth rate in spending was 6 per cent per annum. Admittedly, the scale of this growth was less than the very marked concurrent expansion in national income (consequently, the ratio of public spending was static for most of the Celtic tiger period); from 2003, increases in public spending outpaced growth in national income (Honohan, 2009). Therefore, from politicians' point of view, the beauty of Ireland's version of asset price Keynesianism was that it enabled them to satisfy multiple, competing agendas simultaneously. They could cut taxes and rollback banking regulation in order to satisfy free marketeers and pump prime economic growth, while increasing social spending in order to meet the needs of welfare claimants, keep public servants happy and attract voters with a more social democratic political bent (Murphy, 2016; Kitchen and Bartley, 2007).

The Irish version of asset price Keynesianism was also distinctive because it was shaped by ideological vestiges and practical legacies of the property-based welfare system which preceded it. For instance, the very old tradition of extensive intervention in property markets by successive Irish governments which has been outlined in preceding chapters helped to legitimate much higher levels of public subsidisation of construction and property acquisition that would usually be associated with a neo-liberal policy regime. Although social housing accounted for 11.2 per cent of total housing output in England in 2005 compared to 7.9 per cent in Ireland, public spending on social housing was much lower in the former jurisdiction because the sector was funded almost entirely by loans (half from private banks and half from government), whereas the Irish social housing sector was funded entirely by government grants at this time (Department of Housing, Planning and Local Government, various years a; Whitehead, 2007). Section 23 tax incentives and the similar incentives to support construction of non-residential property introduced during the 1990s and 2000s targeted much larger numbers of districts than the Urban Development Corporations and Enterprise Zones – the main programmes established by the Thatcher governments to encourage "market-led" (as opposed "state-led" approach which was previously the norm) regeneration of declining urban neighbourhoods in the UK. Only 23 areas were designated as Urban Development Corporations and Enterprise Zones, and the boundaries of target areas were tightly drawn to ensure the public subsidies addressed localised and genuine instances where developers faced (non-demand related) barriers to entering specific property markets (Jones and Evans, 2008). Whereas as explained earlier, in Ireland construction tax incentives were used much more broadly as strategy for addressing regional economic underdevelopment rather than dealing with localised housing market failure.

This strategy was also inspired by the long-standing ideological commitment to supporting the rural and agricultural way of life which has been discussed in depth in previous chapters. The continuing influence of this ethos is evident in policymakers' rationale for applying the Section 23 tax incentives to the Rural Renewal Scheme area for instance:

> It has long been recognised that the area designated has suffered long term population decline and less than average economic growth. It is also an area that is without significant urban centres which elsewhere have acted as focusses for economic growth and inward investment. In an effort to address this problem, a tax incentive scheme . . . [will be applied to] this area. Both to encourage people to reside in the area and to promote new economic activity.
>
> (Department of Finance, 1996: 6)

Although the century-long land redistribution project had ceased entirely in the 1980s, it bequeath rural Ireland with a very significant socio-economic legacy – a large number of small, owner-occupied farms particularly in the west of Ireland and therefore a rural population which was high by the standards of the turn of twentieth century but lacked a strong economic foundations. Local government politicians' eagerness to facilitate extensive construction of one-off rural housing can in part be explained by the important role of sales of sites for housing and also the important contribution of off-farm employment in construction in ensuring the economic viability of these farms (Gkartzios and Scott, 2014).

The historical context should also be taken into account when assessing the factors which inspired liberalisation of credit markets in Ireland during the Celtic tiger boom. Krippner's (2012) economic history of the USA suggests that in this case financialisation was the *unintended* consequence of a series of policy reforms such as the deregulation of foreign capital flows and interest rates which were introduced in response to the economic and fiscal crises of the 1970s. American policymakers assumed that capital would always be a scarce resource and were unable to imagine a scenario whereby an oversupply of credit would emerge. In the context of a severe shortage commercial credit since the Irish independence, it is likely that Irish policy reforms were influenced by a similar misapprehension and policymakers' failure to appreciate the risks of credit market expansion may have been reinforced by the fact that, unlike the USA, Ireland never had a strong tradition of credit market regulation in the first place. Ireland did not experience any bank collapses during the Great Depression and, consequently, did not establish the banking regulatory infrastructure commonly introduced elsewhere in the developed world at this time. Ireland managed with a currency board rather than a central bank until 1943, and Honohan (1992: 4) argues that the Irish Central Bank continued with "all intents and purposes" to act primarily as currency board until at least the early 1970s. In a context where government provided most mortgages until the 1980s (directly via SDA mortgages or indirectly via building societies which are subsidised and strongly controlled by government), there was little need to establish an infrastructure to regulate the modest level of commercial mortgage lending provided at this time.

Conclusions

This chapter has described the marketisation of the arrangement for property redistribution which followed the demise of Ireland's property-based welfare system in the 1980s. During the 1990s and 2000s, the system of government loans, grants and tax subsidies which had previously provided most of the capital for housebuilding and purchase and farmland acquisition was replaced by radically increased reliance on commercial lenders and regulation of these lenders was liberalised. The policy regime which emerged from this period of reform had much in common with the asset price Keynesianist model which Brenner (2006) has identified in the USA (and Crouch 2011 and Watson 2010 identify in the UK) in the sense that rising credit availability and the attendant growth in property prices were used to underpin consumer demand and thereby economic growth. These parallels reflected common drivers of policy change because, in Ireland and many other developed countries, liberalisation of credit market regulation reflected the increasing power of the finance industry and a political and regulatory consensus regarding the benefits of commercial provision of almost all credit and the removal of any regulatory barriers which might impede this.

However, the Irish version of asset price Keynesianism had some distinctive features. Most significantly, credit growth was accompanied by high levels of housebuilding and construction of other types of property during the 1990s and early 2000s which was facilitated by a very liberal approach to land use planning by Western European standards and also by unusually high government subsidisation of construction and the property market, more broadly via tax subsidies, supports for low-income homebuyers and subsidisation of private landlords to house low-income renters. The preceding discussion has argued that these distinctive features of the Irish approach to asset price Keynesianism are legacies of the property-based welfare system. In particular, they reflect the very long tradition of government intervention in the property market and of using construction, particularly housebuilding, as an economic stimulus and the legacy of a large rural population and weak rural economy as a result of land reform. They also reflect the economic and political power of the building industry. As explained in preceding chapters, this sector became increasingly powerful from the 1950s, but its economic import increased even further during the early 2000s to the extent that the property developers' interests and the national interest came to be seen as indistinguishable, in the same way as farmers' interests and the common good were viewed as one and the same during the decades after Irish independence. Furthermore, the increase in tax revenue from the property market which was facilitated by asset price Keynesianism also had key efficiency benefits from the perspective of Irish politicians because it enabled them to satisfy multiple, competing political agendas simultaneously. They could cut taxes and rollback banking regulation in order to satisfy free marketeers and pump prime economic growth, while simultaneously increasing social spending in order to meet the needs of welfare claimants, keep public servants happy and attract voters with a more social democratic political bent (Murphy, 2016; Kitchen and Bartley, 2007). In this way, asset price Keynesianism played a key role in underpinning the electoral success of Fianna Fáil during the period under review in this chapter.

As explained earlier, the Irish version of asset price Keynesianism facilitated a distinctive dual credit/house price and housebuilding boom which significantly increased the pace of economic growth during the early 2000s in particular and subsequently accentuated the severity of the economic bust which commenced in 2007–2008 and resulted in the collapse of almost the entire Irish banking system and Ireland's entry into an EU and IMF-sponsored emergency stabilisation programme in 2010 (Norris and Coates, 2014). Asset price Keynesianism is also associated with a far less progressive distribution of capital assets in Ireland than was the case in the past. This is evident in declining rates of homeownership. At the start of the Celtic tiger boom in 1991, 80 per cent of Irish households were owner occupiers, but by the end of the boom in 2006 homeownership rates had declined to 77.2 per cent and they have declined even further to 70.1 per cent by 2011 (Central Statistics Office, various years). A contraction of this scale in home-ownership is almost without precedent in modern developed economies. Homeownership has grown in the vast majority of OECD members since the early 1980s, and the contractions which have occurred have generally been less than 4 per cent. Finland and New Zealand are the only countries which are exceptions in this regard (Andrews and Sánchez, 2011; Boverket, 2005; Statistics New Zealand, 2013). Homeownership in Ireland has contracted across all social classes, but this development has been especially pronounced among low-income households. In 1991, 91 per cent of professional and 64.9 per cent of unskilled manual household heads aged between 35 and 44 were home-owners; the equivalent figures for 2011 are 80 and 49 per cent. The decline in housing wealth among lower earners associated with this development has been amplified by the marked resurgence in private renting since the early 1990s. After decades of decline, the proportion of households living in this tenure increased from 8.1 per cent in 1991 to 18.6 per cent in 2011 (National Economic and Social Council, 2014). This development has obviously resulted in the increased concentration of housing wealth in the hands of the landlords.

This pattern of increasingly regressive distribution of capital asset ownership in Ireland is due in large part to the dismantling of the property-based welfare regime and the associated system of socialised homeownership. As argued in preceding chapters, this policy regime expanded homeownership rates to super-normal levels well above what could be supported by the market; therefore, following its withdrawal homeownership has contracted to levels which can be supported by the market alone. This is evident, for instance, in the decline of sales of local authority social housing to tenants. In 1991, 8.1 per cent of all home-owners were buying their home using this scheme, by 2006 this had declined to just 2.2 per cent and this category of homeowner was not reported at all in the 2011 census – presumably because the numbers involved were too small to merit disaggregation (Central Statistics Office, various years). Furthermore, the replacement of mainly govern-ment-provided mortgages as part of the property-based welfare system with mainly commercial bank-provided mortgages as part of asset price Keynesianism ended the privileged position of homeowners in terms of access to housing credit. The local authorities and building societies which provided the vast majority of mortgages during the property-based welfare period were mandated by government to lend primarily to homeowners and private landlords would have faced significant difficul-ties in securing a mortgage during this period. Whereas the banks which have provided most mortgage credit in recent decades face no such restrictions and, as a result, lending for buy-to-let mortgages rose radi-cally during the Celtic tiger period while the proportion of mortgages granted to homeowners contracted.

References

Addison-Smyth, D., & McQuinn, K. (2009). *Quantifying revenue windfalls from the Irish housing market.* Dublin: Central Bank Paper 10/RT/09.

Andrews, D., & Caldera Sánchez, A. (2011). *The evolution of homeownership rates in selected OECD countries: Demographic and public policy influences.* Paris: OECD.

An Taisce (2012). *State of the nation: A review of Ireland's planning system 2000–2011.* Dublin: An Taisce.

Bacon, P., & Associates (1998). *An economic assessment of recent house price developments.* Dublin: Stationery Office.

Bacon, P., (2009). *Over-capacity in the Irish hotel industry and required elements of a recovery programme, Final Report.* Wexford: Peter Bacon Economic Consultants.

Bacon, P., & Associates (1999). *The housing market: An economic review and assessment.* Dublin: Stationery Office.

Bacon, P., & Associates (2000). *The housing market in Ireland: An economic evaluation of trends and prospects.* Dublin: Stationery Office.

Bannon, M. (1989). *Planning: The Irish experience 1920–1988.* Dublin: Wolfhound Press.

Bieling, H.-J., & Jäger, J. (2009). Global finance and the European economy: The struggle over banking regulation. In B. van Apeldoorn, J. Drahokoupil, & L. Horn (Eds.), *Global finance and the European economy: The struggle over banking regulation* (pp. 87–105). London: Palgrave Macmillan.

Boverket (2005). *Housing statistics in the European Union.* Stockholm: Boverket.

Brenner, R. (2006). *The economics of global turbulence: The advanced capitalist economies from long boom to long downturn, 1945–2005.* New York: Verso.

Brooke, S. (2001). *Social housing for the future: Can housing associations meet the challenge?* Dublin: Policy Institute, Trinity College Dublin.

CBRE (2010). *2010 Q2 Dublin retail market review.* Dublin: CBRE.

Central Bank (various years). *Quarterly review.* Dublin: Central Bank.

Central Statistics Office (various years). *Census of population of Ireland.* Dublin: Stationery Office.

Cheshire, P. (2004). The British housing market: Constrained and exploding. *Urban Policy and Research, 22*(1), 13–22.

Coates, D. (2008). The Irish sub-prime residential mortgage sector: International lessons for an emerging market. *Journal of Housing and the Built Environment, 23*(2), 131–144.

Conefrey, T., & FitzGerald, J. (2010). Managing housing bubbles in regional economies under EMU: Ireland and Spain. *National Institute Economic Review, 211*, 91–108.

Corcoran, M., Keaveney, K., & Duffy, P. (2007). Transformations in housing. In B. Bartley, & R. Kitchin (Eds.), *Understanding contemporary Ireland.* London: Pluto Press.

Crouch, C. (2009). Privatised Keynesianism: An acknowledged policy regime. *British Journal of Politics and International Studies, 11*(3), 328–399.

Crouch, C. (2011), *The Strange Non-death of Neo-liberalism*, London: Policy Press.

Department of Finance (2011). *Economic impact assessment of potential changes to legacy property reliefs: Final report.* Dublin: Department of Finance.

Department of Public Expenditure and Reform (various years). *Revised estimates for public spending.* Dublin: Department of Public Expenditure and Reform.

Department of Social Protection (various years). *Social welfare statistical report.* Dublin: Department of Social Protection.

Department of the Environment and Local Government (1998). *Action on house prices.* Dublin: Department of the Environment and Local Government.

Department of the Environment and Local Government (1999). *Action on the housing market.* Dublin: Department of the Environment and Local Government.

Department of the Environment and Local Government (2000). *Action on housing.* Dublin: Department of the Environment and Local Government.

Department of the Environment and Local Government (2002). *National spatial strategy for Ireland, 2002–2020: People, places and potential.* Dublin: Department of the Environment and Local Government.

Department of Housing, Planning and Local Government (various years a). *Annual housing statistics bulletin.* Dublin: Department of the Environment.

Department of Housing, Planning and Local Government (various years b). *Annual planning statistics.* Dublin: Department of the Environment.

Department of Tourism, Sport and Recreation (1999). *An interdepartmental review of the pilot tax relief scheme for certain resort areas.* Dublin: Department of Tourism, Sport and Recreation.

DKM Economic Consultants (various years). *Review of the construction industry and outlook.* Dublin: DoECLG.

Doyle, N. (2009). Housing finance developments in Ireland. *Central Bank Quarterly Bulletin, 09*(1), 75–88.

DTZ Sherry FitzGerald (2013). *Irish shopping centres and retail parks: A stock analysis.* Dublin: DTZ Sherry FitzGerald.

European Central Bank (2009). *Housing finance in the Euro area.* Frankfurt: European Central Bank.

European Mortgage Federation (various ears). *Hypostat.* Brussels: European Mortgage Federation.

Eurostat (various years). *Population and social conditions database: Employment and social conditions theme.* Luxembourg: Eurostat.

FitzGerald, J. (2005 March). The Irish housing stock: Growth in the number of vacant dwellings. *Economic and social research institute, quarterly economic commentary.*: Dublin: Economic and Social Research Institute.

Goodbody Economic Consultants (2005). *Goodbody review of area-based tax incentive renewal schemes.* Dublin: Goodbody Economic Consultants.

Gkartzios, M., & Norris, M. (2011). If you build it, they will come: Governing property-led rural regeneration in Ireland. *Land Use Policy, 28*(3), 486–494.

Gkartzios, M., & Scott, M. (2014). Placing housing in rural development: Exogenous, endogenous and neo-endogenous approaches. *Sociologia Ruralis, 54*(3), 1467–952.

Honohan, P. (1992), "Fiscal Adjustment in Ireland in the 1980s", *Economic and Social Review, 23*(3), 258–314.

Honohan, P. (2010). *The Irish banking crisis – Regulatory and financial stability policy, 2003–2008.* Dublin: Central Bank of Ireland.

Honohan (2009). *What went wrong in Ireland.* Washington: World Bank, unpublished paper.

Honohan, P., & Leddin, A. (2006). Ireland in EMU: More shocks, less insulation? *Economic and Social Review, 37*(3), 263–294.

Indecon Economic Consultants (2005). *Indecon review of property-based tax incentive schemes.* Dublin: Department of Finance.

Joint Committee of Inquiry into the Banking Crisis (2015a). *Report of the Joint Committee of Inquiry into the Banking Crisis: Volume 1: Report.* Dublin: Stationery Office.

Joint Committee of Inquiry into the Banking Crisis (2015b). *Report of the Joint Committee of Inquiry into the Banking Crisis: Volume 3: Evidence.* Dublin: Stationery Office.

Jones, P., & Evans, J. (2008). *Urban regeneration in the UK: Theory and practice.* Dublin: Sage.

Kearns, A., & Woods, M. (2006). The concentration in property-related lending – A financial stability perspective. In Central Bank (Ed.), *Financial stability report, 2006* (pp. 133–144). Dublin: Central Bank.

Kelly, S. (2014). Light-touch regulation: The rise and fall of the Irish banking sector. In A. Maclaran, & S. Kelly (Eds.), *Neoliberal urban policy and the transformation of the city: Reshaping Dublin* (pp. 37–53). Basingstoke: Palgrave Macmillan.

Kelly, J., & Everett, M. (2004). Financial liberalisation and economic growth in Ireland. *Central Bank Quarterly Bulletin, 04*(03), 91–112.

Kelly, R., McQuinn, J., & Stuart, R. (2011). *Exploring the steady–state relationship between credit and GDP for a small open economy – The case of Ireland.* Dublin: Central Bank.

Keaveney, K., & Walsh, J. (2004). Recent housing trends in rural Ireland. *Paper presented to the single dwellings in the countryside – Informing the debate conference.* Queens University Belfast, 3rd of December.

Kennedy, K., Giblin, T., & McHugh, D. (1988). *The economic development of Ireland in the twentieth century.* London: Routledge.

Kitchen, R., & Bartley, B. (2007). Ireland in the twenty first century. In R. Kitchen, & B. Bartley (Eds.), *Understanding contemporary Ireland* (pp. 1–26). London: Pluto Press.

Kitchin, R., Hearne, R., & O'Callaghan, C. (2015). *Housing in Ireland: From crisis to crisis.* Maynooth: National Institute for Regional and Spatial Analysis, working paper series no. 77 Maynooth University.

Kitchin, R., O'Callaghan, C., Boyle, M., Gleeson, J., & Keaveney, K. (2012). Placing neoliberalism: The rise and fall of Ireland's Celtic Tiger. *Environment and Planning A, 44*(1), 1302–1326.

Kirby, P. (2010). *The Celtic Tiger in collapse: Explaining the weaknesses of the Irish Model.* London: Palgrave Macmillan.

KPMG (1996). *Study on the urban renewal schemes.* Dublin: Department of the Environment.

Krippner, G. (2012). *Capitalizing on crisis: The political origins of the rise of finance,* Harvard, Harvard University Press.

Leahy, P. (2010). *Showtime: The inside story of Fianna Fáil in power.* Dublin: Penguin Ireland.

Mercille, J. (2014). The role of the media in sustaining Ireland's housing bubble. *New Political Economy, 19*(2), 282–301.

MacLaran, A. (2014). Ready money: Over development in the offices sector. In A. Maclaran, & S. Kelly (Eds.), *Neoliberal urban policy and the transformation of the city: Reshaping Dublin* (pp. 93–106). Basingstoke: Palgrave Macmillan.

MacLaran, A., & McCrory, R. (2014). The changing ideology and operation of planning in Dublin. In A. MacLaran, & S. Kelly (Eds.), *Neoliberal urban policy and the transformation of the city: Reshaping Dublin* (pp. 66–92). Basingstoke: Palgrave Macmillan.

McQuinn, K., & O'Reilly, G. (2008). Assessing the role of income and interest rates in determining house prices. *Economic Modelling, 25*(3), 377–390.

Molotch, H. (1976). The city as a growth machine: Toward a political economy of place. *American Journal of Sociology, 82*(3), 309–332.

Monk, S., Pearce, B., & Whitehead, C. (1996). Land use planning, land supply and house prices. *Environment and Planning A, 28*(1), 495–511.

Murphy, G. (2016). *Electoral competition in Ireland since 1987: The politics of triumph and despair*. Manchester: Manchester University Press.

Murphy, E., Fox-Rogers, L., & Grist, B. (2016). The political economy of legislative change: Neoliberalising planning legislation. In A. Maclaran, & S. Kelly (Eds.), *Neoliberal urban policy and the transformation of the city: Reshaping Dublin* (pp. 53–65). Basingstoke: Palgrave Macmillan.

National Economic and Social Council (2004). *Housing in Ireland: Performance and policy*. Dublin: National Economic and Social Council.

National Economic and Social Council (2014). *Homeownership and rental: What road is Ireland on?* Dublin: National Economic and Social Council.

Norris, M. (2006). Developing, designing and managing mixed tenure estates: Implementing planning gain legislation in the Republic of Ireland. *European Planning Studies, 14*(2), 199–218.

Norris, M. (2016). Varieties of home ownership: Ireland's transition from a socialized to a marketised regime. *Housing Studies, 31*(1), 81–101.

Norris, M., & Byrne, M. (2015). Asset price Keynesianism, regional imbalances and the Irish and Spanish housing booms and busts. *Built Environment, 41*(2), 205–221.

Norris, M., & Coates, M. (2010). Private sector provision of social housing: An assessment of recent Irish experiments. *Public Money and Management, 30*(1), 19–26.

Norris, M., and Coates, D. (2014). How housing killed the Celtic tiger: Anatomy and consequences of Ireland's housing boom and bust. *Journal of Housing and the Built Environment, 29*(2), 299–315.

Norris, M., Coates, D., & Kane, F. (2007), Breaching the limits of owner occupation? Supporting low-income buyers in the inflated Irish housing market. *European Journal of Housing Policy, 7*(3), 337–356.

Norris, M., & Shiels, P. (2007). Housing affordability in the Republic of Ireland: Is planning part of the problem or part of the solution? *Housing Studies, 22*(1), 45–62.

Norris, M., Gkartzios, M., & Coates, D. (2013). Property-led urban, town and rural regeneration in Ireland: Positive and perverse outcomes in different spatial and socio-economic contexts. *European Planning Studies, 22*(9), 1841–1861.

Ó Rian, S. (2012). The crisis of financialization in Ireland. *The Economic and Social Review, 43*(4), 497–533.

Ó Rian, S. (2014). *The rise and fall of Ireland's Celtic tiger: Liberalism, boom and bust*, Cambridge: Cambridge University Press.

Redmond, D., Scott, M., & Russell, P. (2011). The politics and governance of rural housing: Insights from local politicians. In M. Scott (Ed.), *Sustainable rural development: Managing housing in the countryside* (pp. 33–36). Dublin: Environmental Protection Agency.

Regling, K., & Watson, M. (2010). *A preliminary report on the sources of Ireland's banking crisis.* Dublin: Stationery Office.

Ranciere, R., Tornell, A., & Westermann, F. (2003). *Crises and growth: A re-evaluation.* Cambridge MA: National Bureau Of Economic Research.

Simons, G. (2003). *Planning and development law.* Dublin: Roundhall.

Statistics New Zealand (2013). *2013 census QuickStats about national highlights.* Wellington: Statistics New Zealand.

Stephens, M. (2003). Globalisation and housing finance systems in advanced and transition economies. *Urban Studies, 40*(5–6), 1011–1026.

Sunday Independent (2010, September 26). Docklands dealings immersed in an incestuous maze. *Sunday Independent*, p. 14.

van der Zwan, N. (2010). Making sense of financialization. *Socio-Economic Review, 12*(1), 99–129.

Watson, M. (2010). House price Keynesianism and the contradictions of the modern investor subject. *Housing Studies, 25*(3), 413–426.

Whitehead, C. (2007). Social housing in England. In C. Whitehead, & K. Scanlon (Eds.), *Social housing in Europe* (pp. 54–69). London: London School of Economics.

Williams, B. (2006). Fiscal incentives and urban regeneration in Dublin: 1986–2006. *Journal of Property Investment and Finance, 34*(6), 542–558.

Williams, B., & Shiels, P. (2002). The expansion of Dublin and the policy implications of dispersal. *Journal of Irish Urban Studies, 1*(1), 1–21.

Williams, B., Shiels, P., & Hughes, B. (2002). *SCS housing study 2002: A study of housing supply and urban development issues in the Dublin area.* Dublin: Society of Chartered Surveyors.

7

Conclusions

Introduction

This book has presented a new and innovative analysis of the development of Ireland's welfare system from its emergence in the late nineteenth century until the early twentieth century. This analysis has challenged the conventional interpretation of Ireland's welfare system as a liberal one which is similar to that operated in other English-speaking countries and characterised by relatively low public spending and means tested rather than universal provision particularly of social security benefits (Esping-Andersen, 1990). Rather than developing *weakly*, the preceding chapters have demonstrated that for most of the twentieth century the Irish welfare system developed *differently* from most other North Western European countries. Ireland's regime was distinctive firstly in terms of focus – which was primarily on property redistribution, while the redistribution of incomes and provision of social services were relegated to a less important role than in neighbouring countries (Castles, 2002). This property-based welfare system was also distinctive in terms of purpose. Whereas welfare states in most other European countries were intended to operationalise the "grand bargain"

© The Author(s) 2016
M. Norris, *Property, Family and the Irish Welfare State*,
DOI 10.1007/978-3-319-44567-0_7

between capital and the urban labour movement, Ireland's system of state subsidised property redistribution was intended to support a rural, agrarian and familist social order in which individual interests, values and prerogatives were subordinated to those of the family (Fahey, 2002; McCullagh, 1991).

This distinctive Irish welfare system was largely dismantled during the 1980s, and since then social policy in this country has converged more closely with the norm in other English-speaking countries – Chap. 6 highlighted particularly strong parallels between Irish policy developments in the 1990s and 2000s and the asset price Keynesianist model which Robert Brenner (2006) identified in the USA. However, this chapter also revealed that the Irish welfare system retained distinctive elements during this period, such as strong government intervention to support construction and property acquisition, which were legacies of the property-based welfare regime.

In this final chapter, these key arguments are explored in more depth and related to some of the most prominent debates in the literature on welfare states and housing policy. In this way, their implications of the Irish case for analysis of welfare systems in other countries and for ways of thinking about social policy are identified.

Property as Welfare

An important implication of the analysis offered in this book is that property redistribution can act as an effective form of welfare provision and therefore as the cornerstone of a welfare state. This is implicit in the discussion of the historical development of the Irish welfare system set out in preceding chapters, but it is worth stating explicitly here because this is not a widespread view among social policy analysts.

As mentioned in Chap. 1, research on welfare states and particularly cross-country comparisons of this sector is focused on social security benefits and, to a lesser extent, social services and polices such as land reform, which this book has identified as a core element of the Irish welfare system, are not conventionally defined as social policies. Furthermore, rather than a cornerstone, housing policy is widely regarded as the "wobbly pillar" under the welfare state because, in contrast to health and education (which in Europe are provided mainly by government and available as of right) for instance, housing services are generally delivered primarily by the market and therefore access is dependent on ability to pay (Torgersen, 1987 coined this phrase). Harloe's (1995) landmark comparative research on social housing in Europe and America links the commodified status of housing its asset value. Private property rights are central to the operation of market economies; consequently, he suggests that proposals that threaten such rights are more strongly resisted than efforts to decommodify health service provision for instance.

This history of the Irish welfare system presented in this book contradicts this consensus. It demonstrates that property redistribution need not be a primarily marketised activity, which is reliant mainly on market forces such as commercial lenders and construction. For most of the twentieth century, homeownership in Ireland was a socialised tenure because, although dwellings were privately owned, most capital for home purchase and construction came from the Irish government and many homeowner dwellings were also government constructed (Norris, 2016). This homeownership regime was also very effective in promoting welfare because it enabled decommodification of housing and thereby insulated homeowners from the vagaries of the market. During the middle decades of the twentieth century in particular, Irish households could acquire a home with little debt, pay off this debt quickly (often helped by rising incomes) and, once they had done so, live mortgage free and therefore survive on a lower income (Fahey and Norris, 2010). The extensive public subsidisation of land redistribution in Ireland had even stronger decommodifying effects because a farm provided both a home and a living. Furthermore, land reform required government intervention in the property rights of landowners which was just as radical as the taxation applied to the incomes and assets of middle and higher earners to establish the social security and social service systems provided by other European welfare states. Ireland's property-based welfare system was also effective in spreading these positive welfare outcomes widely throughout the population by enabling much more progressive distribution of property, particularly homeownership, than of other forms of wealth. During the twilight years of this regime in 1991, more than half of all household heads aged between 34 and 44 in every social class were homeowners. At this time, the proportion of higher professionals in this age group who were homeowners was not substantially higher than their counterparty in the unskilled manual occupational group (91 per cent compared with 64.9 per cent). In contrast, after the dismantling of the socialised homeownership regime and its replacement by marketised arrangements for home purchase in 2011, only 49 per cent of unskilled manual household heads aged between 35 and 44 were homeowners compared to 80 per cent of their equivalents in the higher professional occupational group (National Economic and Social Council, 2014).

Why Property Becomes Welfare

This book has also examined how property came to be defined as welfare in Ireland and why this property-based welfare system expanded and persisted for so long. This element of the analysis focused on the broad themes of power, legitimacy and efficiency, and it revealed that all of these factors played a role in driving the emergence and growth of the property-based welfare system but the distribution of power and efforts to respond to the concerns of different powerful groups and mediate conflict between them were particularly significant. In common with most mainstream welfare states, the Irish welfare system emerged from changes in the distribution of power due to economic change, the extension of the franchise and the emergence of new political movements aimed at mobilising these newly powerful groups and concerns to mediate the associated conflicts. Ideology reinforced these developments as did practical concerns because government support for welfare provision was in part an effort to deal with the effects of economic restructuring. What was different in the Irish case was that these developments were not associated with urbanisation and industrialisation and the associated rise of the urban trade union and social democratic movements and conflicts between labour and capital, rather they were associated with rural socio-economic restructuring and the associated agrarian capitalist economic crisis and the rise of tenant farmers as the numerically and politically dominant class and also with the interlinking of the tenant farmers' cause with the Irish nationalist project, Catholic social teaching and familist ideology. These urban/industrialist factors propelled the emergence and growth of mainstream welfare states focused on the provision of social security benefits and social services; whereas in Ireland, these rural/agrarianist factors drove the emergence of a property-based welfare system focused on the redistribution of land and the promotion of homeownership and because these factors remained powerful until the late twentieth century, they ensured that this welfare regimes expanded and persisted.

As mentioned in Chap. 1, Ireland's property-based welfare system is unusual in Western Europe, but it is not without parallel internationally. Significantly some of the similar welfare models employed in other countries are also rooted in agrarian power struggles and ideologies and rural economic challenges, rather than in urban labourist drivers. For instance, Saunders (1999) points out that farmers were key drivers of early US government socio-economic interventions in the late nineteenth and early twentieth centuries. Although the USA was rapidly urbanising at this time, power was fragmented and farmers were politically influential because they were not only numerous but were skilled political mobilisers. More importantly, they were economically powerful because the USA was a major exporter of agricultural products at this time, to the extent that it contributed to an agricultural depression in Europe which in part inspired the emergence of the Irish Land League and also a government response in the form of the Land Acts. Monica Prasad's (2012) longitudinal study of the US welfare state argues that farmers' power and political led to the emergence of a type of property-based welfare system which she calls a "mortgage Keynesianism". This model was characterised by progressive taxation but also a credit-based economy in which government enabled and regulated the provision of credit which supported consumption and economic growth. These outcomes suited farmers who needed consumers to buy their products and did not want the burden of taxation to impede this and also desperately needed credit to enable them mechanise agricultural production in the context of a labour shortage and bountiful land availability. Notably, she traces the roots of the US credit crunch which commenced in 2007 back to mortgage Keynesian, in a line of argument which echoes the analysis of Ireland's concurrent economic crisis which is set out in Chap. 6.

There is a strong consensus in the literature that a number of developed South East Asian countries operate property-based welfare systems, including Hong Kong, Singapore, South Korea, Taiwan and Japan (Doling, 1999; Swato, 2007). The housing systems in these countries bear a striking resemblance to the property-based welfare system employed in Ireland until recent decades because in all cases governments play a central role in providing credit for housebuilding and purchase; in Hong Kong, Singapore and South Korea, the state is also a major owner and distributor of land for housebuilding and is empowered to compulsorily acquire land for this purpose. The role of familism and developmentalist economic management arrangements and efforts to reinforce loyalty to the state in driving the emergence any growth of property-based welfare in these countries has been widely commented on. Rather surprisingly, despite the fact that extensive land reform programmes were implemented in Japan, Taiwan and South Korea after World War II, the relationship between these developments and the property-based welfare states which these countries operate has not been explored, at least in the English-language literature (Dore, 1959; Fei et al., 1979; Shin, 1998). The analysis of the Irish welfare system presented in this book indicates that this line of analysis would be well worth exploring.

Property and the Mainstream Welfare State

The issue of whether property ownership, particularly homeownership, impedes the development of the mainstream welfare state is a long-running debate in the social policy literature. By correlating public spending and homeownership rates in 19 OECD countries, Francis Castles (1998) famously identified a "really big trade-off" between the two, and in his landmark study of homeownership Jim Kemeny (1981) argued that by increasing housing costs during the family formation years (when households have to save for a deposit and then service a mortgage) this tenure reduces homeowners' appetite to pay the higher taxes required to provide social security and social services. His later work also argues that homeownership-dominated housing regimes are more likely to emerge in countries where the individualist solutions to social problems are supported over collectivist solutions. For this reason, he argues that countries with strong mainstream welfare systems are more likely to be dominated by renters (Kemeny, 1995).

The analysis of the Irish welfare system presented in this book supports the view that a trade-off exists between property ownership or, more specifically, between public subsidisation of this activity and public spending on social security benefits and social services. Indeed, rather than acting as a "wobbly pillar" in many respects the property-based welfare system shaped the mainstream Irish welfare state particularly during the middle decades of the twentieth century (Malpass, 2008, makes the same argument about the influence of housing on the British welfare state). The Irish case also provides some new insights into how this trade-off operates. In this country, the trade-off was manifested in three categories of tensions: financial, structural and political.

The significance of financial tensions is evidenced by the fact that no trade-off between mainstream and property-based welfare was evident before Irish independence when Ireland was part of the UK and crucially therefore cross-subsidised by Britain (although Irish nationalists took the view that the Irish paid more in taxes than they received in subsidies). The late nineteenth and early twentieth century saw unprecedented expansion of both the property-based welfare system (in the form of land reform and rural social housing subsidies) and the mainstream welfare state (all of the social security benefits and social services made available in Britain during this time were extended to Ireland with the exception of the health insurance elements of the 1911 National Insurance Act). Although rural social housing and Poor Law means-tested social security supports were funded primarily by local government rates, land reform, old age pensions and social insurance benefits were heavily subsidised by the central exchequer. The loss of this Westminster government subsidy after Irish independence, coupled with the poor state of the Irish public finances between the 1920s and the 1950s, necessitated difficult choices. Concentration of public investment on property-based welfare after 1922 helped to constrain the growth of other types of welfare spending because, as explained in Chap. 3, the former was prioritised over the latter. This was to an extent for financial reasons because land reform and housing subsidies inspired less worry among the many proponents of fiscal rectitude in the finance ministry because they were formally categorised as part of the national debt and in theory were funded by loans which would be repaid (although in practice land redistribution and social housebuilding loans were rarely repaid in full by their beneficiaries). In addition, housebuilding and small farms also provided employment which was particularly valuable in the context of chronic labour oversupply. The initial investment in land redistribution also necessitated further spending in this area because, as Breathnach (2005: 18) points out, "the greatest flaw in the various land acts" was their failure to acknowledge "the difference between economic and uneconomic holdings, that is those would could afford to pay their rent from the sale of agricultural produce and those who could not". Thus, post-independence governments were moved to redistribute more land by the practical imperative of creating economic farms, but the definition of an economic holding changed over time (the acreage required to provide a satisfactory living was substantially higher in 1950 than in 1920), so this proved to be a long, expensive and ultimately Sisyphean struggle (Dooley, 2004).

The trade-off between property-based welfare and mainstream welfare was also structural. By maintaining an artificially high proportion of the population working in agriculture as farmers, farm labourers and in the informal role of "relatives assisting" on farms, land reform and the labourers' cottage building programme (which effectively subsidised farm labourers' wages) created practical difficulties for the extension of the social insurance system (see Chapt. 3). This is because farmers were unwilling or unable to pay employers' social insurance for their employees and certainly for relatives assisting who were often paid in the form of bed and board rather than in cash. Sophia Carey's (2007) history of the failure of efforts to introduce a universal social insurance-funded social security system for employees during the late 1940s and early 1950s illustrates how this problem played out in practice. Despite significant support for this approach among politicians and the inspiration of the 1942 Beveridge Report which set out a plan for the development of the British social security system and received widespread attention in Ireland, the Irish 1952 Social Welfare Act excluded large sections of the population, including farmers, farm labourers and relatives assisting from coverage – these groups made up 45.2 per cent of the workforce according to the 1946 census (Central Statistics Office, various years). Carey (2007) reveals that the practical objections of farmers' representatives to universal social insurance on the grounds that they could not bear the cost of employers' contributions played a significant role in the decision to restrict coverage.

After Irish independence, many of the proponents of property-based welfare system and the beneficiaries of this regime such as farmers actively campaigned against the expansion of mainstream welfare on ideological or self-interested grounds. For instance, supporters of distributism actively promoted this model as an alternative to the government-provided public service and benefits model they found ideologically objectionable for instance. Similarly, policymakers opposed the extension of social security benefits because of their potential to undermine the familist social model by providing alternative means to secure a living. In this vein, Finance Minister Seán MacEntee (cited in Lee, 1989: 284) claimed that the Unemployment Assistance Act 1933 had undermined parental authority and "Without the firm exercise of such authority a peasant economy such as ours, based on the patriarchal principle, cannot survive" (see also Carey, 2007). Although it was argued in Chap. 3 that the three agrarian parties which emerged and disbanded between the 1920s and 1940s had limited impact on policy, this does not mean that the farmers who they represented also failed to shape policy and these parties' platforms provide a useful insight into famers' policy preferences. Despite the fact that these parties served different farmer constituencies (the Farmers Party and the National Centre Party were supported by large farmers, Clann na Talmhan served small farmers in the west) and consequently had different attitudes to land reform, their attitude to taxation and public spending on mainstream welfare services was strikingly similar. All three campaigned for radical cuts in agricultural rates (the principal tax paid by farmers) and to fund this argued for commensurately large reductions in public spending (Varley, 2010). Although they did not enjoy immediate success in achieving their objectives, they were successful in the longer term and a series of rates remissions granted to various categories of farmers slowly but surely weakened the agricultural rates base as the twentieth century progressed (Daly, 1997). This had a direct and serious impact on the mainstream welfare state because, in the context of the weakness of the central government-funded social security system in Ireland until the 1980s, the means-tested, discretionary "home assistance" system (as Poor Law social security was renamed after Irish Independence) played a key role in supporting low-income households. Remission of agricultural rates reduced the revenue available to local authorities to fund this scheme. As mentioned earlier, lobbying from farmers' representatives was also a key reason why a targeted rather than a universal system of social insurance was introduced by the 1952 Social Welfare Act (Carey, 2007).

The role of farmers in shaping the mainstream Irish welfare state was probably particularly strong in the Western European context, and the influence of this sector was far less than in countries such as the UK which urbanised and industrialised earlier and quicker. However, there is evidence of a significant agrarian influence on the formation of other mainstream European welfare states. For instance, Denmark has remained a primarily agricultural economy until recent decades, and Esping-Andersen (1990: 263) claims that in this case "powerful (liberalistic) farmers insisted on budgetary austerity and a price stabilisation policy in order to maintain agrarian exports. Hence welfare state reforms and full employment in Denmark were not part of the political formula until the late 1950s". In contrast, in Sweden and Norway, where he reports that "farmers were both economically and politically marginal", a comprehensive welfare state was put in place at a much earlier stage in the twentieth century (ibid.).

References

Breathnach, C. (2005). *The congested districts board, 1891–1923*. Dublin: Four Courts Press.

Brenner, R. (2006). *The economics of global turbulence: The advanced capitalist economies from Long Boom to Long Downturn, 1945–2005*. New York: Verso.

Carey, S. (2007). *Social security in Ireland, 1939–1952: The limits to solidarity*. Dublin: Irish Academic Press.

Castles, F. (2002). Developing new measures of welfare state change and reform. *European Journal of Political Research, 41*(5), 613–641.

Castles, F. (1998). The really big trade-off: Home ownership and the welfare state in the New World and the Old. *Acta Politica, 33*(1), 5–19.

Central Statistics Office (various years). *Census of population*. Dublin: Central Statistics Office.

Daly, M. (1997). *The buffer state: The historical origins of the Department of the Environment*. Dublin: Institute of Public Administration.

Doling, J. (1999). Housing policies and the little tigers: How do they compare with the other industrialized countries. *Housing Studies, 14*(2), 229–250.

Dooley, T. (2004). *The land for the people: The land question in independent Ireland*. Dublin: UCD Press.

Dore, R. (1959). *Land reform in Japan*. London: Oxford University Press.

Esping-Andersen, G. (1990). *Three worlds of welfare capitalism*. Princeton: Princeton University Press.

Fahey, T. (2002). The family economy in the development of welfare regimes: A case study. *European Sociological Review, 18*(1), 51–64.

Fahey, T., & Norris, M. (2010). Housing. In F. Castels, S. Leibfried, J. Lewis, H. Obinger, & C. Pierson (Eds.), *The Oxford handbook of the welfare state* (pp. 479–494), Oxford: Oxford University Press.

Fei, J., Ranis, G., & Kuo, S. (1979). *Growth with equity: The Taiwan case*. New York: Oxford University Press.

Harloe, M. (1995). The peoples' home: Social rented housing in Europe and America. Oxfrod: Blackwell.

Kemeny, J. (1995). *From public housing to the social market*. London: Routledge.

Kemeny, J. 1981. *The myth of home ownership*. London: Routledge.

Lee, J. (1989). *Ireland, 1912–1985: Politics and society*. Cambridge: Cambridge University Press.

Malpass, P. (2008). Housing and the new welfare state: Wobbly pillar or cornerstone?. *Housing Studies, 23*(1), 1–19.

McCullagh, C. (1991). A tie that binds: Family and ideology in Ireland. *Economic and Social Review, 22*(3), 199–211.

National Economic and Social Council (2014). *Homeownership and rental: What road is Ireland on?* Dublin: National Economic and Social Council.

Norris, M. (2016). Varieties of home ownership: Ireland's transition from a socialized to a marketized regime. *Housing Studies, 31*(1), 81–101.

Prasad, M. (2012). *The land of too much: American abundance and the paradox of poverty*. Harvard Mass: Harvard University Press.

Saunders, E. (1999). *The roots of reform*. Chicago: University of Chicago Press.

Shin, G.-W. (1998). Agrarian conflict and the origins of Korean Capitalism. *American Journal of Sociology, 103*(5), 1309–1351.

Swato, I. (2007). Welfare regime theories and the Japanese Housing System. In Y. Hirayama, & R. Ronald (Eds.), *Housing and social transition in Japan* (pp. 73–94). London: Routledge.

Torgersen, U. (1987). Housing: The wobbly pillar under the welfare state. In B. Turner, J. Kemeny, & L. Lundqvist (Eds.), *In between state and market: Housing in the post-industrial era* (pp. 116–127). Gavle: Almqvist and Wiksell International.

Varley, T. (2010). On the road to extinction: Agrarian parties in twentieth-century Ireland. *Irish Political Studies, 25*(4), 581–601.

Index

© The Author(s) 2016
M. Norris, *Property, Family and the Irish Welfare State*,
DOI 10.1007/978-3-319-44567-0

Printed by Printforce, the Netherlands